PASSION, VITALITY, AND FOMENT

PASSION, VITALITY, AND FOMENT

The Dynamics of Second Temple Judaism

Edited by
Lamontte M. Luker

TRINITY PRESS INTERNATIONAL

Copyright © 2001 by Trinity Press International

All rights reserved. No part of this book may be reproduced, stored in a retrieval system, or transmitted in any form or by any means, electronic, mechanical, including photocopying, recording, or otherwise, without the written permission of the publisher, Trinity Press International.

Trinity Press International, P.O. Box 1321, Harrisburg, PA 17105
Trinity Press International is a division of the Morehouse Group.

Cover art: *Jonah and the Whale*. Copyright © Culver Pictures/PictureQuest.
Cover design: Laurie Westhafer

Library of Congress Cataloging-in-Publication Data

Passion, vitality, and foment : the dynamics of Second Temple Judaism / edited by Lamontte M. Luker.
    p. cm.
    Includes bibliographical references and index.
    ISBN 1-56338-353-5 (alk. paper)
    1. Judaism – History – Post-exilic period, 586 B.C.-210 A.D. 2. Bible. O.T. – Criticism, interpretation, etc. I. Luker, Lamontte M.
    BM176 .P265 2001
    296′.09′014 – dc21
                               2001027249

Printed in the United States of America

01   02   03   04   05   06   10 9 8 7 6 5 4 3 2 1

Contents

Editor's Preface

This book is dedicated to Walter Harrelson, whose passion for Torah and prophetic vitality has enlivened his long and distinguished career. All of the contributors are his former doctoral students at Vanderbilt University. This book is our way of thanking him and honoring him.

The subject is chosen specifically because Walter spent most of his life lifting up the literature of this period as significant products of a vibrant spirituality. At the beginning of his career, this period was often characterized at worst as sacerdotal legalism and at best as paling in light of the First Temple period. To a degree due to the influence of Walter's teaching and writing, we now view this period as the time when "it all came together," an age with its own robust religious vitality that gave birth to rabbinic Judaism and Christianity. The obvious implication is that the themes elucidated in this book are appropriate to enliven and enlighten church and synagogue today.

Thanks are due to all the contributors who have worked so hard on this project. It is no easy task to compose a multiauthor book on a unified subject. I especially want to thank my friends John Endres and Will Soll for their help and support when I initially conceived the idea for this book. I would also like to thank Bobby Morris for compiling the indexes.

Abbreviations

AB	Anchor Bible
ANET	*Ancient Near Eastern Texts Relating to the Old Testament* (ed. J. B. Pritchard; 3d ed.; Princeton: Princeton University Press, 1969)
CBQ	*Catholic Biblical Quarterly*
Eng.	English verse numbers when they differ from Hebrew versification
JBL	*Journal of Biblical Literature*
JSOT	*Journal for the Study of the Old Testament*
JSOTSup	Journal for the Study of the Old Testament Supplement Series
NJPSV	New Jewish Publication Society Version
NRSV	New Revised Standard Version
OTP	*The Old Testament Pseudepigrapha* (ed. James H. Charlesworth; 2 vols.; Garden City: Doubleday, 1983)
RSV	Revised Standard Version
SBLDS	Society of Biblical Literature Dissertation Series
VT	*Vetus Testamentum*
VTSup	Vetus Testamentum Supplement

– O N E –

Passion for Torah and Prophetic Vitality

– *Lamontte M. Luker* –

Torah

Torah of course means instruction,[1] not law. This is confirmed by noting how much of the Torah is narrative or poetry, not commandments. Torah is God's good gift to God's people to help them live in God's kingdom.[2] The various post-Mosaic statutes and legal collections flow theologically from the Decalogue. This may be true historically if, as is probable, Moses is responsible for the original form of the Decalogue.[3] It is certainly true literarily since both Exod 20 and Deut 5 place the Ten Commandments before all others.

The Decalogue opens with God's gospel[4] announcement: "I am the LORD your God who has set you free from all that would

---

1. The term *torah* is derived from hiphil *yarah* ("to teach").
2. The concept of God's reign is at least as old as the Song at the Sea (Exod 15:18).
3. This is the view of Walter Harrelson, *The Ten Commandments and Human Rights* (rev. ed.; Macon, Ga.: Mercer University Press, 1997), 35 (=pp. 42–43 in 1st ed. [Philadelphia: Fortress, 1980]).
4. I use the term *gospel* generically for the good news of God present throughout the Hebrew Bible.

1

enslave you." Then follow ten guidelines on how to maintain that freedom, since antinomianism is its own enslavement. Each commandment guards a gracious gift that the God of freedom has given humankind: God's identity, unconstrained by images (1–2); God's name (3); rest (4); parents (5); life (6); sexuality, marriage, and family (7); possessions (8); truth and truthful relationships (9); and contentment with what we have (10). Legal collections such as the Covenant Code (Exod 20:22–23:33), the Holiness Code (Lev 17–26), and the Book of Deuteronomy, as well as miscellaneous statues, including among other things guidelines on worship, all help the people of God respond to God's liberating gospel and live in God's kingdom, which is characterized by *mishpat* (justice with compassion), *tsedaqah* (right relationship with God engendering right relationships with human beings), and *shalom* (peace and prosperity for all).

The Torah was finalized in the early postexilic period and reflects centuries of preexilic and exilic interaction between priests and prophets.[5] While this theological masterpiece certainly preserves and reflects preexilic traditions, it is in the postexilic period that the Torah, with such radical concepts as the sabbatical laws, jubilee, and special concern for the poor and oppressed, becomes the "constitution" of Judah. And while the foundational institutions of preexilic religion were messiah (king) and temple, Second Temple Judaism is centered around temple and Torah (with hope for messiah being pushed into the future). In

---

5. This is seen, e.g., in the obvious relationship between Jeremiah and Deuteronomy, the reality that Ezekiel the priest was in exile with his fellow priests who were compiling the Torah, and the preservation of prophets such as Amos, Micah, and Isaiah and their eventual influence on the religious establishment.

fact, so central was the Torah that Judaism was able to survive even the loss of the temple altogether.

Therefore it is also in the postexilic period that torah[6] becomes a way of life. Living torah is living in the kingdom of God. The Torah is the inscribed wisdom of God descended from heaven and dwelling on earth (Sir 24),[7] instructing the faithful in torah living: justice and righteousness and ultimately peace.

The priests in Second Temple Judaism are not only liturgical leaders but teachers of torah. However, God offers assistance. An early version of Deuteronomy had counseled, "Hear, O Israel: The LORD is our God, the LORD alone. You shall love the LORD your God with all your heart, and with all your soul, and with all your might" (6:4–5).[8] Yet preexilic priests and prophets had taught in vain. So the final editors of Deuteronomy, probably influenced by Jeremiah (cf. 31:31–34) and Ezekiel (cf. 36:25–27), add, "Moreover, the LORD your God will circumcise your heart and the heart of your descendants, so that you will [be able to] love the LORD your God with all your heart and with all your soul, in order that you may live [torah]" (30:6). External circumcision is a sign of the covenant, but it does not change human nature. An insight from the late First Temple period is carried into Second Temple Judaism: only God can change the human heart so that we can do torah.

---

6. Here I spell *torah* with lowercase *t* to distinguish the life of torah from the five scrolls.

7. Sir 24 provided the model for the prologue to John's Gospel. For John, Jesus the Christ is the wisdom and torah of God incarnate; he chooses the word *logos* to incorporate both concepts.

8. Unless otherwise noted, biblical quotations are from the NRSV.

Third Isaiah

Also early in the postexilic period a prophet, or succession of
prophets, arose who has traditionally become known as Third
Isaiah and is generally considered to be the author and redactor
of Isa 56–66. From the opening line he is true to his eighth-
century mentor in calling for justice (*mishpat*) and righteousness
(*tsedaqah*) (56:1) even while noting their absence (59:9); this
vital prophetic pair reverberates in his subsequent oracles (e.g.,
58:2; 59:14, 15b–16; 61:8a/11b). Like his preexilic counterparts,
he is critical of sentinels (prophets) who are blind and shepherds (rulers) who have no understanding (56:10–11). Aware
of exclusivistic elements in the religious establishment, he maintains the universalistic prophetic vision that includes foreigners
and eunuchs and a rebuilt temple as a "house of prayer for all
peoples" (56:3–7). Sounding much like Amos, he castigates in-
authentic worship that does not inspire right living (58:1–14;
66:1–4; cf. 1:10–17), and he addresses this recurring problem
with his own prophetic exhortation: authentic shabbat (56:1–8;
58:13–14).[9]

Sounding much like the Suffering Servant of Second Isaiah,
he announces his own role to bring good news to the oppressed
(61:1–3), but with his own postexilic twist. Isaiah of Jerusalem
had responded to God's call with *hineni,* "Here am I; send me!"
(6:8), but his mission ultimately failed. Taking his clue again
from his predecessor Second Isaiah (52:6), Third Isaiah places
First Isaiah's response directly on God's lips, employing the em-

---

9. References to keeping shabbat in 56:2, 4, 6 and 58:13 form an exhor-
tative inclusio around references to unrighteousness, apostasy, and injustice
and suggest, in the prophet's opinion, the means to achieve righteousness,
right worship, and justice.

phatic form (with energic *nun*) *hinneni* (58:9; 65:1 twice): God himself has taken up the mission and says, "Here I am, Here I am, Here I am!" In Second Isaiah the Suffering Servant suffers on behalf of the sinners, but Third Isaiah says, "In their suffering, God also suffered. . . . They . . . grieved God's Holy Spirit" (63:9–10).[10] Third Isaiah seems to continue the insight of Jeremiah (31:31–34), Ezekiel (36:25–27), and Deuteronomy (30:6): prophetic exhortation had not worked, so God must take a more active role in salvific enabling. Isaiah 63:11 speaks of God "who put within them his holy spirit,"[11] and 59:20–21 says:

> And [God] has come/is coming/will come [the form can mean all three] to Zion as Redeemer, and to those in Jacob who turn away from sin (it is an oracle of the LORD). And as for me, this is my covenant with them, says the LORD: My spirit that is upon you and my words that I put in your mouth will not be removed from your mouth or from the mouth of your progeny or from the mouth of the progeny of your progeny, says the LORD, from now on and until eternity (my translation).

This sense of God's intimate role in the task of justice and righteousness is reinforced by Third Isaiah's parent language when speaking to God — "the longing of your heart, your

---

10. The translation is from Walter Harrelson, "'Why, O Lord, Do You Harden Our Heart?' A Plea for Help from a Hiding God," in *Shall Not the Judge of All the Earth Do What Is Right? Studies on the Nature of God in Tribute to James L. Crenshaw* (ed. David Penchansky and Paul L. Redditt; Winona Lake, Ind.: Eisenbrauns, 2000), 163–64. He goes on to comment: "No other text in the Hebrew Scripture expressly affirms that God suffers with the suffering people" (167).

11. Besides these two mentions in Isa 63:10–11, the only other reference to "holy spirit" in the Hebrew Bible is Ps 51:13 (Eng. 51:11).

mother-love" (63:15); "but you — you are our Father...you, O Lord, are our Father" (63:16); "yet, O Lord, you are our Father" (64:7 [Eng. 64:8])[12] — and when God responds: "As a mother comforts her child, so I will comfort you" (66:13).

The entrée for God's enabling grace is confession: "All our righteousness is like a filthy rag"[13] (64:5 [Eng. 64:6]; cf. 66:2b). Now the "sentinels" (prophets) are redeemed and can fulfill their mission (62:6–7); sinners have become "the Holy People" (62:12) and "servants" of the Lord (Isa 65 passim). All of God's people are called "priests of the Lord" (61:6) including some Gentiles (66:21)! Thus First Isaiah's vision (11:6–9) can be fulfilled:

> The wolf and the lamb shall feed together,
>   the lion shall eat straw like the ox;
>   and dust shall be the serpent's food.
> They shall not hurt or destroy
>   in all my holy mountain,
>   says the Lord (65:25 rsv).

> And you shall know that I, the Lord, am your Savior
>   and your Redeemer, the Mighty One of Jacob....
> I will appoint Peace as your overseer
>   and Righteousness as your taskmaster (60:16–17).

Haggai, Zechariah 1–8, and the Chronicler

Haggai and Zechariah are instructive in that, in the tradition of Jeremiah, Ezekiel, and perhaps Isaiah of Jerusalem (prophets who

---

12. Harrelson's translation ("Why, O Lord," 164–65), upon which he comments: "The repeated designation of God as father is...without precedent in the Hebrew Bible" (169).

13. Ibid., 165. Harrelson adds that the rag is "no doubt a reference to cloth used during the menstrual cycle and then discarded" (171).

were also priests), they demonstrate that prophetic and priestly concerns are not necessarily inimical: their main job is to get the temple rebuilt. They display an intimacy of the presence of God: "I am with you" (Hag 1:13; 2:4); "my Spirit abides among you" (2:5); "return to me . . . and I will return to you" (Zech 1:3); "I will return" (8:3). And while they were wrong about Zerubbabel being the Branch (messiah), they ushered in an era in which messianic hope was increasingly eschatological, with the high priest functioning in that role in the meantime.[14]

Torah concerns are central for Zechariah. In 5:1–4 stealing and swearing falsely are evidently references to the Decalogue; perhaps the early postexilic community was having particular problems with these two commandments. Like Third Isaiah 58, Zechariah exhorts that fasting be replaced by right living: "Render true judgments, show kindness and mercy to one another; do not oppress the widow, the orphan, the alien, or the poor; and do not devise evil in your hearts against one another" (7:9–10). Similar is 8:16–17: "Speak the truth to one another, render in your gates judgments that are true and make for peace, do not devise evil in your hearts against one another, and love no false oath."

Likewise Zechariah echoes the universalistic strains of Third Isaiah: "Many nations shall join themselves to the LORD on that day, and shall be my people" (2:15 [Eng. 2:11]); "many peoples and strong nations shall come to seek the LORD of hosts in Jerusalem, and to entreat the favor of the LORD. Thus says the LORD of hosts: In those days ten men from nations of every lan-

---

14. Cf. Zech 6:9–14, where the "crowns," originally one for Zerubbabel and one for Joshua, in the final redaction are both placed on the head of Joshua who is called Branch; cf. 3:8, where Joshua is told to expect the coming of the Branch.

guage shall take hold of a Jew, grasping his garment and saying, 'Let us go with you, for we have heard that God is with you'" (8:22–23).

Chronicles presents a priestly vision of the kingdom of God headed by David as the ideal priestly messiah who leads the people to walk in Torah. The Chronicler gives precedence to the Levites (2 Chr 29:34), who function in the messianic role during the postexilic period. He has prophetic concerns at heart (36:15–21) but the role of prophecy has likewise been taken over by the Levites (20:5–22; cf. 1 Chr 25:1, 5; 2 Chr 29:30); that is, prophecy works through the worshiping community. Concern for Torah is paramount as the way of the kingdom of God (17:7–9; 6:16 cf. 1 Kgs 8:25). In short, for the Chronicler the kingdom of God is initiated by a priestly David and is the worshiping community of Judah. Torah is the constitution of the kingdom, and the messianic and prophetic roles are performed by the Levitical priests.

Malachi

Malachi, on the other hand, condemns corrupt priests who preside at hypocritical liturgies and engender faithlessness. His passion for Torah is obvious, mentioning it four times in as many verses at the beginning of his book (2:6–9) and closing his book with his final injunction: "Actively hold in remembrance [observe, enact, and teach — the verb is the pregnant *zakhar*] the Torah of Moses my servant" (3:22 [Eng. 4:4], my translation). The priest is to live and function "prophetically" as God's "messenger" (2:7)[15] by living and teaching Torah (2:6–7)

---

15. The word *mal'akh* is often used with reference to a prophet. The word *mal'akhi* in 1:1 means "my messenger."

but these priests are doing neither (2:8–9). Malachi probably had the Decalogue in mind when he chastises husbands who are faithless to the wives of their youth and condemns divorce (2:13–16; cf. Mark 10:2–12);[16] certainly he had in mind the welfare of the woman as vulnerable in that society. God's judgment is "against the sorcerers, against the adulterers, against those who swear falsely, against those who oppress the hired workers in their wages, the widow and the orphan, against those who thrust aside the alien, and do not fear [God]" (3:5).[17]

The gospel glue that holds the book together is the fatherhood of God (1:6; 2:10; 3:17), who loves us (1:2). In a statement of radical monotheism that Walter Harrelson calls the most universalistic in the entire Hebrew Bible, this divine Parent announces "from the rising of the sun to its setting my name is great among the nations, and in every place incense is offered to my name, and a pure offering; for my name is great among the nations" (1:11). By the last verse of Mal 1, which began with God saying "I have loved you" (1:2) and "I am a father" (1:6), the metaphor has shifted to the kingdom of God: "I am a great King . . . and my name is reverenced among the nations" (1:14).

It is not by accident that the Book of Malachi concludes with exhortation to remember the Torah of Moses and expect the Prophet Elijah (3:22–24 [Eng. 4:4–6]). The earmarks of true religion are passion for Torah and prophetic vitality.

---

16. This chastisement would also serve as a criticism of one aspect of the campaign of Ezra and Nehemiah, namely, divorce of foreign wives.

17. While there may be some ironic reference to fearing the judgment of God, the last phrase is a technical term for having faith in God and living the faithful life, as the Torah and prophets constantly exhort.

Joel

Addressing hedonistic priests and other groups, Joel interprets a devastating locust plague that has destroyed vineyards and pastures as just punishment upon them: no more wine and meat for them. Unlike his predecessors, Joel says the time for fasting has returned, as long as it is accompanied by true contrition (1:14; 2:12–13, 15). He recounts the Torah's core theology (cf. Exod 34:6–7) of the nature of God:

> Return to the LORD, your God,
>   for he is gracious and merciful,
> slow to anger, and abounding in steadfast love,
>   and relents from punishing (Joel 2:13).

Then God's forgiveness will return, God will restore fertility to the land (2:19–27; 4:13, 18 [Eng. 3:13, 18]),[18] and the nations who had abused Judah will be punished (Joel 4 [Eng. Joel 3]).

Like his predecessors, Joel includes an element of universality. Even as the period of formal Hebrew prophecy is nearing its end, Joel envisions a time when all God's people will be prophets, or at least exhibit prophetic vitality. God says,

> And it shall come to pass afterward,
> that I will pour out my spirit on all flesh;
> your sons and your daughters shall prophesy,
>   your old men shall dream dreams,
>   and your young men shall see visions.

---

18. Milk is a reference to sheep and goats; hence wine and milk mean that vineyards and pastures will return.

Even upon the menservants and maidservants
  in those days, I will pour out my spirit (3:1–2 RSV [Eng.
  2:28–29]).

Then everyone who calls on the name of the LORD shall
be saved (3:5 [Eng. 2:32]).

Compare Moses' passionate statement in the Torah: "Would that
all the LORD's people were prophets, and that the LORD would
put his spirit on them!" (Num 11:29).

Jonah

The Book of Jonah (cf. 4:2) is a midrash on Exod 34:6–7a, a
central passage of the Torah, also alluded to by Joel (see above):

The LORD, the LORD,
a God merciful and gracious,
slow to anger,
and abounding in steadfast love and faithfulness,
keeping steadfast love for the thousandth generation,
forgiving iniquity and transgression and sin.

In my view, the book is a universalistic response to certain exclusivistic elements in some sectors of Second Temple orthodoxy.
The author's prophetic vitality inspires him to write the midrash
on the "gospel" portion of Exod 34:6–7a and omit the "law" portion that follows in 34:7b. There is warrant in the Torah pericope
itself for doing this: God's forgiveness extends for a thousand
generations, his judgment for only three or four.

    The author chooses as the audience for Jonah's mission Nin-
eveh, renowned as the most sinful capital of the most sinful
nation on earth, the very epitome of everything anti-God and

Gentile to boot. Pouting, Jonah preaches the shortest sermon on record (were the book to comprise only the proclamation of the prophet it would be only five words long in Hebrew), "Forty days more, and Nineveh shall be overthrown!" (3:4), but it is the most effective oracle uttered by any prophet in the Hebrew tradition: the entire city repented, even the animals. So God forgives the city; but more concerned about his own reputation than about God's universal love and grace, Jonah is exceedingly displeased and angry. He says in effect, "That's why I didn't want to come here in the first place; I knew you would forgive them!": "I knew that you are a gracious God and merciful, slow to anger, and abounding in steadfast love, and ready to relent from punishing" (4:2b).

The author paraphrases Exod 34:6–7a in almost exactly the same way as Joel 2:13 did; this theological gem on the essential nature of God from the Torah must have been a maxim of Second Temple Judaism. And it must have been a vital religion indeed that could produce a theological book in which Gentile sailors exhibit more faith than the Hebrew prophet and offer a sacrifice and make vows (1:16), and a heathen city like Nineveh can observe an authentic fast of repentance and be forgiven.

Zechariah 9–14

The foment of the postexilic period simmers throughout Zech 9–14, a protoapocalyptic addition to the oracles of the Prophet Zechariah. The messianic branch failed to sprout in Zech 1–8, and circumstances have deteriorated in these latter chapters. The flock of Judah wanders like sheep and suffers for lack of a shepherd (10:2); God's anger is hot against the current shepherds, but the Lord cares for his flock, Judah (10:3; cf. 9:16).

The whole tenor of the composition is that God himself must act decisively to bring about an entirely new reality. With a hint of the Suffering Servant motif, the prophet is told to become the shepherd of the flock doomed to slaughter (11:4, 7), but only in order to destroy only shepherds and prepare for a "worthless shepherd...who does not care for the perishing, or seek the wandering, or heal the maimed, or nourish the healthy, but devours the flesh of the fat ones, tearing off even their hoofs" and "who deserts the flock" (11:15–17).

But there is hope:

> Rejoice greatly, O daughter Zion!
>> Shout aloud, O daughter Jerusalem!
> Lo, your king comes to you;
>> triumphant and victorious is he,
> humble and riding on a donkey,
>> on a colt, the foal of a donkey (Zech 9:9).

There is nothing unusual about a Near Eastern king processing on a donkey; but the salient feature of this messianic oracle is that he is humble. In the tradition of Mic 4:1–4 and 5:1–4a (Eng. 5:2–5a) the humble messianic king ushers in an age of peace:

> He[19] will cut off the chariot from Ephraim
>> and the war horse from Jerusalem;
> and the battle bow shall be cut off,
>> and he shall command peace to the nations;
> his dominion shall be from sea to sea,
>> and from the River to the ends of the earth (Zech 9:10).

---

19. Whether one reads "he" with the Septuagint or "I" with the Masoretic Text, the meaning is the same: God acts through the messiah and the messiah acts for God.

But not before much more foment. Whether this humble king
is (a) "the shepherd who is struck" so that the people are scattered, with the result that one-third are refined in order to renew
the covenant (13:7–9)[20] and/or (b) the one (from the house of
David?) for whom the people mourn "when they look on the
one whom they have pierced" (12:10) is far from clear, but some
heirs of Second Temple Judaism in the first century C.E. certainly
took it that way.[21]

Regardless, much like Joel's universalizing of the prophetic
spirit (3:1–2 [Eng. 2:28–29]), Zech 12:8 democratizes the concept of messiah (cf. Isa 55:3). In the future the feeble inhabitants
of Jerusalem "shall be like David, and the house of David shall
be like God." The prophet envisions a time when the people will
exhibit messianic virtues and the messiah will be transparent to
God (on the divine son, cf. 2 Sam 7; Ps 2; 45; 72; 110; etc.). In
Zech 14 God gathers all the nations to Jerusalem, they take the
city, then God approaches from the Mount of Olives to defeat
them and become King over all the earth, at which time the
Torah's Shema will be universally recognized: "The LORD will
be one and his name will be one" (14:9; cf. Deut 6:4).

The book concludes with a further universalizing of worship
at the temple. With God himself enthroned as universal King,

---

20. Zech 13:9b is widely viewed as "covenant renewal" language; cf. Hos
2:25 (Eng. 2:23); Jer 31:33; Zech 8:8.

21. I refer here to early Christianity. Peculiarities in these Hebrew texts encourage creative exegesis. For example, a literal translation of the Masoretic
Text of Zech 12:10 (where God is speaking) is, "And I will pour out upon the
house of David and upon the inhabitant [note the singular] of Jerusalem a
spirit of grace and supplication, and they will look to me, the one whom they
pierced, and they will mourn for him as one mourns for an only child...a
firstborn son." Similarly, 13:7–9, which begins with reference to the stricken
shepherd, concludes with an inclusio in the singular: "[God will] say, 'He is
my people,' and he will say, 'YHWH is my God'" (my translations).

God's messiah ruling with divine attributes, and the people exercising messianic virtues, all Gentiles will join Israel annually to celebrate the Feast of Booths in Jerusalem.[22] And in a radical democratization of the holy, normal temple pots will be as sacred as altar bowls, and every pot in Jerusalem and Judah (whether owned by Jew or Gentile) will be appropriate for use in sacrificial liturgies. In the midst of the foment of the postexilic period, when common Jews were afflicted by both their Gentile overlords and their own civic and priestly leaders, the prophet's vital hope is for the universal kingdom of God.

What, in the opinion of our author, is the role of prophecy in all of this? It is waning. It is "the dawn of apocalyptic."[23] "The diviners see lies; the dreamers tell false dreams" (10:2). Zechariah 13:2–6 describes prophecy in such negative terms that there can be no doubt that in the opinion of the author it is no longer a viable phenomenon. In a parody of Amos (7:14) through whom classical prophecy had been born, Zech 13:5 pronounces prophecy dead. Joel and Zech 9–14 offer opposite views on the future of Hebrew prophecy, which itself had waxed and waned with the Hebrew monarchy. For the former, prophecy will be universalized; for the latter it will become extinct. God will choose new means to express the prophetic spirit in the Second Temple period and beyond, among them passion for Torah, the vitality of the written prophetic canon, and the apocalyptic vision.

---

22. This is itself a further universalizing of Neh 8:13–18, where all the Jews who had returned from exile (not just the males as in Exod 34:23) celebrate the Feast of Booths. Cf. the flow of the nations to the temple mount in passages such as Mic 4:1–4 // Isa 2:2–4.

23. To use Paul Hanson's well-known phrase in *The Dawn of Apocalyptic* (Philadelphia: Fortress, 1975).

Isaiah 24–27

If the foment simmered in Zech 9–14, it boils over in the "Isaiah Apocalypse." Not since the flood has universal destruction appeared so imminent. The cosmic sea monster, representing chaos, has reared its head as at creation and must be defeated once more (Isa 27:1). It must have been a suffering righteous remnant indeed that penned this vision, which is a montage of various passages from the Prophets and the Psalms, recast and reapplied, and which contains a host of various genres. The issue of theodicy is evident: the humble righteous suffer at the hands of the arrogant wicked. Torah is transgressed (24:5) and the poor and the needy languish (25:4; 26:6): "I pine away, / I pine away. Woe is me! / For the treacherous deal treacherously, / the treacherous deal very treacherously" (24:16).

But within the din of chaos can be heard a strain of persistent faith from those who confidently "wait" on the Lord (25:9; 26:8). Most of the language is communal ("the righteous nation that keeps faith"; 26:2), but occasionally the lone voice of the righteous sufferer breaks forth:

> The confident mind You guard in safety,
> In safety because it trusts in You....
> At night I yearn for You with all my being,
> I seek You with all the spirit within me.
>
> (26:3, 9 NJPSV)

And songs of triumph can be heard in the distance (24:14–16a).

But it is a distant melody indeed. While the prophet is sure of God's eventual victory, he is not sure that every righteous sufferer will see it in his or her lifetime. Hence he envisions God's defeat of the ultimate enemy—death—using the metaphor of a universal banquet on the mountain of God (25:6–9).[24] With this theological insight, he becomes the first biblical writer to put forth a doctrine of the afterlife, the only other being the author of the Book of Daniel (12:1–3), an apocalyptic work from the late postexilic period. Specifically, our prophet's doctrine of the afterlife envisions a "single resurrection." The wicked will remain dead forever (Isa 26:14) but the righteous will be raised (26:19).[25] What unjust suffering must have produced this theological development. In fact, the author compares the suffering of his people to that of a pregnant woman who carries her baby to term, writhes and cries out in birth pangs, but brings forth only wind (26:16–18). If justice does not come in this world, it will come in the next.

So in the end, the Isaiah Apocalypse is hopeful; faith will persevere. Isaiah of Jerusalem had sung a love song about a vineyard, an allegory of God's relationship with God's people. God as the "beloved" plants a vineyard, God's "beloved" Judah. He chose a very fertile hill, dug it, cleared it of stones, planted choice vines, built a watchtower and a wine vat; but instead of the good fruit he expected, it yielded bad fruit. The result is that God removes the vineyard's hedge so that it is devoured, breaks down its wall so that it is trampled down, makes it a waste

---

24. Lit., "on this mountain." The author may have in mind Zion (or the cosmic mountain of the gods common in ancient Near Eastern mythology and referenced elsewhere in the Hebrew Bible) but if so, Zion is a symbol. One could refer to this loosely as a "messianic banquet," though the author does not use that terminology. Clearly it is a vision of the kingdom of God beyond this world; and elsewhere in the Hebrew Bible kingdom and messiah are intimately connected — you do not get one without the other. At any rate, with this poem the author has stepped from prophetic eschatology, which always expects the kingdom of God in this world, to apocalyptic eschatology.

25. Contrast Daniel's doctrine of a "double resurrection" in 12:1–3.

without pruning or hoeing, allows briers and thorns to grow up, and stops the rain upon it. But in a much later and much different setting, the Isaiah Apocalypse sings a new vineyard song, totally reversing his mentor's imagery.

> On that day:
> A pleasant vineyard, sing about it!
>   I, the LORD, am its keeper;
>   every moment I water it.
> I guard it night and day
>   so that no one can harm it;
>   I have no wrath (27:2–4a).

The final vision of the Isaiah Apocalypse (27:12–13) depicts the blast of a great trumpet with the result that all exiled and dispersed Jews come to worship God "on the holy mountain at Jerusalem." Whether he meant Mount Zion in Judah or the New Zion in the world to come is impossible to tell, nor do I think we are supposed to decide for one option or the other. But one fact bears final mention. The image of Jerusalem/Zion is vital in virtually all the postexilic prophets.

Conclusion

The texts we have examined have revealed that at least a significant portion of Second Temple Judaism sought to live out the vitality of Torah with prophetic passion, and vice versa: passion for the spiritual core of Torah produced a prophetic vitality equal to the First Temple period. Lessons learned from the preexilic experience of human nature and the painful experience of the exile led to an emphasis on God's enabling grace to bring about in the hearts of individuals the kingdom of God, symbolically centered at Zion, and universal in scope. Confession and forgiveness characterize a dynamic faith in God, intimate father and loving mother, who is met in authentic worship, including developing traditions of the Sabbath. The experience in faith of the intimacy of God produces messianic virtues, i.e., the daily living out of the ethics of the kingdom of God. Yet sin and evil remain real entities in this world which is, however, not the really real. There is a kingdom beyond, not disparaging but consummating God's rule in this world.

– T W O –

The Social Context
of Postexilic Judaism

– Jon L. Berquist –

Jerusalemite historians wrote accounts of Judah's monarchy, which had flourished for centuries before the Babylonian Empire conquered the political apparatus of the Judean state in the early sixth century B.C.E. The collapse of the monarchy, which never returned in any form remotely resembling its predecessor, stimulated numerous changes within the religion of YHWH. Jerusalemite historians wrote that they and their ancestors were exiled from Jerusalem in 587 B.C.E. and did not return until 539 and afterward. When they reentered the land of Judah, they found a very different situation politically and economically. In fewer than fifty years the world had changed, and the religion had to adapt to a new setting, a situation typically termed postexilic.

Scholars often refer to the time after the exile as the Second Temple period, indicating the time between Zerubbabel's establishment of a new Jerusalem temple (ca. 520 B.C.E.) and the Roman Empire's military destruction of that temple (ca. 70 C.E.), including Persian, Hellenistic, and Roman influences. As such, the postexilic period participates in a wide variety of political forms and economic situations. This wide variety, however, has its roots within the beginning years of the Second Temple, specifically the time of the Persian Empire (539–332 B.C.E.).[1]

Scholarship has greatly reassessed the significance of the Second Temple period for the understanding of the origins of Judaism.[2] The biblical account of exile and restoration is a theological interpretation that expresses the view of those Babylonian-born and Persian-born persons who moved to the Jerusalem area in 539 B.C.E. and afterward. They asserted a prior claim to the land by insisting that it be "returned" to them, and

---

1. The standard history of this era has been A. T. Olmstead, *History of the Persian Empire* (Chicago: University of Chicago Press, 1948). This has been largely supplanted by newer works, the best of which are Pierre Briant, *Histoire de l'Empire Perse: De Cyrus à Alexandre* (Paris: Fayard, 1996); Muhammad A. Dandamaev, *A Political History of the Achaemenid Empire* (Leiden: Brill, 1989); and Muhammad A. Dandamaev and Vladimir G. Lukonin, *The Culture and Social Institutions of Ancient Iran* (Cambridge: Cambridge University Press, 1989). Also of vital importance for scholars are John Boardman et al., eds., *The Cambridge Ancient History*, vol. 4: *Persia, Greece and the Western Mediterranean, c. 525 to 479 B.C.* (2d ed.; Cambridge: Cambridge University Press, 1988); Maria Brosius, *Women in Ancient Persia (559–331 B.C.E.)* (Oxford Classical Monographs; Oxford: Clarendon, 1996); W. D. Davies and Louis Finkelstein, eds., *The Cambridge History of Judaism*, vol. 1: *Introduction; the Persian Period* (Cambridge: Cambridge University Press, 1984); Lester L. Grabbe, *Judaism from Cyrus to Hadrian*, vol. 1: *The Persian and Greek Periods* (Minneapolis: Fortress, 1992); and Heleen Sancisi-Weerdenburg et al., eds., *Achaemenid History: Proceedings of the Achaemenid History Workshop*, 8 vols. (Leiden: Nederlands Instituut voor het Nabije Oosten, 1987–94).

2. Introductions to the period with a specific focus on biblical issues can be found in Gösta W. Ahlström, *The History of Ancient Palestine from the Paleolithic Period to Alexander's Conquest* (ed. Diana Edelman; JSOT-Sup 146; Sheffield: JSOT Press, 1993), 812–906; Jon L. Berquist, *Judaism in Persia's Shadow: A Social and Historical Approach* (Minneapolis: Fortress, 1995); Charles E. Carter, *The Emergence of Yehud in the Persian Period: A Social and Demographic Study* (JSOTSup 294; Sheffield: Sheffield Academic Press, 1999); and Norman K. Gottwald, *The Hebrew Bible: A Socio-Literary Introduction* (Philadelphia: Fortress, 1985), 409–39.

they portrayed their religious innovations as "restoring" a faith that others had abandoned or corrupted. This perspective remained unchallenged by most histories of Israel until the last decades of the twentieth century.

Now, an emerging consensus depicts Jerusalem as a site of conflict in the late sixth century and beyond as native inhabitants sought to continue traditional ways of life while new immigrants from the imperial core began a new life within Jerusalem. As part of the expansion of the Persian Empire, these immigrants built the colony Yehud as a new social, cultural, and political entity. They created for themselves a new society within the context of local contests and imperial intrusion.[3] Within this consensus, there remain controversial questions about how much continuity existed between this new social reality and the previous societies of Jerusalem, in particular regarding religious practices and a sense of identity.[4] What is becoming clear, however, is that Persian Yehud was a creative and innovative society with a major impact upon the development of the documents that became the Hebrew Bible and the religion that became known as Judaism.

This Persian period was one of the most energetic times for the Jewish religion. Change abounded in the context of local

---

3. For examples of this approach, see Samuel E. Balentine, *The Torah's Vision of Worship* (Overtures to Biblical Theology; Minneapolis: Fortress, 1999); Berquist, *Judaism in Persia's Shadow;* Philip R. Davies, *In Search of "Ancient Israel"* (JSOTSup 148; Sheffield: Sheffield Academic Press, 1992); and Paula McNutt, *Reconstructing the Society of Ancient Israel* (Library of Ancient Israel; Louisville: Westminster John Knox, 1999).

4. See, e.g., Davies, *In Search of "Ancient Israel";* Niels Peter Lemche, *The Israelites in History and Tradition* (Library of Ancient Israel; Louisville: Westminster John Knox, 1998); Thomas L. Thompson, *The Mythic Past: Biblical Archaeology and the Myth of Israel* (New York: Basic Books, 1999); and Keith Whitelam, *The Creation of Ancient Israel* (London: Routledge, 1996).

dissent, imperial interest, and social innovation. Many earlier studies concentrated on how disruptive this period was, but it was also a time of great vitality, as the religion adapted to a wide range of historical events and cultural situations. The religion developed many new forms and engendered a wide variety of new literary genres with which to express its faith and life. This vitality meant passion, especially the passion of persuasion. Different aspects of the faith empowered persons in ways never before imagined under the monarchic cult. At the same time, various adherents to the faith sought ways to convince each other that their increasingly divergent forms of the religion were valid or preferable; the resultant foment served only to increase the vitality and passion of religious life in the postexilic period.

Jerusalem in the Persian Period

The sixth century began with the Babylonian Empire firmly entrenched as the world's great superpower. Increasingly, Babylonian hegemony influenced the kingdom of Judah, a small yet still independent state. By 597 B.C.E., Babylonia had deported a large segment of Judah's elite from its main city of Jerusalem, including King Jehoiachin and many of the officials of state (2 Kgs 24). The empire was content for a time to control Judah through less direct political means, but in 587 B.C.E. Babylonia was militarily victorious over Jerusalem after an eighteen-month siege (2 Kgs 25). This invading force took apart Jerusalem's walls and burned the city. They killed many of the remaining ruling class and deported many others into exile in the central regions of Babylonia. Despite the severity of the destruction, there were limits to Babylonian action against Judah. The empire disassembled Judah's institutions of political autonomy, but not Judean culture.[5] The sixth century represented not a total exile of Judean society but its bifurcation. One group remained in the traditional Judean countryside, bereft of ethnic leadership and under imperial control. The other, smaller group of former elites began a very different pattern of life in central Mesopotamia.[6]

Within the former nation-state of Judah, life may have continued with remarkable similarity. The biblical text indicates that Babylonia "carried away all Jerusalem" (2 Kgs 24:14a NRSV), but the passage immediately corrects this impression: "no one remained, except the poorest people of the land" (24:14b NRSV; cf. 25:12). The Babylonian Empire replaced an entrenched elite (the Davidic monarch and others) who had ruled the area for centuries. The imperial government's concerns were the maintenance of a peaceful community that would produce taxes to support their elite, and thus their goals of government were not very different from the former monarchy. Scholars have often made the argument of ethnicity, that the Judean monarchs were preferable because they had ethnic ties to the rural population. However, the social differences between the rulers and the ruled may have overwhelmed any perception of affinity. The Babylonian Empire may have fostered a greater sense of alienation than did the Judean monarchy, but the economic and social separation did not greatly change.

Instead, the greater change came for the Judean rulers who

---

5. For further discussion, see Berquist, *Judaism in Persia's Shadow*, 3–19. This perspective is in contrast to an emphasis on the complete removal of Judean culture, as present in earlier scholarship's historiography. See, e.g., John Bright, *A History of Israel* (3d ed.; Philadelphia: Westminster, 1981), 331.

6. See Daniel L. Smith, *The Religion of the Landless: The Social Context of the Babylonian Exile* (Bloomington, Ind.: Meyer-Stone, 1989).

faced deportation into Mesopotamia. These exiles were the former elite from Judah's government, military, religion, and economy. They had experienced life as middle management and as high authorities in autonomous structures. The Babylonian Empire sought two results from its policy of deportation. First, they removed from Judah the class that could most easily foment rebellion, replacing them with persons who were more trusted by the imperial authorities. Second, the Babylonian Empire valued the exiles' contributions. These persons were trained in Judean governmental service; and the expanding Babylonian Empire required additional bureaucrats, in larger numbers than their own training would produce.

Ezekiel depicts exile as a rural affair, and certainly many of the exiles were employed as manual farm labor or as agricultural supervisors and experts.[7] On the other hand, Deutero-Isaiah concentrates on the religious practices of the exiles and their Babylonian captors. The prophet's focus on Babylonian cult, especially idolatry, locates the writing in proximity to a temple. This matches the location of the deported king, who lived in the imperial palace (2 Kgs 25:11, 27–30). These exiles were probably involved in the chief business of the capital: governmental service.[8] The empire's need for bureaucracy grew at such a rate that it required the addition of new government servants to operate the expanding holdings of the empire. The elite from Judah had previously collected taxes, prepared censuses, performed accounting, created scribal records, translated documents, negotiated trade, and performed religious practices. All of these functions were just as necessary within the empire

---

7. Ezekiel's inaugural vision was located near the irrigation canal Chebar (Ezek 1:1).

8. See Dandamaev, *Political History of the Achaemenid Empire*, 61.

as they were within the former small monarchy.[9] The Babylonian Empire gathered these former elite in the city of Babylon
to work in these same capacities, albeit under strict supervision.

Judeans during the Babylonian period lived in separate groups,
in at least three distinct social groups. A rural contingent in
Babylonia served the empire through their food production.
Within the capital of Babylon, many Jews were employed within
the palace and the temple, where they served the government
in a variety of ways. Most Judeans still lived in the same countryside, however, and conducted their lives in much the same
way as before, despite the presence of a ruling power that was
ethnically different and nationally foreign. This divergence of
Judeans began in 597 B.C.E., was furthered by the conquest of

---

9. A chief concern in the acquisition and development of bureaucrats is
literacy. Scribes and accountants needed writing and counting skills. Furthermore, the regulation and promotion of intra-imperial commerce required
proficiency in multiple languages, which would have been an extremely
valuable skill. Also, as imperial size increased, it is likely that the imperial
bureaucracy grew more reliant upon sending messages rather than traveling
personally to locations. If so, the need for written communication, and thus
for more scribes to write and read, would have grown at perhaps exponential
rates. As long as overall literacy rates within the population were low, the
value of retaining and retraining literate foreigners would have been high.
For related studies of literacy in the ancient world, see Alan K. Bowman
and Greg Woolf, eds., *Literacy and Power in the Ancient World* (Cambridge:
Cambridge University Press, 1994); Richard Lee Enos, ed., *Oral and Written
Communication: Historical Approaches* (Written Communication Annual 4;
Newbury Park, Calif.: Sage, 1990); Jack Goody, *The Logic of Writing and the
Organization of Society* (Studies in Literacy, Family, Culture, and the State;
Cambridge: Cambridge University Press, 1986); William V. Harris, *Ancient
Literacy* (Cambridge: Harvard University Press, 1989); Dan Lacy, *From Grunts
to Gigabytes: Communications and Society* (Urbana: University of Illinois Press,
1996), 9–20; Henri-Jean Martin, *The History and Power of Writing* (trans.
Lydia G. Cochrane; Chicago: University of Chicago Press, 1994), 1–115;
and Wayne M. Senner, ed., *The Origins of Writing* (Lincoln: University of
Nebraska Press, 1989).

Jerusalem itself in 587 B.C.E., and continued throughout the rule of the Babylonian Empire. Soon, the inhabitants of the traditional land and of Babylonia were second generation, with no direct experience of unity under the previous Judean monarchy. This new generation had experienced only their own situations and probably had little contact with or affinity for members of the other groups.

This was the situation in 539 B.C.E., when the Persian Empire conquered the Babylonians and began their own hegemony over the former empire's sphere of influence and beyond. As early as 555 B.C.E., the ruling family of Persia had revolted against the Median Empire, to the north of the Babylonians. Persia and Babylonia formed a successful alliance against Media, but by 547 B.C.E. Persia had completely defeated Media and surrounded the Babylonian Empire. Emperor Nabonidus led Babylonia in a strategic retreat into Arabia, but by 539 B.C.E., the Babylonian army fell to Cyrus and his fledgling Persian Empire. Cyrus not only commanded the relatively small holdings that were historically Persian, but also the combined expanse of the Babylonian and Median empires. This vast area included Judah, which experienced a change in its administration. Whereas Babylonia had pursued a policy of removing local elites, the Persian Empire used such populations as liaisons to their colonial periphery. In 539 B.C.E., Cyrus issued a decree allowing all imperial residents of Judean ancestry to emigrate to Jerusalem, a city seen (in most cases) only by their grandparents.

The Beginning of Persia's Influence

Cyrus's edict at the beginning of his reign in 539 B.C.E. only allowed emigration, but the Persian Empire did nothing to

encourage it. Instead, the Persian Empire administered former Judah as a small colony, which the empire called Yehud.
Throughout the reign of Cyrus and his successor, Cambyses
(530–522 B.C.E.), any emigration was slow for a population influx, as reflected in Ezra and Nehemiah's small numbers. The
reasons for this slowness are straightforward. The Jews in Babylonia had grown up there; it was the only life that they had
known. In Babylonia they had their families, their homes, their
work; in Jerusalem were none of those things. Furthermore,
Babylonia was the core of the empire, the center of civilization,
whereas Jerusalem was underpopulated, impoverished, and distant. Though some people moved from Babylonia to Jerusalem,
the social and economic conditions at the time hardly made it
attractive for large numbers to move.[10] Movement was slow and
gradual, and the emigrants found a culture quite unlike what
they had experienced before.

The Babylonian Empire's intrusion into Jerusalem's politics
had created at least two separate Jewish cultures: those who
had remained in Judah and those who were deported to Babylonia. With each successive wave of immigration into Yehud, the
culture there underwent a transformation as it struggled to integrate these separate cultures. Because immigration stretched
over decades, this was a protracted process. Perhaps the most
important characteristic of this slow immigration was that very
little changed. Even though Yehud was not well populated, the

---

10. One might surmise that those who did move were the more marginal
members of Babylonian Jewish life, those with the least to lose from a move.
Though there is no evidence to prove this possibility, it would follow the pattern by emigrants in most societies. See Berquist, *Judaism in Persia's Shadow*,
3–19; cf. Grabbe, *Judaism from Cyrus to Hadrian*, 1:20–25; and Smith, *Religion
of the Landless*, 179–200.

newcomers were a small proportion of the population. During the reigns of Cyrus and Cambyses, the immigrants included few wealthy or powerful persons, and so their arrival in the Jerusalem area did not increase the economic resources or greatly affect the power structures of the society. From 539 to 520 B.C.E., most life in Yehud remained unchanged: most of the population was still a peasant class that changed only the nation to whom taxes were paid.[11] Cyrus's administrative patterns retained Babylonian bureaucrats in many of the colonies, and so Jerusalem still operated within the same structures of imperial economic domination.[12]

Within this context of relative stability under two imperial administrations, Jerusalem's religion also remained stable. The Babylonian conquest in 587 B.C.E. destroyed the temple, and scholars have often interpreted that building's devastation as signaling the end to independent religious practice.[13] In reality, sacrifices continued in Jerusalem throughout the period of the so-called exile. Those who remained in the Jerusalem area used the site where the temple had once stood, erecting some sort of temporary, non-enclosed altar that sufficed for sacrificial worship.[14] This practice probably mirrored the long-standing reality in Judah's outlying areas, where communities worshiped YHWH (and other deities) on the high places of the countryside.[15] In fact, the rural forms of religion may have flourished

---

11. Eric R. Wolf, *Peasants* (Foundations of Modern Anthropology; Englewood Cliffs, N.J.: Prentice-Hall, 1966).

12. Berquist, *Judaism in Persia's Shadow*, 23–44.

13. Ibid., 17–18.

14. Smith, *Religion of the Landless*, 34–35.

15. Jacques Berlinerblau, *The Vow and the "Popular Religious Groups" of Ancient Israel: A Philological and Sociological Inquiry* (JSOTSup 210; Sheffield: Sheffield Academic Press, 1996).

with the removal of the centralizing influences from an official, state-supported Jerusalem temple.

These practices during the Babylonian administration of Jerusalem changed little once the dominance passed to Persia. Just as Babylonia allowed local worship to continue using its old forms, so did Persia, even from the start of Cyrus's reign. Former residents of Babylonia who had recently moved to Jerusalem were accustomed to any form of Jewish religion beyond local worship, since temple-based sacrifice did not exist in Babylonia. Perhaps some of these immigrants had shifted their own beliefs to some sort of syncretism, and they persisted in a combination of Jewish and Babylonian practices, alongside the many other forms of local (and perhaps partly syncretized) religion in exilic Judah.[16] Without a centralizing temple, many forms of worship grew, with little distinction and few boundaries between them.

Many scholars argue that the original impetus for Jewish emigration from Babylonia to Jerusalem after Cyrus's edict was a strong desire to build a temple and to return to monarchic forms of worship.[17] This hypothesis has withstood numerous challenges and has enjoyed a great influence upon subsequent scholarship, and yet it struggles to explain the evidence at hand.[18] In reality, the situation contraindicates a desire to build a Jerusalem temple.[19] From 587 B.C.E. onward, there is no evidence that the Babylonians blocked the construction of the Jerusalem temple

---

16. Berquist, *Judaism in Persia's Shadow,* 15–17.

17. See, e.g., Gerhard von Rad, *Old Testament Theology* (trans. D. M. G. Stalker; New York: Harper & Row, 1962–65), 2:281; and Bright, *History of Israel,* 360–68.

18. A judicious appraisal can be found in Ahlström, *History of Palestine,* 841–42.

19. Of course, a population's desire remains impossible to prove. Instead, the analyst can focus on what a society did with its available resources and

or of any other public building in Jerusalem. Babylonian imperial policy often allowed conquered areas to build facilities, as
long as the central administration maintained control and taxes
were paid on schedule. Had the residents of the Jerusalem area
in the middle of the sixth century wanted to build a temple,
there was no known impediment. They chose not to construct
one.[20] Certainly, by 539 B.C.E., the Persian imperial conquest removed any fears about temple construction that had arisen over
the previous five decades; the Persian Empire soon undertook a
variety of construction projects throughout its borders. Furthermore, there was now a gradual influx of new inhabitants, yet
they did not initiate any known temple construction projects
for seventeen years. Not only was construction expensive, but
it would have allowed Persia to exercise further influence in
the Jerusalem area. The residents of Jerusalem continued worship practices that were not temple based, even though they
included at least some sacrificial elements.

On the other hand, Cyrus wanted to develop a strong periphery.[21] His own direct military campaigns were conducted
toward the empire's east, and included conquest and annexation
in the direction of India. His approach toward the management
of the western colonies focused strictly on encouraging local
government, possibly through providing them with some additional leadership. The Book of Ezra lists some of the Babylonian
Jewish notables who moved to Jerusalem at this time.[22] Accord-

---

on the paths that were unblocked (as far as the historical distance allows one
to see) but unchosen.

20. Berquist, *Judaism in Persia's Shadow*, 147–59.

21. Ibid., 24–26; and Dandamaev, *Political History*, 54, 64.

22. Of course, Ezra also narrates Samaritan opposition to the construction plans (Ezra 4), and many scholars have interpreted a strong Jewish
desire to build a temple followed by a strong opposition that shuts down the

ing to Ezra 2:64–65, a total of 49,897 persons arrived with the
Persian governor Sheshbazzar in Jerusalem as a result of Cyrus's
ordered emigration.[23] However, Ezra's historiography should be
considered suspect at best. The books of Ezra and Nehemiah
contain records from the middle of the fifth century as well as
recollections from the late sixth century; the memories of the
earlier time of Cyrus seem to be much less accurate. Ezra's assertion of nearly fifty thousand emigrants may be correct for the
number who had moved by the completion of the temple construction, but the thought of one large caravan at a single point
in history cannot be accurate.[24] Still, these emigrants changed
the direction of Judean cultural development. They provided a
cultural influence that had not been felt in the Jerusalem area
previously, since they were much more aware of the world at
large than were most of the rural natives. This group of immigrants grew slowly in influence throughout the time of Persia's
first two emperors, until its numbers were significant by the end
of this period.

Cambyses' reign included substantial military activity in the
west. Whereas Cyrus attacked India, Cambyses turned to Egypt
and conducted a major military campaign there. This brought a
large military force into this part of the empire for the first time

---

construction project for over a decade and a half. Ezra's account, however,
contradicts itself, first proposing that Emperor Artaxerxes stopped the construction that Darius later restarted, even though Artaxerxes reigned after
Darius (Ezra 4–5), and then asserting that the construction never actually
stopped (Ezra 5:16). Overall, the historiography of Ezra appears to argue ten-
dentiously to defend the nonconstruction of the temple before Darius. Cf.
H. G. M. Williamson, *Ezra and Nehemiah* (Old Testament Guides; Sheffield:
JSOT Press, 1987), 51–54.

23. A mostly parallel list in Neh 7:66–67 indicates a slightly larger
number: 49,942 persons.

24. Grabbe, *Judaism from Cyrus to Hadrian*, 1:122–23.

in Persian rule. The army never reached Jerusalem, however. Cambyses' forces wintered along the Mediterranean coast far to the north, and then in spring launched a surprise attack against Egypt by boat. Egypt expected the Persian army to take a long march through Palestine and the Sinai, arriving in Egypt from its east only after its energy had been depleted through travel. Instead, the Persians arrived from the unexpected and undefended north, months earlier than they would have otherwise been able to press the attack. Persia quickly conquered Egypt, and Cambyses ruled there for a few years with an iron hand, imposing Persian customs and violating Egyptian sensitivities. Unsurprisingly, Egypt revolted shortly after the departure of the Persian army.[25] No one, however, had counted on Cambyses' sudden death on the way back from the Egyptian occupation.[26] While still in the Mediterranean area, the Persian army was without military or political command. It returned to Mesopotamia frag-

25. Dandamaev, *Political History*, 70–82.

26. History recounts a number of stories about Cambyses' death. It may have been accidental, the suicide of a deranged and weak leader, or the treacherous assassination of an incumbent emperor by dissident forces within the government's highest echelons. Obviously, it was a story much loved by the ancients, who represented it with such grand folkloric motifs that historical reality has become hopelessly obscured. Whatever the cause(s) of Cambyses' death, it threw the imperial government into sharp but short-lived distress. See Ahlström, *History of Ancient Palestine*, 817–20; Berquist, *Judaism in Persia's Shadow*, 45–50; Dandamaev, *Political History*, 70–102; Grabbe, *Judaism from Cyrus to Hadrian*, 1:124; Ephraim Stern, "The Persian Empire and the Political and Social History of Palestine in the Persian Period," in *The Cambridge History of Judaism*, vol. 1: *Introduction; the Persian Period* (ed. W. D. Davies and Louis Finkelstein; Cambridge: Cambridge University Press, 1984), 70–71; and T. Cuyler Young Jr., "The Early History of the Medes and the Persians and the Achaemenid Empire to the Death of Cambyses," in *The Cambridge Ancient History*, vol. 4: *Persia, Greece and the Western Mediterranean, c. 525 to 479 B.C.* (ed. John Boardman et al.; 2d ed.; Cambridge: Cambridge University Press, 1988), 47–52.

mented, and it was not until 522 B.C.E. that the next emperor was firmly in place.

The empire ignored Yehud, allowing it to develop its own identity and its own goals. Cambyses had continued Cyrus's policies, giving Yehud significant freedom in internal affairs. Immigration, reorganization, and construction were all possible, but Yehud chose not to construct a temple. Despite imperial permission for construction, the residents continued their old religion, in whatever new forms imported by the immigrants, including the sacrificial worship of YHWH among the ruins of the monarchic temple. They resisted centralization.[27]

Cambyses' reign produced a time of continued calm and little change in Yehud. The passing army did not come close enough to Jerusalem. Instead, the chief factor was the slow immigration, which did not produce any noticeable cultural changes during this time. For the first seventeen years of the postexilic period, there was little difference from the time of the exile itself. The change of Persian imperial dynasties in 522 B.C.E., however, changed that situation forever.

Vitality: Imperial Intervention

The reign of Darius (522–486 B.C.E.) brought a highly interventionist style to Yehudite society, especially in the early years.[28] Darius was a distant member of the Achaemenid family, and so his accession to the imperial throne after Cambyses' death

---

27. Berquist, *Judaism in Persia's Shadow*, 25–26, 51–86; and John Manuel Cook, "The Rise of the Achaemenids and Establishment of Their Empire," in *The Cambridge History of Iran*, vol. 2: *The Median and Achaemenian Periods* (ed. Ilya Gershevitch; Cambridge: Cambridge University Press, 1985), 200–291.

28. Dandamaev, *Political History*, 103–87.

was, at least in some respects, an usurpation. Certainly, the circumstances surrounding Darius's rise to power from outside the imperial core were questionable; there were other contenders to the throne, and Darius became emperor after no little struggle. Histories of the period usually concentrate on the political intrigue around Darius's accession, but of greater importance were the changes in administrative style that he brought to the empire.

Cyrus and Cambyses had managed the empire in fluctuation between two modes of rule: conquest and maintenance. Cyrus, for example, had conquered territories to the east and had left the west rather neglected; Cambyses did much the opposite. Where the armies were, there was strict imperial control, and the conquest of new territories (with resultant looting) fed the imperial coffers. In the rest of the empire, taxes were relatively low and the local areas enjoyed a fairly high degree of autonomy under minimal administrative structures. Within the first few years of his reign, Darius changed all of that. His own administrative structures were much more highly involved in the micromanagement of the colonies and the periphery. In economic terms, the empire's income derived from maximizing economic production in the colonies and collecting moneys from those areas to fund imperial projects. The army did not conquer as much, at least at the start of Darius's reign. Expansion of the empire was more economic and political than military and geographic.[29]

Darius's political apparatus for this economic intensification was a satrapy system. He divided the empire into twenty satra-

---

29. Berquist, *Judaism in Persia's Shadow,* 53–65; and Olmstead, *History of the Persian Empire,* 119–33.

pies, each with its own government and with separate economic goals for each. Through a newly created formalized bureaucratic structure, Darius controlled production and trade and thus was far more influential in the lives of the imperial subjects.

Egypt provides the clearest example.[30] Cyrus ignored Egypt; Cambyses conquered it, but did not put into place any lasting administrative structures that would have enabled the maintenance of Egypt as a functioning part of the Persian Empire once the army left. Darius used the military to recapture Egypt, but he used much more than the army. Under his command, the Persian Empire used propaganda, combined with funding for construction projects and the support of partial local autonomy in religious and regional affairs, and this policy won the allegiance of Egypt's priestly school at Sais.[31] Part of the propaganda campaign involved advance announcement of the army's approach, including marching the army very slowly and deliberately through the intervening countryside. By the time the army reached Egypt, the Egyptians knew how huge that army was, and they decided to capitulate rather than fight. As a result, Darius took Egypt without military losses, and Persia developed in Egypt a native ruling class with historic ties and loyalty to

---

30. Edda Bresciani, "Egypt and the Persian Empire," in *The Greeks and the Persians from the Sixth to the Fourth Centuries* (ed. Herrmann Bengtson; trans. Phyllis Johnson; New York: Delacorte, 1968), 333–53; Torben Holm-Rasmussen, "Collaboration in Early Achaemenid Egypt: A New Approach," in *Studies in Ancient History and Numismatics Presented to Rudi Thomsen* (Copenhagen: Aarhus University Press, 1988), 29–38; Heleen Sancisi-Weerdenburg and Amélie Kuhrt, eds., *Achaemenid History*, vol. 6: *Asia Minor and Egypt: Old Cultures in a New Empire; Proceedings of the Groningen 1988 Achaemenid History Workshop* (Leiden: Nederlands Instituut voor het Nabije Oosten, 1991).

31. Cf. Joseph Blenkinsopp, "The Mission of Udjahorresnet and Those of Ezra and Nehemiah," *JBL* 106 (1987): 409–21.

the Persian emperor.[32] Darius not only gained Egypt as a colony, but was able to keep it as a productive and tax-paying part of the empire for decades to come with relatively little additional investment of military resources. Though this strategy did not expand the imperial borders as quickly or visibly as military conquest, it produced more revenue with less expenditure and with more secure borders over a much longer period of time.

Under Darius's reign, the Persian Empire undertook the same policies toward the much smaller province of Yehud. Even though the imperial army was much larger than anything little Yehud could muster, there was no need for military conquest or for that sort of violent control. Instead, Persia managed Yehud through rhetoric and investment, producing a ruling class with ties both to the land and to the Persian Empire, which put them in place and gave them such privilege to rule. Darius's administrative contacts with Yehud included the installation of local governors (such as Zerubbabel and his helpers) and rhetorical support for the Persian Empire (such as that offered by Haggai and Zechariah). Yehud was no victim of Persian aggression; it participated in an imperial system that was to its benefit as well.

Perhaps the greatest change in Persia's treatment of Yehud came at the time of the campaign against Egypt. Even though Darius created structures of much more intense management throughout the empire, small colonies such as Yehud still did not receive attention, except for short periods of time. Whereas Cambyses' attack on Egypt required surprise for military advantage, Darius's conquest necessitated the slow approach of a loud, visible army, which would maximize the psychological and political impact upon Egypt. The Persian army had to march

---

32. Berquist, *Judaism in Persia's Shadow*, 57–58.

through Palestine. While there is no evidence that the army went through Jerusalem, it went within miles of Yehud, and the near passage of such a massive army would have certainly had impact upon Yehud. In 519 B.C.E., the army was passing through, but the effects upon Yehud began even before that. The army would have taken possibly as long as two years to march from Persia through Mesopotamia to Egypt. For these two years, the approach of the army would have been known, and the fear of the army would have been felt. Beyond the psychological effects, there were also specific economic ramifications. Armies eat, and large armies require extensive logistical support to supply them with food. Planning for moving that much food into the army's path would have begun as soon as the army's path was decided and the army itself left Persia in 521 B.C.E. No army could have carried years of provision with them; they had to eat what they found along the way. The imperial administration gave Yehud two years to prepare for feeding the army. This preparation had several components: establishment of an administration to run the process, increased grain production, increased taxation of produce so that more grain would be available for the army, and storage of the grain until the army's arrival. Of course, storage requires facilities, and that means construction as well.[33]

Thus, the years immediately after 521 B.C.E. were a time of much activity in Yehud. Zerubbabel, the governor, prepared the people for the army's arrival, and he found support in the rhetorical discourse of contemporary prophets such as Haggai and Zechariah. Production and taxation both increased. Haggai described it this way: "You have sown much, and harvested little;

---

33. Jon L. Berquist, "Haggai," in *Mercer Commentary on the Bible* (ed. Watson E. Mills et al.; Macon, Ga.: Mercer University Press, 1995), 789–92.

you eat, but you never have enough; you drink, but you never have your fill; you clothe yourselves, but no one is warm; and you that earn wages earn wages to put them into a bag with holes" (Hag 1:6 NRSV). Such deliberate deprivation required motivation, and the administration's job was to provide that motivation. Part of the reason for doing this was negative: the fear of the army's wrath if they did not do it. But there was also a positive element: Yehud anticipated the wealth and the freedom that would result, politically and culturally.[34]

These factors came together in the powerful symbol and important reality of the Jerusalem temple. The Persian Empire paid for the construction of a temple in Jerusalem, and this temple would serve many functions. It would be the place of the worship of YHWH, led by a group of priests who would have the privilege of sacrificing once more in a large, formal sanctuary. The temple would be a base of operations for the political administration (cf. Neh 13); and it would also serve as storage for grain. Whereas Cyrus allowed temple construction, Darius paid for it and mandated it. In 521 B.C.E., the same year that preparations for feeding the army began, Yehud started temple construction in Jerusalem.

The temple provided economic impetus to the province, along with political identity and social cohesion. It was a symbol for the people, as well as for Persian rule and its beneficence. The temple's most enduring value, of course, was as a center for the religion of YHWH. In this second Jerusalem temple, the priestly worship of YHWH continued for almost six hundred years. Since the temple also focused the wealth and power of the people, the religion could make use of these advantages to grow for itself.

---

34. Olmstead, *History of the Persian Empire*, 135–41.

The construction of the Second Temple, even though rooted in short-term political concerns, had the most long-lasting religious ramifications. With a new temple and a new group of priests to care for it, the religion of Yhwh enjoyed a massive resurgence in its own vitality and thus in its ability to reflect and guide the faith of the people in and around Jerusalem. With this religious vitality at the center of Yehud's public life, the faith in Yhwh that was expressed in the ancient Torah experienced a renewed ability to transform life.[35]

The Persian army came near Jerusalem and left it unscathed, and the people rightly understood this as causally connected to the construction of the new temple. Shortly after the army returned to Persia, the people finished construction and dedicated the temple in 516 B.C.E. The temple's construction and the safety of Jerusalem had proved God's favor on the Jews gathered there, and the temple allowed new possibilities for the religious practices of the people. At the same time, there was no local monarchy to control the temple and its worship. The Persian Empire's influences were economic and political, but the empire left the religions of the provinces to develop with little input. Temple leadership was not limited by political concerns in most cases and so came a new freedom. Religion lacked the political connections that could restrict it or enforce it. In freedom and responsibility, there was vitality and growth.[36]

Another change during Darius's reign was that the empire funded each province's codification of existing laws. Rather than establish common law by imperial fiat, the Persians allowed each local group to make its own traditions official, at least within

---

35. Berquist, *Judaism in Persia's Shadow,* 147–59.
36. Ibid., 87–103.

some broad framework.[37] This triggered a new initiative to cod-
ify laws, and thus the priests of the Second Temple and other
Jews of the period became much more interested in texts, including the canonization of the official texts. Torah as a fixed,
written document may have first been promulgated at this time,
and the religious traditions stemming from this small temple
community have never experienced any source of more contin-
uous and significant vitality than that expressed and embodied
in their Scriptures. With temple and the book as centers for the
faith and for life, the Second Temple period was full of religious
vitality.

Passion: Laity, Diversity, and Persuasion

Under Darius's rule, the Persian Empire changed many of its
administrative structures, placing much more economic power
and political authority in the hands of local bureaucrats. This
allowed the rise of governors such as Zerubbabel, along with
the prophets and other figures who supported his rule. At the
same time, the Persian Empire funded construction projects such
as Jerusalem's Second Temple. In this context, the priests who
managed the temple gained power and ability to influence the
society gathered around this new, central symbol for public life.
With the rise of these priests in position and esteem, the religious
dimensions of life took on a renewed character, offering a vital
element to both individual and corporate existence. The temple
and its priests provided a focus for vitality within the community
of Yehud.

---

37. Dandamaev and Lukonin, *Culture and Social Institutions of Ancient Iran*,
116–21.

Darius's reign lasted three and a half decades, during which
Yehud enjoyed long-term stability that allowed priestly vitality
to flourish. Imperial political intervention was low, and the Persian army remained absent from the southeastern Mediterranean
during the latter half of Darius's imperium, since the army was
busily pressing a series of failing attacks against Greece. Still,
the political system in Yehud stayed in place. Egypt remained
a loyal colony within the Persian Empire, and so Yehud was a
trade corridor instead of an endangered border colony. In Yehud,
the empire appointed local leaders (including priests) to collect
taxes. Both taxes and threats of military loss were low enough
to encourage slow economic growth, improving the lot of most
inhabitants of the city of Jerusalem and perhaps some of the
surrounding peasants as well. A large portion of the collected
taxes remained in Yehud to provide income for the rulers and
the priests and to maintain the operation of the temple, including its sacrificial system. This balanced political situation, along
with the absence of the Persian army from the region, allowed
a stable time for the priesthood to renew its energy and to re-
assert its authority in realms of faith, morality, and other aspects
of common life.[38]

Upon Darius's death in 486 B.C.E., Xerxes assumed the Persian throne. Darius had groomed his son Xerxes for this post for
decades, and Xerxes mostly continued the policies set by his father in administering the empire. Xerxes quickly led the army in
marches against most of the furthest outlying colonies, including a campaign against Egypt in 485–484 B.C.E. that brought the

---

38. Jon L. Berquist, "Malachi," in *Mercer Commentary on the Bible* (ed.
Watson E. Mills et al.; Macon, Ga.: Mercer University Press, 1995), 799–802;
idem, "The Social Setting of Malachi," *Biblical Theology Bulletin* 19 (1989):
121–26.

army through the area around Yehud.[39] But the army was not at battle; there were only minor skirmishes to be settled in some areas, none of which seem to have affected Yehud at all. Instead, the army's presence merely served to show the might of the empire and to remind the colonies that opposition to Xerxes would be as fruitless as opposition to Darius had been. Certainly, Yehud showed no signs of revolt or dissension throughout Xerxes' reign, and most other colonies also remained loyal to the empire.

With control of the borders firmly in place, Xerxes turned attention to the one area that his father had been unable to conquer: Greece. By 480 B.C.E., Persia was entrenched in a war of attrition against Greece that produced a few short-term gains but no long-term victories. By the end of his reign, the Delian League was well established in Greece and even in westernmost Asia.[40] In many ways, Xerxes' persistent losses against Greece sealed the fate of the Persian Empire, resulting in its eventual destruction more than a century later.

Within the time of Xerxes' reign itself, however, there was no obvious sign that Persian military or political might was waning. But the imperial government faced a problem on another front. In the ancient world, most battles were funded from the tribute income received at the end of a victorious war.[41] Xerxes never actually lost the war against Greece, but he did not win it, either. This stalemate proved to be expensive, and the war never became a source of income. Having proved incapable of locat-

---

39. Olmstead, *History of the Persian Empire*, 234–35. Cf. Ezra 4:4–6.

40. See P. J. Rhodes, "The Delian League to 449 B.C.," in *The Cambridge Ancient History*, vol. 5: *The Fifth Century* B.C. (ed. D. M. Lewis et al.; 2d ed.; Cambridge: Cambridge University Press, 1986), 34–61.

41. Likewise, many soldiers were paid with booty, with slaves taken from captured people, or with land seized from the vanquished. A losing army, on the other hand, would have lost everything.

ing new funding outside the imperial borders, Xerxes turned to the only remaining option: he increased income from internal sources. In other words, he raised tax rates sharply throughout the empire, changing the economies of the colonies.[42]

Xerxes brought one other significant change to the government of the imperial bureaucracy. Darius's policy was to find local rulers or administrators with ethnic ties to a region who could work for the Persian Empire and its goals (Zerubbabel had been one of these locally connected rulers). This meant that much of Darius's governmental middle-management had been ethnically non-Persian. Xerxes reversed this policy and placed Persian administrators in most key areas throughout the empire. This seems to be a part of an antiprovincial attitude on Xerxes' part; resources were shifted to the imperial core at the expense of the peripheries.[43]

Yehud suffered economically under the combination of these two trends: the increase in taxes charged to the colonies and the shift of political and economic resources to ethnic Persians at the imperial core. The tax increases brought economic stagnation to Yehud. Local temples and religious practices were left without income from collected taxes, since the funds available went to core Persian functions instead. This left the Jerusalem temple without any guaranteed source of funds.[44]

---

42. Berquist, *Judaism in Persia's Shadow,* 87–91.

43. Ibid., 91–101.

44. Olmstead (*History of the Persian Empire,* 235–37) argues that Xerxes physically destroyed temple sites in Babylonia (and other areas of the Persian Empire). Matthew W. Stolper ("The Governor of Babylon and Across-the-River in 486 B.C.," *Journal of Near Eastern Studies* 48 [1989]: 296) understands the temple sites to exhibit dilapidation during Xerxes' time, rather than outright destruction. This latter position is consonant with a decrease in imperial funding for provincial temple sites throughout the empire, though it does not prove it.

With a shortfall of funding, the temple priests had few options, all of them grim. By the beginning of Xerxes' rule in 486 B.C.E., these priestly families had experienced three and a half decades of vitality, which was in part due to the imperial income that allowed the temple's programs to expand. One solution to this financial crisis was to cut costs and curtail programs; the other was to find new sources of funds that did not depend upon imperial largesse. As one might expect, both solutions had their proponents, and both were probably enacted to varying degrees. Certainly, public expectation for the temple declined over time; when Ezra and Nehemiah arrived in the latter half of the fifth century, they experienced a situation far different from Zerubbabel's period of expansion.

On the other hand, the Jerusalem temple did not stop functioning during Xerxes' reign. Not all programs were curtailed due to the lack of funds. Certainly, the other option was also operative; other resources were found to finance some temple activities. The priests had no income aside from the temple, and there would be no additional funding from the empire to support politicians or priests. Therefore, the new source of temple support was the laity. When Persia no longer funded the temple, at least some of the loss was compensated by the willingness of Jerusalem's inhabitants to support their religion out of their own free will. This was not taxation, since Xerxes' imperial policy did not allow local entities to impose their own taxes. In fact, Xerxes continued and increased the taxes levied by his predecessor; the only difference was that the temple did not receive any of these increased taxes. Temple priests succeeded in convincing laity to give money and goods to the temple over and above what they owed the Persian administration.

The Prophet Malachi represents the interplay of these responses to the decreased financial status of the Jerusalem temple. Malachi derides priests who let the condition of the temple sacrifices suffer. Some of the priests were bringing into the temple whatever animals they could find, at the lowest prices, even blind animals forbidden by the Priestly Code (Mal 1:7–8). The prophet calls the priests to obey their own laws and to teach the instructions that they know to be true (2:6). Malachi thus opposes the priestly solution of decreasing sacrificial quality.

But at the same time, Malachi also has words against the laity who do not support the temple. He condemns those who find it wearying to serve God and who cheat by bringing lesser animals from their own flocks (1:13–14). The prophetic condemnation attacks both the priest who conducts the sacrifice and the layperson who brings the deficient animal to the temple in the first place. Both should hold themselves to a loftier goal — that of proper temple worship — and such worship is possible only with the cooperation of priests and laity together. Malachi calls the inhabitants of Yehud to bring God both tithes and offerings (3:8), juxtaposing these two words for the only time in the Hebrew Bible. It may well be that the first of these words refers to taxes, which would still be collected within the temple itself, and the second refers to freewill offerings, which Malachi argues that the laity should bring to support the religious aspects of the temple. Even if the etymology is more obscure than that, Malachi clearly expected all of Yehud's inhabitants to support the temple activity financially and to do so at a level that allows a high level of sacrificial quality according to the regulations of the Torah.[45]

At the same time, the temple's increased reliance on the laity

---

45. See Berquist, "Social Setting of Malachi"; and idem, "Malachi."

compromised the power of the priesthood. No longer could the priests do as they chose without lay support from within their own society. Priestly accountability shifted away from the hierarchy in two directions: Torah and people. Priests were increasingly involved in accountability to their own traditions as embodied in the Torah, and the ancient canon became an ever more vibrant source of authority for their actions, calling them to a high standard of behavior. The Torah was justification for all of their actions, and their obedience to the Torah was a sign of God's blessing. No longer could the priests do anything they chose to do without explanation.[46] They were seen at least as partners if not as servants of the worshipers, who through their own expenditures could shape the direction of the temple's work. Thus, priestly religion became persuasive, arguing for its own validity and necessity in an increasingly pluralistic religious setting.

As the priests lost some of their ability to enforce social norms, some of that authority went to the Torah and some to the people. In other words, the people gained in their ability to choose for themselves modes of responsiveness to the Torah. Following the directions of the priests was one way, and it remained the dominant means of obedience to the Torah throughout the Second Temple period. The priesthood, however, no longer asserted the only correct way to follow God through the Torah. Other interpretations arose, as various groups chose different means of living Torah within their own living situations. The priesthood

---

46. This may be very closely connected to the canonization of the Torah, and especially to its promulgation as official law by Darius. With the Priestly legislation of the Torah published for all to read, the priests were justifying themselves to the laity and were allowing the laity to act as critics of whether the priests were following their own rules. See Berquist, *Judaism in Persia's Shadow*, 51–86, 131–46; and Grabbe, *Judaism from Cyrus to Hadrian*, 1:124–26.

did not have the economic leverage, the undisputed moral authority, or the political connections to enforce a monolithic religion in Yehud. The result was a pluralism that flourished throughout the postexilic period, with some of its deepest roots planted during Xerxes' reign.

The modern interpreter understands pluralism to be affected by current situations, but ancient Yehud's pluralism was perhaps a much more limited affair. Malachi points to a time of greatly enhanced lay involvement in the worship of YHWH, in no small part as a result of greater public access to the text of the Torah. The vitality of the priesthood under Darius allowed the construction and dominance of the temple form of worship; Xerxes' lack of support triggered lay involvement that expressed a passion for the faith. As more and more people knew the Torah and made their own commitments about their own responses to it, their passion for religion grew. Of course, it did not all grow in the same direction, and so there was pluralism, but at the root of this variety was passion. The Second Temple period created an environment where more and more people found an excitement in their faith, which caused them to become fervent supporters of their own particular responses to the Torah. This passion proved the driving force for the expansion and diversity of faith in YHWH throughout the postexilic era.

Foment: Imperial Abandonment

Xerxes' reign was a time when the Persian Empire began to pull back to the imperial core. Persia lost its wars against Greece, and Egypt's revolt left Yehud as one of the few Persian colonies on the Mediterranean, Persia's far western border. Fewer resources were available to the outlying areas, and Yehud's inhabitants discovered that their own passion for faith pushed for the perseverance of Torah religion, in a growing number of forms. What the people lacked in economic power through the first half of the fifth century was more than compensated by their excitement and their commitment. During the century's second half, new emperors worried more about the western periphery. At times, such as during the governorships of Ezra and Nehemiah, Persia tried to strengthen Yehud as a resource to protect the core against enemies such as Egypt and Greece.[47] But over the span of decades, Yehud felt the abandonment of an increasingly absent empire, and the more influential factor was Greece's growing economic might.

Perhaps at this time more than at any since Babylonia's incursions, Yehud experienced life on the periphery. Persia still maintained firm control on the inner workings of Jerusalem society, but there was no interest in helping Jerusalem to be more connected to the cultural centers of the empire. Persia exercised great economic influence, especially through the variation in rates of taxation, but Persia was no longer the only economic influence. The same case held in military matters; Persia was still the largest army in the world, but it was spread out over such a large geographic area that it rarely affected Yehudite life. On the other hand, there were other Mediterranean powers, such as Egypt and Greece, that may well have proved more of a regular threat to the physical safety of Jerusalem.[48]

Yehud's peripheral status showed in its politics. At times, there are records of strong governors, such as Ezra and Nehemiah.

---

47. See Kenneth G. Hoglund, *Achaemenid Imperial Administration in Syria-Palestine and the Missions of Ezra and Nehemiah* (SBLDS 125; Atlanta: Scholars Press, 1992).

48. Berquist, *Judaism in Persia's Shadow,* 105–27.

Both of them seem to have been career bureaucrats in the Persian administrative structure. Nehemiah claims to have seen service in the imperial court itself; Ezra's scribal credentials are more vague. The presence of figures such as these shows that at times Persia still desired to invest resources in Yehud to keep it as a stable part of the empire. Perhaps Persia wanted a strengthened and fortified Yehud to help defend against enemies such as the Greek-Phoenician alliance in 458 B.C.E.[49] Soon after the Persian victories, however, this attention declined, and Persia once more abandoned border areas such as Yehud. Inconsistency characterized Persian administrative policies toward Yehud, creating a deep instability within the populace.

Life on the periphery manifested itself clearly in economic matters. Though Persia maintained political and military control over parts of its western border, the empire was no longer wealthy enough to integrate the whole region economically. Persian trade declined sharply in the Mediterranean basin during the second half of the fifth century. In its place, Greece became the significant trading partner for Yehud, even though Greece was a political enemy of the Persian Empire. Yehud needed a steady supply of goods (the colony was rarely if ever in a position to be financially independent). With Persia less economically active in the area, Yehud began to trade with Greece. In all probability, Yehud traded grain to Athens and other Greek city-states for olive products and wine, as early as the reign of Artaxerxes I. Though at first this may well have been simply an economic move, trade soon brought cultural exchange. By the

---

49. Othniel Margalith, "The Political Role of Ezra as Persian Governor," *Zeitschrift für die alttestamentliche Wissenschaft* 98 (1986): 111. See also Fritz M. Heichelheim, "Ezra's Palestine and Periclean Athens," *Zeitschrift für Religions- und Geistesgeschichte* 3 (1951): 251–52.

year 400 B.C.E., if not sooner, Yehud was a political vassal of Persia and an economic dependent of Greece, placing the colony in a politically dangerous situation. More important than the dangers, however, was the shift in identity. Yehud was a destabilized colony of the world empire, but it was also a nonfavored trading partner and potential enemy of the growing economic influence in the region. Between the two, Yehud was trapped without respect or protection from either of these conflicting spheres.[50]

As a result, Yehud experienced exploitation and depletion from both sources. Texts such as Neh 5:5 show some of the crushing effects of this economic decline, even to the point of selling children into slavery to pay debts. As early as 455 B.C.E., interest rates were normally surpassing 12.5 percent, with occasional references in the following decades to rates in the 40–60 percent range.[51] Economic collapse was imminent, but it did not arrive soon; instead, the balance of power between Persia and Greece continued this destructive stalemate throughout most of the fourth century.

The degradation was also cultural. The growing Greek influences set the stage for the widespread cultural changes of Hellenization. Yehud's unique language was under assault, and other cultural productions were sure to follow. The loss of political security and of economic stability combined with a decline in cultural solidity and identity. This was much more

---

50. Jon L. Berquist, "The Shifting Frontier: The Achaemenid Empire's Treatment of Western Colonies," *Journal of World-Systems Research* 1/17 (1995): 1–25 (available on the internet at http://csf.colorado.edu/wsystems/jwsr/vol1/v1_nh.htm).

51. E. Neufeld, "The Rate of Interest and the Text of Nehemiah 5:11," *Jewish Quarterly Review* 44 (1953–54): 196–202.

than the vibrant pluralism of the preceding decades; Yehudite culture underwent a dissolution from external sources. Internally, there were many responses over generations and centuries. The culture experienced substantial foment over a long period of time.

The responses to the foment varied. Some groups urged acceptance of cultural pluralism; others condemned it as antithetical to the ways of the ancestors and the desire of God. The first set of groups may well have been responsible for the propagation of some of Yehud's most loved short stories. The Book of Ruth tells of the possibilities for salvation inherent in the acceptance of foreigners; Esther's novella recounts Jews who look very Persian and work within imperial systems. The dividing lines between cultures blur in these short stories, and their authors seem to revel in the different combinations that are possible. At the same time, this period saw the rise of apocalyptic movements that called forth God's wrath upon all who deviated from the single path of God's will. The latter chapters of Daniel, for instance, express a desire that foreign rule be abolished and that the non-Jews face destruction. Such apocalypticists preached an intolerance very alien to the short stories, but both participated in the foment of the period.[52]

Yehud continued its peripheral existence throughout the rest of the Persian period. Economic fortune varied throughout the Hellenistic and Roman periods, but there was substantial foment throughout the Second Temple's existence. Jerusalem's political institutions and Judaism's religious leaders faced the threats of waves of dissidents, rebels, insurgents, and separatists, including groups as diverse as Qumran, the Zealots, and a never-ending

---

52. Berquist, *Judaism in Persia's Shadow*, 221–32.

wave of messianic contenders.[53] This foment embodied both the earlier pluralism of expanding diversity and the period's intense vitality and vibrancy of religious expression. These groups cared deeply about their faith and their ways of life. As they felt the call of God upon their lives in contradistinction to the ways of the world imposed by the successions of empires, they reacted strongly and sometimes violently to defend and continue their own responses to the Torah that enlivened them.

Life on the Pluralistic Edge

The period of Judaism's Second Temple, then, was a time of living on the edge. Politically, it was life on the edge of huge empires, which sometimes served Yehudite interests well and sometimes oppressed the people, but never failed to impact daily life. It was also life on a cultural edge, as Israelite, Babylonian, Egyptian, Persian, Greek, and Roman cultures clashed within the city gates. Vitality, passion, and foment all characterize the religion of this period.

Throughout this time, many people took a greater interest in their religion than ever before. They pursued their own perceptions of faith with great energy, responding to the Torah in increasingly diverse ways and sometimes contesting the differences with their lives. The people who followed the Torah possessed great diversities of geography, language, and ethnicity; this produced theological variation at the same time that it brought the love of the Torah to new populaces throughout the imperial world. The faith, in all of its forms, was intimately

---

53. See Richard A. Horsley and John S. Hanson, *Bandits, Prophets, and Messiahs: Popular Movements at the Time of Jesus* (San Francisco: Harper & Row, 1985).

connected with lived experience, arising in reaction to new situations, and so this period produced forms of religion with a
remarkable ability to adapt. It is not surprising, then, that forms
of this religion are still extant today, and that these forms of
faith are still vibrant, still diverse, and still capable of motivating
energies in human life.

THREE

"Alas, She Has Become a Harlot," but Who's to Blame? Unfaithful-Female Imagery in Isaiah's Vision

— *Katheryn Pfisterer Darr* —

Ancient Israel's prophets and other poets drew from women's lives and experiences, as well as stereotypical associations with females (whether accurate or not), toward a variety of strategic ends. When the author of Isa 3:16–17 wishes to depict human haughtiness and its consequences, for example, he gives it a female face and form:

> Because the daughters of Zion are haughty
> and walk with outstretched necks,
> glancing wantonly with their eyes,

Early versions of portions of this essay were presented to the Israelite Prophetic Literature Section ("How Are Women Made to Help? The Functions of Females in Isaiah 1–39 and Ezekiel") at the 1995 annual meeting of the Society of Biblical Literature in Philadelphia and to the Biblical Criticism and Literary Criticism Section ("'Alas, She Has Become a Harlot' But Who's to Blame?") at the 1996 annual meeting of the Society of Biblical Literature in New Orleans. I offer this reading of the great scroll of Isaiah, completed in the vital postexilic period, in honor of Walter J. Harrelson. My title is taken from Isa 1:21a NJPSV.

mincing along as they go,
 tinkling with their feet;
the Lord will afflict with scabs
 the heads of the daughters of Zion,
 and the LORD will lay bare their secret parts.[1]

In Isa 4:1, desperate females illustrate the social repercussions when warfare decimates the male population: "Seven women shall take hold of one man in that day, saying, 'We will eat our own bread and wear our own clothes; just let us be called by your name; take away our disgrace.'"

Travailing-woman similes regularly function to illumine human anguish in the face of impending doom:

Damascus has become feeble, she turned to flee,
 and panic seized her;
anguish and sorrows have taken hold of her,
 as of a woman in labor (Jer 49:24).[2]

Both Gomer and Isaiah's unnamed wife birth babies bearing message names (Hos 1:3–5, 6–7, 8–9; Isa 7:3; 8:3–4). King Hezekiah "performs" a metaphorical proverb about childbirth complications, correlating himself and his advisers with women

---

1. Unless otherwise indicated, biblical quotations are from the NRSV.

2. Also, e.g., Isa 13:7–8a; 21:3; 42:14; Jer 6:23–24; Ps 48:7 [Eng. 48:6]. See my "Like Warrior, Like Woman: Destruction and Deliverance in Isaiah 42:10–17," *CBQ* 49 (1987): 560–71; idem, "Two Unifying Female Images in the Book of Isaiah," in *Uncovering Ancient Stones: Essays in Memory of H. Neil Richardson* (ed. Lewis M. Hopfe; Winona Lake, Ind.: Eisenbrauns, 1994), 17–30; idem, *Isaiah's Vision and the Family of God* (Louisville: Westminster John Knox, 1994), 100–105.

lacking the strength to bring forth their babies (2 Kgs 19:3 [=Isa 37:3]).[3]

Ezekiel condemns "the daughters of your people, who prophesy out of their own imagination," and exploits stereotypical associations linking females with sorcery and witchcraft (13:17–23). In Ezek 22:2–5, references to women flesh out the prophet's accusations against the male inhabitants of "Bloodshed City," as Jerusalem is called. These men treat their fathers and mothers contemptuously and oppress aliens, widows, and orphans. They commit adultery, participate in incestuous acts with daughters-in-law and half-sisters, and engage in sexual intercourse with women who are in their menstrual periods.

Unfaithful-Female Imagery

From at least the days of Hosea, certain of Israel's prophets took up the metaphorical vehicle of "unfaithful female" imagery to depict the tenor of Israel's religious and political apostasies. Hosea charges that Israel has cuckolded her husband, Yhwh, by "playing the harlot";[4] and he threatens "her" with the punishments ostensibly due an adulterous wife: public stripping; withdrawal of life's necessities; abandonment; even death (Hos

---

3. Hezekiah's proverb performance functions both as a penitent confession and as an invitation to perceive Assyria's impending siege against Jerusalem in a way most likely to move Isaiah and Yhwh to pity and action on the city's behalf. See chap. 6 ("No Strength to Deliver: Bringing to Birth") in my *Isaiah's Vision*, 205–24; and idem, " 'No Strength to Deliver': A Contextual Analysis of Hezekiah's Proverb in Isaiah 37:3b," in *New Visions of the Book of Isaiah* (ed. M. Sweeney and R. Melugin; JSOTSup 214; Sheffield: JSOT Press, 1996), 219–56.

4. In descriptions of illicit female sexual activity, biblical authors employ not only *na'af* ("to commit adultery") but also *zanah* ("to commit fornication, be a harlot"). See my *Isaiah's Vision*, 119–21, and the literature cited there.

2:4–15 [Eng. 2:2–13]). In Jer 3:1–2, Yʜᴡʜ accuses Judah of "whor[ing] with many lovers":

> Look up to the bare heights, and see:
> Where have they not lain with you?
> You waited for them on the roadside
> Like a bandit in the wilderness.
> And you defiled the land
> With your whoring and your debauchery (ɴᴊᴘsᴠ).

Leave it to Ezekiel, however, fully to exploit unfaithful-female imagery. His lengthy, lewd indictments of adulterous Jerusalem and sister Samaria in Ezek 16 and Ezek 23 take shame (not pride) of place among examples of biblical pornography and bristle with difficulties, since imagery, especially biblical imagery, that details the degradation and humiliation of women, that describes female sexuality as the object of male possession and control, that displays women being battered and mutilated, and that presents such violence as a means toward healing a broken marital relationship can have murderous consequences.[5]

A Synchronic Reading of Isaiah's Vision

For most modern critics, a diachronic reading of Isaiah is not second nature — it is first nature.[6] So accustomed are we to seeing at least three complex collections within its sixty-six chapters that reading the scroll as what it purports to be, "the vision of

---

5. See Katheryn Pfisterer Darr, "Ezekiel's Justifications of God: Teaching Troubling Texts," *JSOT* 55 (1992): 115; and idem, "Ezekiel," in *The Women's Bible Commentary* (ed. Carol A. Newsom and Sharon H. Ringe; Louisville: Westminster John Knox, 1992), 183–90.

6. Unless otherwise indicated, the terms *Isaiah*, *Isaian*, and *Isaianic* refer to Isa 1–66, rather than to the eighth-century prophet.

Isaiah son of Amoz" (1:1), seems downright difficult, if not a betrayal of what we learned in graduate school. Why operate as if we, like over two millennia of previous readers, were ignorant of those methods that enabled the discovery that Isa 1–39 has a complex composition history, that Isa 40–55 is the product of an anonymous exilic prophet, and that Isa 56–66 reflects the religious, political, and social foment of the postexilic period?

Some specialists, though steeped in historical-critical methods, have created serious synchronic readings of Isa 1–66,[7] their literary approaches focusing either upon the text as an object as "solid and material as an urn or icon"[8] or upon its relationship to the audience or reader.[9] "A changing view on the Book of Isaiah," writes R. Rendtorff, "should allow, and even require studies on topics, themes, expressions, and . . . ideas characteristic [of]

---

7. See, e.g., B. W. Anderson, "The Apocalyptic Rendering of the Isaiah Tradition," in *The Social World of Formative Christianity and Judaism* (Festschrift for H. C. Kee; ed. Jacob Neusner et al.; Philadelphia: Fortress, 1988), 17–38; B. S. Childs, *Introduction to the Old Testament as Scripture* (Philadelphia: Fortress, 1979), 311–38; R. E. Clements, "The Unity of the Book of Isaiah," *Interpretation* 36 (1982): 117–29; idem, "Beyond Tradition History: Deutero-Isaianic Development of First Isaiah's Themes," *JSOT* 31 (1985): 95–113; R. J. Clifford, "The Unity of the Book of Isaiah and Its Cosmogonic Language," *CBQ* 55 (1993): 1–17; P. D. Miscall, "Isaiah: The Labyrinth of Images," *Semeia* 54 (1991): 103–21; idem, "Isaiah: New Heavens, New Earth, New Book," in *Reading between Texts* (ed. D. N. Fewell; Literary Currents in Biblical Interpretation; Louisville: Westminster John Knox, 1993); R. Rendtorff, *The Old Testament: An Introduction* (trans. J. Bowden; Philadelphia: Fortress, 1991), 190–200; A. Van Selms, "L'unité du livre d'Isaïe," in *The Book of Isaiah — Le Livre d'Isaïe* (ed. J. Vermeylen; Bibliotheca ephemeridum theologicarum lovaniensium 81; Louvain: Peters, 1989), 11–53.

8. T. Eagleton, *Literary Theory: An Introduction* (Minneapolis: University of Minnesota Press, 1983), 47.

9. "Object" and "audience" equate to "objective theories" and "pragmatic theories" in M. H. Abrams, *The Mirror and the Lamp: Romantic Theory and the Critical Tradition* (New York: Oxford University Press, 1953), 6.

the book as a whole or significant parts of it, without at the same time discussing the questions of redaction or composition. A synchronic reading, if carried out with the necessary sophistication, should have its own right."[10] In *Isaiah's Vision and the Family of God*, I have undertaken such a synchronic reading, showing how my ancient, sequential reader, a heuristic construct, construes significant themes in Isaiah's unfolding vision.[11]

Female Imagery in Isaiah 1

Christopher Seitz observes that in the Book of Isaiah "the second major character alongside God is Zion."[12] Our sequential reader

10. R. Rendtorff, "The Book of Isaiah: A Complex Unity; Synchronic and Diachronic Reading," in *Society of Biblical Literature Seminar Papers* (1991): 20.

11. In chap. 1 of *Isaiah's Vision*, I set out a reader-oriented method (23–35; for application to Isa 1, see 135–40), acknowledging my indebtedness to J. A. Darr's own approach as detailed in " 'Glorified in the Presence of Kings': A Literary-Critical Study of Herod the Tetrarch in Luke-Acts" (Ph.D. diss., Vanderbilt University, 1987) and further refined in *On Character Building: The Reader and the Rhetoric of Characterization in Luke-Acts* (Literary Currents in Biblical Interpretation; Louisville: Westminster John Knox, 1992) as well as in subsequent essays. I also identify my "reader" that I, as critic, construct. So too, in this current essay, my reader "belongs to post-exilic Israel's cognoscenti, a scribe or religious leader and educator enjoying such legal rights and social standing as were possible at the beginning of the fourth-century B.C.E., and under Persian rule. Culturally-literate and fully at home within his society, he knows — or at least thinks he knows — basic facts . . . related to Israel and its world. Though this is his first reading of Isaiah [1–66], he is familiar with other of Israel's [texts and traditions]. . . . For the vast majority of his contemporaries, of course, access to Isaiah consists only of listening to brief excerpts in contexts of worship. . . . But [my] reader, a minority in his society, enjoys the opportunity, access, expertise, and time to read and interpret the unfolding Isaiah scroll on other than just a pericope by pericope basis" (Darr, *Isaiah's Vision*, 30).

12. Christopher Seitz, "Isaiah 1–66: Making Sense of the Whole," in *Reading and Preaching the Book of Isaiah* (ed. Christopher R. Seitz; Philadelphia:

first glimpses "Fair Zion" in 1:8, a passage that invites pity, since the sins of her inhabitants (detailed in 1:2–6) have left her as fragile and vulnerable as a rickety harvest hut.[13] Some verses later, she reappears within a lament: "Alas," we read in Isa 1:21a, "the (once-)faithful city has become a harlot" (my translation). Behind this line stands the traditional metaphor of Jerusalem as YHWH's wife. The statement that she has become an habitual fornicator might remind readers of similar slurs by earlier prophets, especially if they suspect that the so-called lament is actually a piece of prophetic mockery.

Careful inspection confirms, however, that this lament is the genuine article — an earnest expression of grief and anger to which God immediately responds with the promise that Zion's current condition will be reversed (1:24–26).[14] Isaiah 1 does not portray Jerusalem behaving in harlotrous ways. We search in vain for the brazen "hussy" of Hosea, Jeremiah, and Ezekiel. Rather, it focuses upon those elements that have caused her present, debased state: her rebellious and sinful inhabitants, and especially their leaders. Once she was filled with justice, and righteousness

---

Fortress, 1988), 122. See also his *Zion's Final Destiny: The Development of the Book of Isaiah* (Minneapolis: Fortress, 1991); and Barry G. Webb, "Zion in Transformation: A Literary Approach to Isaiah," in *The Bible in Three Dimensions* (ed. D. J. A. Clines et al.; Sheffield: JSOT Press, 1990), 65–84.

13. The precariousness of the *melunah*, a temporary booth constructed to shelter guards watching a ripening crop, is clear from Isa 24:20. See also the Sumerian "Lamentation over the Destruction of Ur" (quoted in F. W. Dobbs-Allsopp, *Weep, O Daughter of Zion: A Study of the City-Lament Genre in the Hebrew Bible* [Biblica et orientalia 44; Rome: Pontifical Institute Press, 1993], 69), where Ningal mourns the destruction of her temple using related imagery: "My house founded by the righteous, / Like a garden hut, verily on its side has caved in... / My faithful house... /...like a tent, like a pulled-up harvest shed, / like a pulled-up harvest shed indeed / was exposed to wind and rain."

14. For a fuller discussion of these verses, see Darr, *Isaiah's Vision*, 135–40.

dwelt in her. Now murderers are her lodgers (1:21b).[15] Her silver has become dross, her fine wine watery. Said differently, her
princes are rebels and cronies of thieves who pursue bribes and
pervert justice (1:22–23). Like many a woman of the ancient
Near Eastern world, it seems, Zion has become a harlot through
a tragic reversal of her circumstances.[16]

How shall she again be the "faithful city?" Through the
purging of her contaminants: "Ah," Yhwh declares:

> I will vent my wrath on my enemies [mpl],
>   and avenge myself on my foes [mpl].
> I will turn my hand against you [fsg]
>   and will smelt away your [fsg] dross as with lye
>   and remove all your [fsg] alloy (1:24b–25 rsv).

Metallurgy required lengthy exposure to extreme heat inside the
smelting furnaces, and the reader who knows how Jerusalem
has suffered (most terribly in 587 b.c.e.) will not downplay the
fierce intensity of the process she must endure.[17] God's purpose,
nonetheless, is separating slag from silver. Once the dross and

---

15. These phrases are suggestive, given the immediately preceding lament
over Zion's harlotry. Yet the notion that justice and righteousness once spent
the night in Jerusalem can hardly be construed pejoratively, while the observation that murderers are her present lodgers itself underscores her current,
imperiled plight. How could this vulnerable woman rid herself of murderers?

16. See R. Harris, "Independent Women in Ancient Mesopotamia?" in
Women's Earliest Records from Ancient Egypt and Western Asia (ed. B. S. Lesko;
Atlanta: Scholars Press, 1989), 145–56; S. Rollin, "Women and Witchcraft
in Ancient Assyria," in *Images of Women in Antiquity* (ed. A. Cameron and
A. Kuhrt; London: Croom Helm, 1983), 34–45; and Darr, *Isaiah's Vision*,
115–18.

17. In Isa 48:10, furnace imagery reappears in Yhwh's description of the
"refining" punishment that Israel experienced in exile on account of its
long-lived history of rebelliousness (48:8). Ezekiel also used this imagery;
see 22:17–22.

alloy have been removed, that is, once Jerusalem's rebellious and sinful authorities have been replaced by a just and righteous leadership class, she will again be called "City of Righteousness" and "Faithful City" (1:26).

To summarize: Isa 1, the reader's entrée into Isaiah's vision, laments that Zion has become a harlot. But the text does not detail her sins by further exploiting the metaphorical vehicle of unfaithful-female imagery. Rather, its prompt shift to pointed indictments of Jerusalem's wicked leaders places the blame for Zion's decline on their heads and encourages readers to perceive her as the victim of their defiling ways. Isaiah 1:27–28, which presages the outcome of Isaiah's entire vision, further reassures our reader of her fate:

> Zion shall be saved in the judgment;
> Her repentant ones, in the retribution.
> But rebels and sinners shall all be crushed,
> And those who forsake the LORD shall perish (NJPSV).[18]

How great are the differences between the use of unfaithful-female imagery in Isa 1 and Ezekiel's own! Ezekiel 16 portrays Jerusalem in hot pursuit of lovers (e.g., 16:15–16, 23–25), accuses her of fornicating with Egyptians, Assyrians, and Chaldeans (16:26–29), and charges her with sacrificing to idols the children she has borne for YHWH (16:20–21). Isaiah 1 laments her fall from faithful city to harlot and portrays her as a victim of the consequences of sins committed by YHWH's rebel-

---

18. On Isa 1:27–28 as a summary of the course the Book of Isaiah will take, see Darr, *Isaiah's Vision*, 58–60, 68, 103. Barry G. Webb ("Zion in Transformation," 69) also discerns the significance of these verses for Isaiah as a whole.

lious children (1:2–3, 5, 20, 28). In Ezek 16, God oversees her exceedingly violent execution. The Isaian tradition never depicts the "death" of personified Zion. To be sure, Ezekiel looks beyond Jerusalem's mutilation and murder to proclaim in YHWH's name, "I will remember the covenant I made with you in the days of your youth, and I will establish it with you as an everlasting covenant" (16:60 NJPSV). In his scenario, however, shame and silence will be her responses (16:61–63). In Isa 40–66, Zion is urged to put away "the shame of [her] youth" (54:4), to raise her voice in songs and shouts (54:1). When the Ezekielian tradition envisions the restored city (Ezek 40–48), female imagery has no place. "The only use of … feminine imagery occurs," Julie Galambush observes, "in Yahweh's vehement denial that this city will be like the former one. In 43:7–9, Yahweh explains that the divine presence will be able to remain in the new temple forever because 'the house of Israel will never again defile my holy name … by their prostitution [*zenut*]. … Now they will put their prostitution far away.'"[19] In Isa 40–55, positive female images of restored Jerusalem abound.

Meir Sternberg observes that the beginning of a literary work is especially programmatic for readers.[20] Were the harlotry imagery of Isa 1 further developed along the lines of, for example, Hos 2; Jer 3; and Ezek 16, 23, readers might well enter the world of Isaiah's vision with an extremely negative perception of personified Jerusalem, rather than with hope for her eventual restoration. Isaiah 1–39 will include many an indictment

---

19. Julie Galambush, *Jerusalem in the Book of Ezekiel: The City as Yahweh's Wife* (SBLDS 130; Atlanta: Scholars Press, 1992), 149.

20. See Sternberg's discussion of "the primacy effect" in *Expositional Modes and Temporal Ordering in Fiction* (Baltimore: Johns Hopkins University Press, 1978), 93–96.

against God's people, as well as scathing threats and pronounce-
ments of doom. Time and again, however, our sequential reader
encounters texts that reinforce the promises of Isa 1 (see, e.g.,
4:2–6; 12:6; 18:7). Even 29:1–8, which anticipates Yhwh's siege
against Jerusalem, her demise at the hand of her God-turned-
foe, and her scarcely audible whispering from "deep in the earth"
(29:4, my translation), concludes on a hopeful note:

> And suddenly, in an instant,
> She shall be remembered of the Lord of Hosts
> With roaring, and shaking, and deafening noise,
> Storm, and tempest, and blaze of consuming fire.
> Then, like a dream, a vision of the night,
> Shall be the multitude of nations
> That war upon Ariel,
> And all her besiegers, and the siegeworks against her,
> And those who harass her.
> Like one who is hungry
> And dreams he is eating,
> But wakes to find himself empty;
> And like one who is thirsty
> And dreams he is drinking,
> But wakes to find himself faint
> And utterly parched —
> So shall be all the multitude of nations
> That war upon Mount Zion (29:5b–8 njpsv).

Female Imagery in Isaiah 40–55

Sequential readers arrive at Isa 40 with certain expectations already in place: Yhwh has a plan; that plan concerns not only

Israel, but also all other nations.[21] Thus far, it has included the
punishment of arrogant rulers, sinful cities, presumptuous empires, and also of YHWH's own people. But beyond Assyria's
day, beyond the boasts of arrogant Babylon, lie restoration,
reconciliation, honor, status, and prosperity for Zion.

Female-city imagery was not a pervasive feature of Isa 5–
39.[22] In Isa 40–66, however, it plays a signal role in certain
rhetorical strategies by which both Second Isaiah and the Third
Isaiah community invite their audiences to perceive the world,
YHWH's work, and Jerusalem's role in both, in this way, rather
than in some other way.

While the Second Isaiah corpus supports the claims of earlier prophets that Israel had earned YHWH's punishments (e.g.,
42:24–25; 43:22–24), it persistently moves beyond judgment to
speak of divine grace, forgiveness, and love. I need not quote too
extensively from those poems in which personified Zion plays a
pivotal role, for they are well known. Suffice it to say that they
are filled with the positive female imagery of their culture. Jerusalem is a mother whose children are coming home (49:19–21,
22; 54:1–3). Even nursing mothers might forget their infants,
but God will never forget Jerusalem (49:15). In the past, she
was abandoned like a forsaken and grieved wife (54:6). Now
YHWH, her husband (54:5), comes to her seeking reconciliation
and even acknowledging that perhaps he went too far:

> For a brief moment I abandoned you,
>   but with great compassion I will gather you.

---

21. On YHWH's "plan" in the Book of Isaiah see, e.g., E. Conrad, *Reading
Isaiah* (Minneapolis: Fortress, 1991); J. Jensen, "Yahweh's Plan in Isaiah and
in the Rest of the Old Testament," *CBQ* 48 (1986): 443–55.

22. See my discussion of passages in which female-city imagery appears in
Isaiah's Vision, 143–64.

> In overflowing wrath for a moment
>> I hid my face from you,
> but with everlasting love I will have compassion on you,
>> says the LORD, your Redeemer (54:7–8).[23]

J. F. A. Sawyer attempts to capture the tenor of these lines:

> The last four verses of the poem are apologetic in tone:
> "It was just for a moment — I lost my temper. . . . I won't
> do it again. . . . I promise. . . . I love you." She is physically
> weaker than he is and socially dependent on him. He has
> the power to give her happiness and dignity and freedom;
> she knows he also has the power to punish, humiliate and
> abuse her. So he has to convince her that he really loves
> her and that she can trust him. To do this he sets aside
> all hardness and pomposity, the frightening manifestations
> of his power and his status as "God of all the earth," and
> comes to her, on bended knee as it were, to plead with her
> to let bygones be bygones and start again.[24]

Does Sawyer's interpretation do justice to the author's intent?
Neither our ancient reader nor we can know the answer to that
question. Clearly, however, the text invites us to perceive the
bond between YHWH and Jerusalem through the metaphorical
lens of marriage — a union that, God elsewhere asserts, never
was severed by divorce (50:1). Because Jerusalem is blameless
and no formal divorce decree exists, YHWH can reclaim her as

---

23. Should we discern also in the words of Isa 40:2 ("she has received
from the LORD's hand / double for all her sins") YHWH's acknowledgment
that the punishment has exceeded the crime?

24. J. F. A. Sawyer, "Daughter of Zion and Servant of the Lord in Isaiah:
A Comparison," *JSOT* 44 (1989): 95–96.

his wife. Nowhere in Isa 40–55 is she charged with having been unfaithful to him, or depicted in "compromising positions."

Moreover, the oracles of Second Isaiah do not focus upon the wicked authorities of Israel's past. In Isa 1–39 its rebels, and particularly its corrupt and intemperate leadership, were frequently decried.[25] Isaiah 40–55 frankly acknowledges Israel's rebellious and sinful past, and present-day idolaters elicit ridicule and scorn on more than one occasion (40:18–20; 41:5–7; 42:17). Nonetheless, its poems offer a "clean start" to all of the exiles — whose ranks, we recall, included a disproportionate number of Jerusalem's leaders: "I, I am he who blots out your transgressions for my own sake," YHWH says, "and I will not remember your sins" (43:25; see also 44:22). The people need only accept God's offer and step out in faith to begin the journey home (48:20; 52:11–12; 55:12).

Unfaithful-Female Imagery Returns

Immediately following the jubilant scene of Isa 55:12–13, Isa 56 issues an imperative and a promise:

> Thus says the LORD:
>   Maintain justice, and do what is right,
> for soon my salvation will come,
>   and my deliverance be revealed (56:1).

With Isa 56:9, however, the text's tone changes radically. Carnivorous beasts are summoned to dine on the community's oppressive, intemperate leaders. Yes, Israel's authorities, the class so frequently threatened and condemned in Isa 1–39, reemerge

---

25. See my discussion in chap. 2 ("Child Imagery and the Rhetoric of Rebellion") of *Isaiah's Vision*, 46–84.

within the Trito-Isaiah corpus, a product of the tumultuous post-exilic period, despite God's promises of forgiveness in Isa 40–55. But in 57:3–4, these leaders are derided with phrases similar to the modern, crude "son of a bitch": they are "children of transgression" and "offspring of deceit." Both the modern and ancient slurs intend to insult one's foes by charging that their progenitors are in some sense perverse. "From so poisonous a pedigree, no good issue can come. Depicted metaphorically as the birth products of transgression and deceit, these community leaders epitomize the proverbial 'like mother, like daughter' of Ezek 16:44."[26]

Isaiah 57:3–13 merits special attention, for it is crucial to our reader's understanding of how harlotry imagery functions in Isaiah's vision. Isaiah 57:3–5 casts its accusations in masculine plural grammatical forms. In 57:6–13, however, the poem shifts to almost uniformly feminine singular forms:

> On a high and lofty hill
> You have set your couch;
> There, too, you have gone up
> To perform sacrifices.
> Behind the door and doorpost
> You have directed your thoughts;
> Abandoning Me, you have gone up
> On the couch you made so wide.
> You have made a covenant with them,
> You have loved bedding with them;
> You have chosen lust (57:7–8 NJPSV).[27]

---

26. Ibid., 70.

27. S. Ackerman analyzes Isa 57:3–13 as a finely crafted literary unit ("Sacred Sex, Sacrifice and Death: Understanding a Prophetic Poem," *Bible*

This poem, of which I've quoted only a portion, adopts unfaithful-female imagery, addressing the leaders it condemns metaphori-cally as a fornicating, sorcery-dabbling, child-sacrificing woman. Not a few critics assert that charges lodged against the "wanton woman" of 57:6–10 reflect actual practices of the postexilic cult. J. L. McKenzie, for example, relies on arguments from silence, speculation, and presuppositions concerning the "primitive" nature of that cult to support a literal interpretation:

> That fertility rites of some kind are described seems to ad-mit no doubt. There are also allusions to necromancy.... There are no explicit references to these superstitions in other post-exilic literature; but there is no difficulty in sup-posing that the theological and cultic condition of the early post-exilic community was primitive.... Such rites could well have been practiced by those who lived in the land after the Babylonian wars; there seems to have been no

---

Review 6 [1990]: 38–44) with the following structural pattern: references to the fertility cult, child sacrifice, and the cult of the dead recur twice, in that order, in 57:5a–9b. "Clearly," she avers, "this structure indicates that in the prophet's mind an organic unity exists among sexual fertility rituals, child sacrifice and cults of the dead" (42). As the following summary of her work demonstrates, Ackerman discerns how these activities are linked through the use of polyvalent vocabulary and wordplays: "In verse 5, *'elim* can plausibly be construed to mean either 'terebinths' or 'gods....' The noun *mishkab*, 'bed,' recurs three times in verses 7 and 8 (twice). It refers... to the site of the wanton woman's repeated fornications. But... *mishkab* can also refer to one's grave or resting place [see Isa 57:2].... Again, the word for 'symbol' (*zikkaron*; v. 8) signifies some sort of fertility cultic object. Because it puns the Hebrew word *zakar*, 'male,' it also suggests a phallic image (see also Ezek 16:17). But *zikkaron* can refer to a memorial stela as well. And the reference to *yad*, usually translated 'hand,' but possibly referring in this context to the phallus, elsewhere denotes a monument for the dead.... Hence, these and other word plays bind the woman's activities into an inextricable morass of iniquity" (Darr, *Isaiah's Vision*, 186–87).

center in the country which would have preserved genuine Yahwism.[28]

Paul Hanson, by contrast, correctly reminds his readers that "the description of their activity in [these verses] is to be taken no more literally than is the designation 'sons of a witch, off-spring of the adulterer and the whore' [57:3]. . . . This is no objective description of a cultic practice, but rather a highly sardonical paronomasia used to ridicule the cult of those being attacked."[29]

Although Hanson does not say so, the activities attributed to these civil/cultic leaders were especially associated with women, and so are particularly appropriate to the author's use of feminine grammatical forms and imagery. Ezekiel also knows of women's propensity toward sorcery, witchcraft, and other practices lying beyond the Hebrew Bible's brand of "orthodox Yahwism" (13:17–23). He too describes Jerusalem and Samaria's "relations" with foreign nations as sexual intercourse (e.g., 23:5–23) and depicts Jerusalem's assent to her lofty bed (e.g., 16:24, 31). And like the wanton woman of Isa 57:9, Oholah and Oholibah send envoys afar, in their case explicitly to seek out new paramours (Ezek 23:40–42). But while Ezekiel's personified-city passages excoriate his people as a whole, in Isa 57 one group of Israelites, who regard themselves as YHWH's faithful servants, castigates another. Imagery exploited by earlier prophets to depict the sins of cities, people, and nations as defiled and defiling, shameless, promiscuous, idolatrous, ar-

---

28. J. L. McKenzie, *Second Isaiah* (AB 20; Garden City: Doubleday, 1968), 158.

29. Paul Hanson, *The Dawn of Apocalyptic* (Philadelphia: Fortress, 1975), 198.

rogant, cruel, and unnatural here functions to express the oppressed servants' disgust toward a powerful subgroup within the larger community — a subgroup whose power and practices they experience as oppression.

In commentaries devoted to (only) Isa 40–66, some critics express surprise that harlotry imagery should appear amid the plethora of positive female images of Jerusalem. C. Westermann, for example, surmises that the harlot has found her way into Isa 57 because a redactor discerned at this point an opportunity to slip in some snippets of preexilic prophecy, now reinterpreted by virtue of their redactional framework.[30] In *Isaiah's Vision and the Family of God,* by contrast, I show that for sequential readers of Isa 1–66, the reappearance of harlotry imagery both recalls and reinforces a crucial theme first introduced in the lament of Isa 1: the destruction of Jerusalem is — on account of Israel's long-lived rebelliousness — an unavoidable tragedy, but YHWH's world-embracing plan has, as a central component, her future restoration and elevation to a position of preeminence among the nations. The wanton woman of Isa 57 is intimately related to the unfaithful-female imagery of Isa 1 (see below). But an important innovation has occurred: the Jerusalem of Isa 1 became a harlot on account of her debased inhabitants; here, her perverted residents appear in the guise of a personified, harlotrous female. In fact, 57:6–13 can be construed as a vivid illustration of the accusation that was lodged, but not sustained through sexual metaphors, in Isa 1:21–26. Moreover, female personification, harlotry imagery, and Jerusalem's corrupt leadership are not the only elements linking Isa 1 and Isa

---

30. C. Westermann, *Isaiah 40–66* (trans. D. M. G. Stalker; Old Testament Library; Philadelphia: Westminster, 1969), 323–25.

56–57. Each passage also contains trial speeches, key words, poisonous epithets, a lament, and charges of heinous cultic acts.[31]

Two females, then, appear in the Trito-Isaiah corpus: the harlot who, in a single, graphic appearance, embodies Israel's evil leadership; and the beloved wife and mother who embodies YHWH's faithful servants — those who have repented of Israel's history of rebelliousness, are living obediently according to God's laws, and anticipate the fulfillment of YHWH's plan (Isa 58–59).[32] In Isa 60 this subgroup is addressed as Zion using feminine grammatical forms:

> Lift up your eyes and look around;
>> they all gather together, they come to you;
> your sons shall come from far away,
>> and your daughters shall be carried on their nurses'
>> arms.
> Then you shall see and be radiant;
>> your heart shall thrill and rejoice,
> because the abundance of the sea shall be brought to you,
>> the wealth of nations shall come to you (60:4–5).

Subsequent verses detail the supra-extravagant conditions she will enjoy: the wealth of nations; absolute security; an abundance of children; the abiding presence of God's glory. Indeed, Isaiah's Zion shall forever bask in the sort of extravagant care that Ezekiel's God once lavished upon his bride (16:8–14), who, alas, became a harlot.

---

31. See Darr, *Isaiah's Vision*, 185, 188, 204.
32. Ibid., 69–84, 183–204.

"Zion Shall Be Saved in the Judgment....
But Rebels and Sinners Shall All Be Crushed"

In *A Manual of Hebrew Poetics*, Luis Alonso Schökel writes: "The book of Isaiah is enclosed in a huge inclusion: about fifty words of chapter 1 are repeated in chapters 65–66. This means that the final author desired to edit the work as a book; it does not mean that the inclusion has brought about a unity of composition throughout the book."[33] Both of Alonso Schökel's observations bear some truth, but neither adequately describes what readers encounter in the Isaiah scroll.

Connections between the work's beginning and its ending are not restricted to Isa 1 on the one hand and Isa 65–66 on the other; and they entail a great deal more than shared vocabulary. We should rather say that at the beginning of the Isaiah scroll, the final authors/redactors have both introduced and shaped in strategic ways certain themes that will (1) recur at significant junctures along the way, transcending the modern-day demarcations of First, Second, and Third Isaiah; (2) be developed, such that they attain their (proleptic) resolution by vision's end; and (3) contribute to the sequential reader's construal of Isaiah as a coherent literary work.

Historical critics have long suspected that Isa 1, perhaps as much as Isa 1–4, introduces not only Isa 1–39, but also the Book of Isaiah as a whole. Marvin Sweeney, for example, shows with painstaking care that an understanding of the redactional formation of Isa 1–4 requires that it be read in relation to Isaiah's entire vision, that is, as a component of the book as a whole.[34]

---

33. Luis Alonso Schökel, *A Manual of Hebrew Poetics* (Subsidia Biblica 11; Rome: Pontifical Biblical Institute, 1988), 192.

34. Marvin Sweeney, *Isaiah 1–4 and the Post-Exilic Understanding of the Isa-*

The results of such diachronic analyses, coupled with a synchronic reading of Isaiah's vision, convince me that Isa 1–4 in its final form is the product of the postexilic Trito-Isaian community that not only composed a considerable corpus of new material and engaged in the final shaping of the entire Isaian tradition, but also created an introduction that set up in content and tone a major Isaian theme: the destruction of Jerusalem was, on account of Israel's long-lived rebelliousness, an unavoidable tragedy, but Yhwh's world-embracing plan includes her future elevation to a position of preeminence among the nations. Although the Trito-Isaian community may, in constructing the introduction, have cobbled together older oracles from various periods in the scroll's composition history, its authors/redactors were not, as Sweeney reminds us, "scissors and paste" editors, but "creative theologians who [not only gave] a 'new interpretation' to the older materials which they transmit[ted],"[35] but also placed into the work's prelude, and at other points along the way, particular perspectives on themes and motifs that were crucial to their own, postexilic situation and that built upon elements already present within the earlier Isaian tradition. "Alas! She has become a harlot!" Who's to blame? Her defiled and defiling leaders are at fault. But they can never have the final say about Yhwh's plan. Remember Isa 1:27–28:

> Zion shall be saved in the judgment;
> Her repentant ones, in the retribution.
> But rebels and sinners shall all be crushed,
> And those who forsake the Lord shall perish (njpsv).

---

ianic Tradition (Beihefte zur Zeitschrift für die alttestamentliche Wissenschaft 171; Berlin: de Gruyter, 1988).
35. Ibid., 2.

When all is said and done, and YHWH's new heavens and earth have been unfurled, Zion will enjoy "prosperity . . . like a river, / and the wealth of the nations like an overflowing stream." She will bear her children quickly and without pain, and they will "nurse and be carried on her arm, / and dandled on her knees" (66:12). But those who have rebelled against God shall indeed be destroyed, and YHWH's repentant, obedient servants will go out and gawk at their smoldering corpses (66:24).

Conclusion

The Isaiah scroll is, in its final form, a product of the tumultuous postexilic period. The ongoing Trito-Isaiah community exploited both the positive and the negative possibilities inherent in female (city) imagery in order to portray their community's leaders of various stripes, including the priests, as harlotrous and immoral defilers of Jerusalem and oppressors of YHWH's faithful servants. But God's plan, (now) announced already in Isa 1:27–28, provides hope both for Zion's redemption and for the destruction of those rebels and sinners who have defiled her.

The Vitality of
the Apocalyptic Vision

– Paul L. Redditt –

One of the most significant developments during the period of the Second Temple was the appearance of apocalyptic literature. Sometimes limited for discussion purposes to the period 165 B.C.E. to 100 C.E., it actually rose earlier (by the late third century B.C.E.) and lasted centuries later, in both Judaism and Christianity. While a number of the later works lie outside the parameters of this volume, they stand as testimony to the enduring viability of early Jewish apocalyptic thought. This study, however, will focus on Jewish apocalyptic literature during the period of the Second Temple and the aftermath of its destruction, and it will adopt the widely held view that apocalyptic writings arose in periods of perceived stress. It will show that apocalyptic literature lasted for centuries as a means for people to maintain their faith in God in spite of conditions around them. In developing this thesis, attention will first be given to the issue of definitions and to the scope of this study, followed by a discussion of the origin of apocalyptic literature. Then the essay will narrow its focus to hopes surrounding Jerusalem and the Second Temple, which it will trace through the protoapocalyptic literature of the Old Testament and into full-blown Jewish apocalypses and related literature.

Definitions of Terms and Scope of This Study

The term *apocalypticism* refers to "the ideology of a movement that shares the conceptual structures of the apocalypses."[1] To be sure, the term *movement* has been contested, since Jews and Christians of various sorts seem to have espoused theologies like those found in apocalypses.[2] Even so, the extensive reuse of traditions, lists, and symbols from earlier apocalyptic writers by later ones, both Jewish and Christian, suggests an ongoing way of thinking outside of any single organization or structure. Further, Jewish and Christian contributions to a given work are sometimes difficult to separate, so dedicated were the authors to their shared symbolic representations of the universe. Such distinctions often must be made on the basis of the presence or absence of distinctive Christian doctrines rather than on the basis of the apocalyptic symbols themselves.

One of the chief features of apocalyptic thought is eschatology, which is used with a variety of meanings.[3] On the one hand, it can be limited to a complex of ideas surrounding the end of the old world and the coming of the new.[4] On the other hand, the term has been defined more broadly to include any view of

---

1. John J. Collins, *The Apocalyptic Imagination* (New York: Crossroad, 1984), 10.

2. Indeed, James H. Charlesworth (*OTP* 1:3) warns against the use of the term *movement* at all, since apocalypses are so diverse.

3. Gunther Wanke, "Eschatologie: Ein Beispiel theologischer Sprachverwirrung," *Kerygma und Dogma* 16 (1970): 300–312.

4. Hugo Gressmann, *Der Ursprung der israelitisch-jüdischen Eschatologie* (Göttingen: Vandenhoeck & Ruprecht, 1905), 1.

the future in which the conditions of history or the world are so changed that one must speak of a new state of things that is "wholly other."[5] While the term *eschatology* must be used in the broader sense in connection with the Old Testament prophets, it may be used in its narrower sense in connection with apocalyptic literature. Eschatology is not, however, the sole topic of apocalyptic literature. It looks to the past as well.

The term *apocalypse* refers to a genre of literature. Since there is enough similarity among the apocalypses to speak of a system of thought and symbols,[6] scholars often try to describe them. Literary characteristics include the prevalence of discourse cycles, including visions and/or auditions, the revelation of secrets, dialogue, spiritual turmoil, or other reactions on the part of the seer, the activity of an interpreting angel, pseudonymity, coded speech, parenesis, and narration. Themes characteristic of apocalypses include the periodization of history, the expectation of the imminent end of the age, determinism, dualism, the triumph of good over evil, judgment, a royal mediator, heaven and/or hell, angelology, demonology, astrology, the catchword *glory*, and others.[7]

---

5. Johannes Lindblom, "Gibt es eine Eschatologie bei den alttestamentlichen Propheten?" *Studia theologica* 6 (1952): 81. See also Theodore C. Vriezen, "Prophecy and Eschatology," in *Congress Volume: Copenhagen 1953* (ed. G. W. Anderson et al.; VTSup 1; Leiden: Brill, 1953), 199–229; and Donald Gowan, *Eschatology in the Old Testament* (Philadelphia: Fortress, 1986), 1–2.

6. Walter Schmithals, *The Apocalyptic Movement* (Nashville: Abingdon, 1975), 13.

7. This list was culled from Schmithals, *Apocalyptic Movement*, 13–29; Klaus Koch, *The Rediscovery of Apocalyptic* (Studies in Biblical Theology 2/22; London: SCM, 1970), 24–33; and John J. Collins, "The Jewish Apocalypses," *Semeia* 14 (1979): 28. Good summaries of the history of research on apocalyptic literature can be found in John J. Collins, "Apocalyptic Literature," in *Early*

These characteristics are not unique to apocalypses, nor do all apocalypses contain all of them. Some scholars, therefore, reduce the list to one essential characteristic. For Paul Hanson that characteristic is the failure of apocalypticists to translate their vision for the future "into the terms of plain history, real politics, and human instrumentality due to a pessimistic view of reality growing out of the bleak post-exilic conditions" surrounding the visionaries.[8] For Gerhard von Rad knowledge is "the nerve-center of apocalyptic literature." Consequently, he draws his famous conclusion that apocalypticism derived from the wisdom tradition.[9] For Walter Schmithals the essence of apocalyptic is its "loss of history."[10] And for E. P. Sanders an apocalypse is a genre that combines revelation with the promise of reversal and restoration.[11]

These attempts to enumerate the characteristic(s) of apocalypses left scholars with the uneasy feeling that the genre still eluded description. In 1979 the Apocalypse Group of the Society of Biblical Literature Genres Project offered a formal definition, further elaborated in 1986:

Judaism and Its Modern Interpreters (ed. Robert A. Kraft and George W. E. Nickelsburg; Philadelphia: Fortress/Atlanta: Scholars Press, 1986), 345–70; and Paul D. Hanson, "Prolegomena to the Study of Jewish Apocalyptic," in *Magnalia Dei, the Mighty Acts of God: Essays on the Bible and Archaeology in Memory of G. Ernest Wright* (ed. Frank M. Cross, Werner E. Lemke, and Patrick D. Miller Jr.; Garden City: Doubleday, 1976), 389–401.

8. Paul D. Hanson, *The Dawn of Apocalyptic* (Philadelphia: Fortress, 1975), 11. Cf. Arthur P. Mendel, *Vision and Violence* (Ann Arbor: University of Michigan Press, 1992), 31.

9. Gerhard von Rad, *Old Testament Theology* (trans. D. M. G. Stalker; New York: Harper & Row, 1962–65), 2:306.

10. Schmithals, *Apocalyptic Movement*, 29–49.

11. E. P. Sanders, "The Genre of Palestinian Jewish Apocalypses," in *Apocalypticism in the Mediterranean World and the Near East* (ed. David Hellholm; Tübingen: Mohr, 1983), 457. Sanders himself admits (458) that his definition is inadequate for the composite nature of apocalyptic.

"Apocalypse" is a genre of revelatory literature with a narrative framework, in which a revelation is mediated by an otherworldly being to a human recipient, disclosing a transcendent reality which is both temporal, insofar as it envisages eschatological salvation, and spatial, insofar as it involves another, supernatural world, ... intended to interpret present, earthly circumstances in light of the supernatural world and of the future, and to influence both the understanding and the behavior of the audience by means of divine authority.[12]

Apocalypticism is not, however, confined to apocalypses. It appears in other types of literature as well, notably testaments,[13] *Sibylline Oracle* 4, and some of the sectarian texts at Qumran. Also, the Old Testament contains materials that should be called protoapocalyptic because they exhibit some of the characteristics of later apocalypses.

The Origin of Apocalyptic

The mention of protoapocalyptic literature in the Old Testament raises the next question to be faced: the origin of apocalyp-

---

12. John J. Collins, "Introduction: Towards the Morphology of a Genre," *Semeia* 14 (1979): 9; and Adela Yarbro Collins, "Introduction: Early Christian Apocalypticism," *Semeia* 36 (1986): 7.

13. The distinction between apocalypse and testament may be expressed succinctly: in an apocalypse, the ancient worthy receives information; whereas in a testament, he discloses it, ostensibly in his last words. Anitra Bingham Kolenkow ("Testaments, I: The Literary Genre 'Testament,'" in *Early Judaism and Its Modern Interpreters* [ed. Robert A. Kraft and George W. E. Nickelsburg; Philadelphia: Fortress/Atlanta: Scholars Press, 1986], 262–64) says a testament includes a life history, material learned from above by the testator, and authoritative urging as the last gift from the testator in the form of blessing and curses or exhortations.

tic. Scholarly opinion is divided over whether apocalypticism is an import from outside Judaism or an indigenous development. Scholars who think it was imported often see its source as Mesopotamia or Greece. Among those who think it was indigenous, its roots are said to be either prophecy or wisdom literature.

Apocalypticism as an Imported Movement

It is widely accepted today that Iranian religious thought influenced apocalyptic thinking, an opinion argued first by R. Reitzenstein, H. S. Nyberg, Alfred Bertholet, and others of the German history of religions school. Some of these scholars viewed this borrowing negatively. Wilhelm Bousset, for example, treats apocalypticism as evidence that "late" Jewish religion had lost its vitality. Rather than finding theological clarification in foreign thinking, it found only magical folk religion with nothing to offer but fallen angels, primitive myths, and cosmological speculation.[14] If other scholars viewed apocalypticism less pejoratively, they were just as certain that it was an import. Rudolf Otto sees its origin in Iran in the time before Persian and Indian religions separated.[15] T. F. Glasson argues just as strongly for Greek influence on Jewish apocalypticism.[16]

Scholars are now content to speak of foreign influence with-

---

14. Wilhelm Bousset, *Die Religion des Judentums in neutestamentlicher Zeitalter* (2d ed.; Berlin: Reuter & Reichard, 1906), 459–60. Norman Cohn (*Cosmos, Chaos and the World to Come: The Ancient Roots of Apocalyptic Faith* [New Haven: Yale University Press, 1993]) argues anew for a Zoroastrian origin.

15. Rudolf Otto, *The Kingdom of God and the Son of Man* (Boston: Starr King, 1957), 20–29.

16. T. F. Glasson, *Greek Influence in Jewish Eschatology* (London: SPCK, 1961).

out claiming that those influences were the sole inspiration for the movement. The International Colloquium on Apocalypticism, meeting in Uppsala in 1979, included papers on Akkadian, Egyptian, Etruscan, Greek, Persian, and Roman apocalypticism.[17] The consensus of contemporary scholarship seems to be that "most of the features by which apocalyptic is usually distinguished from prophecy...are found throughout the Hellenistic world and must be considered representative of the *Zeitgeist* of late antiquity."[18] Even so, such borrowing began with a point of contact in Jewish tradition. In addition, apocalypticism also developed answers simultaneously with other peoples in the Hellenistic world addressing conditions common to them all.[19] It will not do, then, to dismiss the "inner-Jewish" features of apocalyptic literature.[20]

Those inner-Jewish features include, among others, the following: (1) it is the God of the Jews — not of the Greeks, Egyptians, Persians, or Etruscans — who holds the future; (2) that future will be markedly better for those whom the Jewish God blesses; (3) it is the Scriptures, however defined, of the Jews that reveal the word of that God; and (4) the ethics and the piety of apocalypticists derive from those Scriptures, particularly the Torah.

---

17. See David Hellholm, ed., *Apocalypticism in the Mediterranean World and the Near East* (Tübingen: Mohr, 1983).

18. John J. Collins, "Jewish Apocalyptic against Its Hellenistic Environment," *Bulletin of the American Schools of Oriental Research* 220 (1975): 33.

19. Ibid., 34.

20. Michael E. Stone, "Lists of Revealed Things in the Apocalyptic Literature," in *Magnalia Dei, the Mighty Acts of God: Essays on the Bible and Archaeology in Memory of G. Ernest Wright* (ed. Frank M. Cross, Werner E. Lemke, and Patrick D. Miller Jr.; Garden City: Doubleday, 1976), 438.

Apocalypticism as an Indigenous Movement

Among scholars who see apocalypticism as an essentially home-grown phenomenon, its origin is said to be either prophecy or wisdom. Representative of the first group is the British trio of R. H. Charles, H. H. Rowley, and D. M. Russell, who argued that apocalypticism was the "child of prophecy." Charles, for example, thought that one source of apocalypticism was unfulfilled prophecy that was rewritten or reedited.[21] Rowley likewise understands apocalypticism as the child of prophecy, but thinks the movement owed much to the social strife of the Maccabean period.[22] Russell claimed that apocalypticism was "prophecy in a new idiom," which arose out of prophecy by developing and universalizing the conception of the Day of the Lord.[23] More recently, Hanson emphasized the connection between Old Testament prophecy and apocalyptic literature, tracing concepts often attributed to foreign influence to ancient Canaanite mythology mediated through hymns and the royal Israelite cult.[24]

Gerhard von Rad challenged this view, arguing instead that the apocalyptic understanding of history was deterministic and, thus, incompatible with the view of history in the prophets. He also argued that the nerve-center of apocalyptic literature was

---

21. R. H. Charles, *A Critical History of the Doctrine of a Future Life* (London: Black, 1913), 108. See F. C. Porter, *The Messages of the Apocalyptic Writers* (New York: Scribner, 1905), 47–48.

22. H. H. Rowley, *The Relevance of Apocalyptic* (2d ed.; London: Lutterworth, 1955), 14.

23. D. S. Russell, *The Method and Message of Apocalyptic* (Old Testament Library; Philadelphia: Westminster, 1964), 92, 94.

24. Hanson, "Prolegomena to the Study of Jewish Apocalyptic," 404. This is the position he argues in *Dawn of Apocalyptic*.

knowledge. Hence, apocalypticism should be understood as the child of wisdom literature.[25]

Reaction to von Rad was swift and often negative. Philipp Vielhauer objected that eschatology and the imminent expectation of the end are characteristic of apocalypticism, but incompatible with wisdom thought.[26] Peter von der Osten-Sacken argued that von Rad based his views on later apocalypses and that Daniel, for example, does not exhibit historical determinism.[27] H.-P. Müller has since modified von Rad's position by arguing that apocalypticism derived not from the school or courtly wisdom of the Old Testament but from mantic or divinatory wisdom of which Daniel was the example par excellence.[28]

---

25. Von Rad, *Old Testament Theology*, 2:302–6. See J. C. H. Lebram, "The Piety of Jewish Apocalyptists," in *Apocalypticism in the Mediterranean World and the Near East* (ed. David Hellholm; Tübingen: Mohr, 1983), 190–91.

26. Philipp Vielhauer, "Apocalyptic and Related Subjects," in *New Testament Apocrypha* (ed. Edgar Hennecke, Wilhelm Schneemelcher, and R. McLean Wilson; Philadelphia: Westminster, 1965), 2:587–88.

27. Peter von der Osten-Sacken, *Die Apokalyptik in ihrem Verhältnis zu Prophetie und Weisheit* (Theologische Exitenz Heute 157; Munich: Kaiser, 1969), 11–12, 32–33. See also, Friedreich Dingermann, "Die Botschaft vom Vergehen dieser Welt und von den Geheimnissen der Endzeit: Beginnende Apokalyptik in alten Testament," in *Wort und Botschaft* (ed. Josef Schreiner; Würzburg: Echter, 1967), 329–42.

28. H.-P. Müller, "Mantische Weisheit und Apokalyptik," in *Congress Volume: Uppsala 1971* (VTSup 22; Leiden: Brill, 1972), 268–93. Cf. P. R. Davies, "The Social World of Apocalyptic Writings," in *The World of Ancient Israel: Sociological, Anthropological, and Political Perspectives* (ed. Ronald E. Clements; Cambridge: Cambridge University Press, 1989), 260–64. Davies paraphrases Ernst Käsemann's famous dictum to the effect that "manticism is the mother of Jewish apocalyptic" (263). Cf. Jonathan Z. Smith, "Wisdom and Apocalyptic," in *Visionaries and Their Apocalypses* (ed. Paul D. Hanson; Issues in Religion and Theology 4; Philadelphia: Fortress, 1983), 101–20.

Apocalypticism as a Peripheral Movement

The search for the origin of apocalypticism concentrated on literary matters until recently. Both sides could point to evidence in their favor: apocalypticism shared many characteristics with its larger, Hellenistic environment and seemed to develop trends in the Old Testament as well, particularly the prophets, but at times from wisdom also. So, to break the impasse, scholars began to investigate its social milieu. Otto Plöger developed the view of Charles and Rowley that apocalypticism originated among the Hasidim.[29] According to Plöger, apocalypticism had a long prehistory, dating back into the Persian period, perhaps as early as 400 B.C.E. Joel, Trito-Zechariah, Isa 24–27, and Daniel were the literary deposits of the Hasidim, an eschatological group that opposed the priestly, theocratic party.[30]

Martin Hengel also argued that the Book of Daniel, along with the *Damascus Document* and *1 (Ethiopic) Enoch,* derived from the Hasidim, described as an essentially closed community that indicted postexilic Judaism, including the temple cult, for succumbing to the influence of Hellenism.[31] The apocalyptic worldview was a response to Hellenism by Jews who perceived it as a threat to their way of life. On the other hand, of course, apocalypticism itself could not escape influence from Hellenism.[32] George W. Nickelsburg observes, however, that Hengel built his reconstruction on two unproven assumptions:

---

29. Charles, *Future Life,* 173; Rowley, *The Relevance of Apocalyptic,* 14, 41.

30. Otto Plöger, *Theocracy and Eschatology* (trans. S. Rudman; Richmond: John Knox, 1968). Hanson (*Dawn of Apocalyptic*) argues for a similar theocratic/eschatological split in the early postexilic period, with Trito-Isaiah and Zech 9–14 as products of the eschatological group.

31. Martin Hengel, *Judaism and Hellenism* (trans. John Bowden; Philadelphia: Fortress, 1974), 1:175–80.

32. Ibid., 196, 252–53.

"(a) that the people slaughtered in the caves (1 Macc 2:29–38) were Hasidim — an identification the text does not make; and (b) that the refusal of these people to defend themselves on the Sabbath indicates that they were *thoroughgoing* pacifists."[33] According to Nickelsburg, Hengel has not proved his thesis; the origin of apocalypticism has not been shown to be among the Hasidim.

Robert R. Wilson's study of Daniel noted a movement toward alienation in the stories of Dan 2, 4, and 5, in contrast with those of Dan 3 and 6. Further, the court setting of those stories suggests that a wisdom circle stood behind them. Daniel 7–12, however, stands much closer to the prophetic traditions of the Old Testament, suggesting a change within the composition of the group responsible for the Book of Daniel.[34] Wilson concludes, therefore, "that apocalyptic groups may develop whenever the required social conditions are present and that the *shape* of a particular group's religion and literature will depend on the group's social and religious background."[35] In

---

33. George W. Nickelsburg, "Social Aspects of Palestinian Jewish Apocalypticism," in *Apocalypticism in the Mediterranean World and the Near East* (ed. David Hellholm; Tübingen: Mohr, 1983), 647. See also J. Collins, "Apocalyptic Literature," 356–57.

34. Robert R. Wilson, "From Prophecy to Apocalyptic: Reflections on the Shape of Israelite Religion," *Semeia* 21 (1981): 88–92. By contrast, Davies ("Social World of Apocalyptic Writings," 261–63) claims that apocalypticism derives from mantic circles.

35. Wilson, "From Prophecy to Apocalyptic," 93. Cf. Davies, "Social World of Apocalyptic Writings," 268; J. Collins "Apocalyptic Literature," 358–59; Russell, *Method and Message,* 27; and Hanson, *Dawn of Apocalyptic,* 20. Christopher Rowland (*The Open Heaven: A Study of Apocalypticism in Judaism and Early Christianity* [New York: Crossroad, 1982], 214–47) emphasizes the role of visionary prophets in the rise of apocalyptic, but declines to assign apocalypticism to one narrow group.

other words under the right circumstances, any group, prophetic or wisdom, can become apocalyptic. This view seems to have gained favor and will be adopted here.

The circumstances may vary; the move to the periphery may be caused by internal or external stimuli;[36] but the crucial issue is that a group perceives itself to be at least relatively deprived and out of power. It may well project the causes for its deprivation on the establishment, design a new set of assumptions about power and how to get it, and propose a new social order.[37] The details of that program will vary from group to group and offer the members a practical means, active or passive, for realizing the group's programs.[38] Further, the program will look not just to the future, but also to the past and present to make sense out of the group's situation.

Vitality in Apocalyptic Literature

Vitality may be understood as the capacity of an individual or a movement to live and develop and remain viable in the face of change or opposition. Clearly apocalypticism lived and devel-

---

36. Peter Worsley (*The Trumpet Shall Sound* [2d ed.; New York: Schocken, 1968], 225) lists four types of societies where these conditions occur: (1) "stateless societies" with no central political institutions, (2) agrarian or feudal societies, (3) societies that have suffered a crushing military defeat, or (4) from societies impacted by internal stimuli. Stephen L. Cook (*Prophecy and Apocalypticism: The Postexilic Social Setting* [Minneapolis: Fortress, 1995], 57–71 and 214) argues that apocalyptic groups may be central or peripheral in their own society due to endogenous or exogenous conditions.

37. Sheldon R. Isenberg, "Millenarism in Greco-Roman Palestine," *Religion* 4 (1974): 35–37. Isenberg prefers the term *millenarism* to *apocalypticism* to avoid confusing the movement with the literary genre *apocalypse*. Cf. Davies, "Social World of Apocalyptic Writings," 253.

38. Wilson, "From Prophecy to Apocalyptic," 86.

oped for centuries. The task now at hand is to demonstrate its viability as well. One word of caution needs to be said: the "viability" in question is first of all its viability for the communities for which the literature was written.

Walter Harrelson demonstrated this viability in two studies of intertestamental literature. In the first study, he points to the well-known threats against Jewish life during the Greek period. In confronting those threats, the apocalyptic *Testament of Moses* "turned to individual ethics and emphasized the motives of human conduct and the attitudes of persons."[39] By contrast, if the danger of such individualism in some apocalyptic pieces seemed too great to some of their contemporaries, "the ethics of the Testaments of the Twelve Patriarchs served well to place a communal frame around the remarkably penetrating individual ethic commended by the author."[40]

Harrelson's second study, of the figure of Ezra in 2 Esd (=4 *Ezra*) 3–10, offers another demonstration of the viability of an apocalypse. Harrelson is struck by Ezra's repeated identification of himself as wicked, despite the contrary arguments of an angel who converses with him. When Ezra confronts a grieving widow who has lost her son, he sternly counsels her to quit crying and to go home. Harrelson rejects the usual explanation that the author spoke through Ezra. Instead, Harrelson reads the admonition as ironic: she is no more capable of ceasing to mourn than Ezra had been. Remarkably, the woman is transformed into the Zion of the future, a Zion whose capacity

---

39. Walter Harrelson, "The Significance of 'Last Words' for Intertestamental Ethics," in *Essays in Old Testament Ethics: J. Philip Hyatt, In Memoriam* (ed. James L. Crenshaw and John T. Willis; New York: Ktav, 1974), 209.

40. Ibid., 211.

is limitless, not simply the Zion of Jews or a small party within the community. In that Zion a vast multitude, including Gentiles, will "learn the meaning of Torah and find peace and life and wholeness."[41]

Given the breadth of apocalyptic literature and the limits of this study, it will be helpful, indeed necessary, to focus on one particular issue. Harrelson's reflections on Zion point to the importance of the city of Jerusalem and its temple in apocalypticism and suggest it as an acceptable focus. The significance of Jerusalem for that literature can be quickly summarized. Its restoration stood at the center of postexilic, protoapocalyptic prophecy, and it functioned as the center of the universe in the earliest apocalypse, 1 (*Ethiopic*) *Enoch* (26:1). The desolation of Jerusalem at the hands of Antiochus Epiphanes prompted the writing of the apocalyptic portions of the Book of Daniel. It played an important role in many of the ensuing apocalypses. Opposition to the Jerusalem priesthood motivated the covenanters at Qumran. The destruction of Jerusalem by the Romans produced another flurry of apocalyptic writing at the end of the first century. Even apocalypses that ignored or downplayed the significance of the city and its sanctuary found themselves having to explain its destruction, and they often depicted heaven as a heavenly sanctuary or an idealized Jerusalem. In short, Jerusalem and the temple are pervasive in apocalyptic literature. Further, since rabbinic and other perspectives on Jerusalem during that time have become a topic of considerable interest in

---

41. Walter Harrelson, "Ezra among the Wicked in 2 Esdras 3–10," in *The Divine Helmsman: Studies on God's Control of Human Events Presented to Lou H. Silberman* (ed. James L. Crenshaw and Samuel Sandmel; New York: Ktav, 1980), 36–37.

scholarship,[42] investigation of their use in apocalyptic literature is timely.

Jerusalem and the Temple in the Protoapocalyptic Sections of the Old Testament

Isaiah 40–55

Georg Fohrer argues that Deutero-Isaiah, with his promise of a better tomorrow, provided the point where Old Testament prophecy turned toward eschatology.[43] The prophet portrayed the difference between the conditions of the exiles and the coming new day by means of the contrast between a forlorn, childless widow and a happily married mother with a tent full of children (Isa 54).[44] The nations would even carry the exiles back home (49:22–23).

---

42. See Marcel Poorthuis and Chana Safrai, eds., *The Centrality of Jerusalem: Historical Perspectives* (Kampen: Kok Pharos, 1996); Julie Galambush, *Jerusalem in the Book of Ezekiel: The City as Yahweh's Wife* (SBLDS 130; Atlanta: Scholars Press, 1992); Gerhard Langer, *Von Gott erwählt — Jerusalem* (Österreichische biblische Studien 8; Klosterneuberg: Österreichisches Katholisches Bibelwerk, 1989); Ben C. Ollenberger, *Zion: The City of the Great King* (JSOTSup 41; Sheffield: JSOT Press, 1987); Josef Schreiner, *Sion — Jerusalem: Jahwes Königssitz; Theologie der heiligen Stadt im Alten Testament* (Studien zum Alten und Neuen Testaments 7; Munich: Kösel, 1963); and Norman W. Porteous, "Jerusalem-Zion: The Growth of a Symbol," in *Verbannung und Heimkehr: Beiträge zur Geschichte und Theologie Israels im 6. und 5. Jahrhundert v. Chr.: Festschrift für W. Rudolph* (ed. Arnulf Kuschke; Tübingen: Mohr, 1961), 235–52.

43. Georg Fohrer, "Die Struktur der alttestamentlichen Eschatologie," *Theologische Literaturzeitung* 85 (1960): 403.

44. See Gottfried Glassner, *Vision eines auf Verheissung gegründeten Jerusalem* (Österreichische biblische Studien 11; Klosterneuberg: Österreichisches Katholisches Bibelwerk, 1991).

Ezekiel

No less important for setting expectations for the postexilic period was the Book of Ezekiel, culminating as it does with the
Gog of Magog oracles (Ezek 38–39) and the vision of the new
temple (Ezek 40–48). The vision passages that can be assigned
to Ezekiel with the most confidence are 40:1–2; 43:4–7a; and
perhaps part of 47:1–12.[45] Perhaps some, maybe even much, of
the rest of the temple vision was from Ezekiel also. Regardless of the specific dates of some of this material, the book
was at least in large measure completed before the end of the
exile.[46]

The Book of Ezekiel developed expectations for the future in
terms of a number of contrasts with the past. In the past, foreign
conquerors had run roughshod over Jerusalem and Judah; in the
future that would not be so. Ezekiel 38–39 seems to envision
a period of time after the exiles returned home.[47] It portrays
Gog of Magog as a world emperor who rallies the armies of the
world for one last great attack against Jerusalem, which does not
succeed. Gog seems not to be a specific person, but a symbol for
any and every would-be conqueror in the future. Moreover, the
image of Gog left a legacy for later apocalypticists: the motif of
a future war against Jerusalem. In the past foreign invaders had

---

45. See, e.g., Aelred Cody, *Ezekiel* (Old Testament Message 11; Wilmington, Del.: Glazier, 1984), 192; G. A. Cooke, *The Book of Ezekiel* (International
Critical Commentary; Edinburgh: Clark, 1936), 425. On the other hand,
Walther Zimmerli (*Ezekiel* [trans. Ronald E. Clements and James D. Martin;
Hermeneia; Philadelphia: Fortress, 1979–83], 2:329 and passim) also con-
siders authentic the long vision of the man who conducted Ezekiel through
the city.

46. Zimmerli (*Ezekiel*, 2:552–53) argues that at most 42:1–14 and 41:5–
15a might have been written with a view toward Zerubbabel's temple.

47. Ibid., 304.

been hugely successful, but in the future God would see that they failed.

Other contrasts that impinge on Jerusalem may be sketched quickly:

1. Solomon's temple lay in ruins. Ezekiel 40–42 gave a floor plan for a new one.

2. In 11:22–23 Ezekiel depicted God's departing the temple and Jerusalem, leaving them defenseless before Nebuchadnezzar. In 43:1–9 God returns to the new temple to make it his throne upon earth and to rule the world from it.

3. In the past foreigners could enter and defile the temple, but not in the future (44:9).

4. In the past, Levites had been allowed to offer sacrifice, but no more. The offering of sacrifices would now be limited to the Zadokite priesthood (44:10–31).

5. In the past provisions for the temple had come from the king, giving the monarchy control over the temple. In the future the priests would have their own land to farm, and so also would the king, who would therefore not need to tax the people for his upkeep (45:1–9).

6. In the past water had been a serious problem for farmers in Palestine. In the future, though, water would flow from under the temple (the throne of God and source of all blessing) and supply the whole land, turning even the Dead Sea into freshwater, except for marshes and swamps, which would remain for obtaining salt from evaporation (47:1–12).

It is fairly clear that in these passages the temple is functioning as the navel of the earth, the source of God's blessing on the land. In 40:2, Ezekiel emphasizes the height of the mountain, and 48:15 makes clear that Jerusalem will lie at the center of the land, both common features of the earth's navel (cf. 5:5; 38:12).

Failed Expectations

The problem, of course, was that the reality of life in postexilic Jerusalem did not match the predictions of Second Isaiah or Ezekiel. The country of Judah, a tiny subprovince in the Persian Empire, included only the city and four small areas of settlement.[48] The population of Judah and Jerusalem was very small. W. F. Albright estimates the entire population of Judah at twenty thousand in the sixth century and at fifty thousand in the time of Nehemiah; Magen Broshi estimates the population of Jerusalem to have been only forty-five hundred as late as the time of Nehemiah.[49] Some scholars place the figures even lower.

The rebuilding of the temple apparently began under Sheshbazzar, but soon floundered (Ezra 1:11; 5:16). Under the urging of Haggai and Zechariah, the struggling community began again. Haggai acknowledged that the new temple seemed as nothing in comparison with Solomon's, but promised in effect that if they would rebuild the temple, God would come (Hag 2:3–7). Further, he predicted that God would overturn the political order of the day and install Zerubbabel as his new king (2:20–23).[50]

---

48. Charles E. Carter, *The Emergence of Yehud in the Persian Period: A Social and Demographic Study* (JSOT Supp 294; Sheffield: Sheffield Academic Press, 1999), 90–100.

49. W. F. Albright, *The Biblical Period from Abraham to Ezra: An Historical Survey* (New York: Harper & Row, 1963), 110–11 n. 180; Magen Broshi, "Estimating the Population of Ancient Jerusalem," *Biblical Archaeology Review* 4 (June 1978): 12–13.

50. Wolter H. Rose (*Zemah and Zerubbabel: Messianic Expectations in the Early Postexilic Period* [JSOTSup 304; Sheffield: Sheffield Academic Press,

Zechariah 1–8

The Prophet Zechariah also confronted the bleak conditions of the early exile. His first effort may have been to send an early version of his visions (1:7–6:15 minus 3:1–10; 4:6b–10a; and 6:11b–13) to Babylon in an effort to recruit more help in rebuilding the temple.[51] Next, he seems to have updated his visions in light of the experiences of 520, naming Zerubbabel as the one who had founded and would complete the temple (4:6b–10a). He also had a vision of God's cleansing the high priest Joshua. Ezekiel 44:10–31 speaks of the Zadokite/non-Zadokite distinction within the priesthood, but knows nothing of a high priest.[52] Thus, Zech 3 seems to go a step farther. Also of importance to this study is the structure of the vision sequence in Zech 1:7–6:15 in alternating between vision and admonition, which became characteristic of later apocalypses. It is this feature of Zech 1–8, more than its theology, that warrants calling those chapters protoapocalyptic.

Isaiah 56–66

When the promised monarchy failed to materialize, the Second Temple and its priesthood emerged as virtually the only institution in preexilic Judah with any power. Consequently, control

---

2000], 208–43) challenges this reading of Hag 2:20–23, arguing that the term *seal* (*khotam*) designates someone for whom one has special care or high esteem, and not royalty. That conclusion is part of Rose's larger study of the Hebrew term *tsemakh*, which Rose thinks does not designate Zerubbabel, but a future ruler. Rose's arguments notwithstanding, Hag 2:20–23 looks like a deliberate revision of Jer 22:24; i.e., Haggai deliberately designates a descendant of Jehoiachin as ruler.

51. Paul L. Redditt, "Zerubbabel, Joshua, and the Night Visions of Zechariah," *CBQ* 54 (1992): 250–55.

52. Zimmerli, *Ezekiel*, 2:551.

of the temple became an early point of conflict. Hanson argues that behind Trito-Isaiah stood a group comprised of disciples of Deutero-Isaiah and disenfranchised Levites who lost out to the Zadokites in the struggle over the temple.[53] He understands references to God's people as sectarian,[54] for example: "Thy holy people possessed thy sanctuary a little while; / our adversaries have trodden it down" (63:18 RSV).[55]

In many ways Trito-Isaiah shows a democratization of the cult that stands in marked contrast with the earlier sentiments of Ezekiel and the later efforts of Ezra and Nehemiah. The opening verses (56:1–8) call foreigners and eunuchs to worship and to minister on the holy mountain, and 61:6 speaks of the people of Zion as the priests of the Lord. To be sure 63:1–6, with its description of God's coming from Edom soaked in the blood of nations, seems poles apart from 56:1–8, but the prophet perhaps sees them as unrepentant. In any case Trito-Isaiah bears testimony that the new Zion, even with its temple, does not yet measure up to the promises of Deutero-Isaiah. Even so, God had promised that it would. Consequently, Trito-Isaiah twice depicts Zion as paradise revisited (65:17–25; 66:22–23). These verses speak, in language similar to 11:6–9, of the renewal of Jerusalem as the renewal of the earth. Hanson calls this type of eschatological hope apocalyptic in the sense that it fails to translate its hope into the terms of plain history, real politics, and human instrumentality.[56] Moreover, the author of these sentiments was convinced that God would ultimately see to it that righteousness

---

53. Hanson, *Dawn of Apocalyptic*, 209.
54. Ibid., 96.
55. Unless otherwise noted, biblical quotations are from the NRSV.
56. Ibid., 11.

prevailed in Jerusalem, thus resolving the discrepancy between past prediction and present reality.

Central and Peripheral Writings

Hanson's reconstruction of the postexilic period plays off the dissidents against the hierocratic priestly party represented in Ezekiel, Haggai, Zechariah, Ezra, Nehemiah, and Chronicles. That all six of these books arose from the same milieu is doubtful. Scholars often question whether Haggai spoke to Joshua at all, since he appears only in redactional introductions. Also, it can be argued that Zechariah's vision was inclusive rather than being a program for Zadokite control; there is certainly no mention of the split in the priesthood. Zechariah saw a role for the king and functioned as a prophet himself. On the other hand, both Haggai and Zechariah emphasized the building of the Second Temple and were no doubt well thought of later by the priests for that reason.

Isaiah 24–27

Nor was there only one peripheral group. Both Isa 24–27 and the Book of Joel probably arose during the sixth or early fifth centuries,[57] but neither of them appears to have been priestly.

---

57. A date for Isa 24–27 during the exile (see Dan G. Johnson, *From Chaos to Restoration: An Integrative Reading of Isaiah 24–27* [JSOTSup 61; Sheffield: JSOT Press, 1988]) or shortly after (Hanson, *Dawn of Apocalyptic*, 314) is preferable to the later dates offered by Plöger and other scholars. If the traditions were exilic, they would reflect the sentiments of people left behind during the exile. A date just before or after 539 and a setting among people having to survive in and around Jerusalem with no king, no official priesthood, and no temple might best explain both the failure of these chapters to mention any of the three and the concern of the chapters over the future of the city. On the date for Joel, see Paul L. Redditt, "The Book of Joel and Peripheral Prophecy," *CBQ* 48 (1986): 234–35.

In contrast with Zech 1–8, Isa 24–27 saw no role for the king or the priesthood and never mentioned the temple explicitly. The city of Jerusalem, however, plays a prominent role. According to Isa 24:23 Yhwh will reveal his glory on Mount Zion (in the temple?). Further, 25:6–10a celebrates God's ultimate elevation of his people on Zion. Moreover, the haughty "city" of 25:1–5 and 26:5–6 functions as the foil to the present lowly Jerusalem. In the future their roles would be reversed.[58] In the absence of a king, God himself would reign directly. It is likely that 27:7–11 also has in view the late exilic or early postexilic city of Jerusalem, whose altar stones had to be crushed and whose Asherim and incense altars had to be removed before God could usher in his glorious day.[59] Then, all the exiles would return to Zion to worship.

The sentiments of these chapters are not so much those of disenfranchised priests as of some other peripheral group in Jerusalem who had given up on cult and state alike. On the other hand the author often quoted earlier prophecy,[60] suggesting that he thought of himself as a prophet or an interpreter of the prophetic tradition. The group for whom such a program would have meaning would have been simultaneously pro-Jerusalem and antiestablishment. They reacted to dashed hopes and internal pressure with passivity, preferring to wait for God to act rather than initiating activity themselves.[61]

---

58. Paul L. Redditt, "Once Again, the City in Isaiah 24–27," *Hebrew Annual Review* 10 (1986): 332.

59. Ibid., 329–32.

60. See the list of quotations prepared by Egge Simon Mulder, *Die Teologie van die Jesaja-Apokalipse* (Groningen: Wolters, 1954), 74–77.

61. Redditt, "City in Isaiah 24–27," 327–28, 331–32.

Joel

In the Book of Joel, the movement to the periphery left a "paper" trail. The book opens, of course, with Joel's warnings of an impending calamity, described in terms of a locust/military invasion, followed by calls to hold a solemn assembly at the temple. It appears that Joel had access to the temple and its priests and expected them to heed what he said. The turning point of the book is 2:18, where suddenly one reads that "the LORD became jealous for his land, / and had pity on his people." In the following verses the punishments predicted in 1:5–20 are reversed.[62] Then, in 3:1–4:21 (Eng. 2:28–3:21) one can detect a steady movement away from the center toward the periphery. That movement is especially clear in 3:1–5 (Eng. 2:28–32), which portrays a future in which God's charisma is freely available to young and old, men and women, servants and (by implication) masters. In short, the cult is democratized in a way unthinkable for the central elite, but quite in keeping with the typical programs of peripheral groups.[63] The best explanation for the appearance of this peripheral program is that Joel or his community was pushed more and more to the periphery of Jerusalemite life.

While Joel 3–4 is eschatological, it nowhere looks beyond history. In particular, 3:1–5 (Eng. 2:28–32) employs the concept of the Day of YHWH and speaks of "portents in the heavens," but G. W. Ahlström argues that the book simply reflects the prophetic use of an old cosmogony employed in the liturgy in Jerusalem. Accordingly, the Day of YHWH was the day of

---

62. Redditt, "Book of Joel and Peripheral Prophecy," 228.
63. Ibid., 232–33.

epiphany, the day when God delivered his people from chaos and disaster.[64]

The vision focused on Jerusalem, but also included the surrounding countryside. The restoration of the fortunes of Jerusalem specifically included Judah (4:1 [Eng. 3:1]), as did also the picture of restoration (4:18–21 [Eng. 3:18–21]) and God's revenge against the Sabeans (4:4–8 [Eng. 3:4–8]). The future attack against Jerusalem (4:2–3 [Eng. 3:2–3]) would include Judah too, which is also promised God's protection. It is from Zion itself, however, that the LORD roars (4:16 [Eng. 3:16]), which emphasizes that people on Mount Zion would survive the final day (3:5 [Eng. 2:32]).

Zechariah 9–14

The remaining protoapocalyptic book in the Old Testament is Zech 9–14. The opening chapter celebrates the coming of God to restore the old Davidic kingdom (9:1–8), the coming of the king to Jerusalem (9:9–10), and God's victory over its enemies and the enemies of Judah (9:11–17). In 10:3b–12 God promises to bring home the exiles of both the northern and southern tribes. In short, these verses look forward to the reunion of north and south under the Davidic monarchy. Precisely these two hopes, however, proved futile. Hence, a different spirit permeates much that follows. Especially in the Shepherd Allegory (11:4–17), a prophet (presumably the redactor of Zech 9–14) breaks his staff that symbolizes the union between north and south and in doing so reverses the prediction of Ezek 37:15–23 that God would reunite the divided monarchy. Nor were the shepherds fulfilling the role of David described in Ezek

---

64. G. W. Ahlström, *Joel and the Temple Cult* (VTSup 21; Leiden: Brill, 1971), 73, 66. See also, Redditt, "Book of Joel and Peripheral Prophecy," 238.

37:24–28; Zech 11:17 pronounces a woe against the worthless shepherd, and 12:10–13:1 looks to the cleansing of Jerusalem. In 12:1–9 and 14:1–21 the author uses the tradition of the nations against Jerusalem, but with two twists: (1) according to 13:9 two-thirds of the people would be destroyed, and (2) according to 12:6–7 Judah would have victory first, thus precluding the preeminence of Jerusalem predicted in 12:8.[65]

Two observations need to be made here. In the first place this revision of the traditions constitutes a classic case of cognitive dissonance. Political reality did not match the traditional expectations. In such cases it becomes necessary "to construct a system of explanation showing how failed predictions can be rescued by reinterpretation and explanation."[66] Blame for failure lay precisely with the shepherds, the leading families in Jerusalem castigated in the shepherd materials and in 12:10–13:1 (or

---

65. See Paul L. Redditt, "Israel's Shepherds: Hope and Pessimism in Zechariah 9–14," *CBQ* 51 (1989): 631–42; and idem, "The Two Shepherds in Zechariah 11:4–17," *CBQ* 55 (1993): 676–86. Two studies attack this position. The first, by Stephen L. Cook ("The Metamorphosis of a Shepherd: The Tradition History of Zechariah 11:17 + 13:7–9," *CBQ* 55 [1993]: 453–66), fails to recognize that priestly families too are criticized (12:13). The second, by Raymond F. Person (*Second Zechariah and the Deuteronomic School* [JSOTSup 167; Sheffield: Sheffield Academic Press, 1993], 153–54), says this position falls into the "simplistic" trap of seeing two, well-defined competing groups. Actually, only the central group is well defined. Around that group were various peripheral groups who defined themselves over against the people in power.

66. Robert P. Carroll, "Ancient Israelite Prophecy and Dissonance Theory," *Numen* 24 (1977): 141. On the concept of cognitive dissonance, see Leon Festinger, *A Theory of Cognitive Dissonance* (Stanford: Stanford University Press, 1957). Simon J. De Vries (*From Old Revelation to New* [Grand Rapids: Eerdmans, 1995], 10–11) questions the applicability of this concept to postexilic prophecy, preferring instead to emphasize a growing prophetic awareness of the person and work of God. Those two positions are not mutually exclusive.

maybe through 13:6). In the second place this revision reflects a conflict between Jerusalem and Judah, not just parties within Jerusalem.

The revision makes clear the real issue facing the postexilic community: who was the real Israel? Was it the priests and their followers? the Davidides and the urban elite? this or that peripheral group? The protoapocalyptic prophets apparently represented a series of voices claiming that each group constituted the real Israel. No one prophet spoke for all groups; in pressing their own cases, each inevitably slighted other groups and perhaps even excluded the ruling group. None of them individually saw the whole picture, but collectively they approximated it.[67]

Jerusalem and the Temple in Jewish Apocalypses

The transition from Old Testament prophecy, Old Testament wisdom,[68] or mantic wisdom[69] is gradual with no single, decisive

---

67. Redditt, "Israel's Shepherds," 641. The date of Zech 9–14 is uncertain, but a date during the Persian period is likely, perhaps in the last half of the fifth century. See Paul L. Redditt, *Haggai, Zechariah and Malachi* (New Century Bible; Grand Rapids: Eerdmans, 1994), 94–100; and, more fully, idem, "Nehemiah's First Mission and the Date of Zechariah 9–14," *CBQ* 56 (1994): 664–78.

68. It is impossible to point to wisdom books in the Old Testament that share the same kind of protoapocalyptic thinking that the postexilic prophets exhibited. It is possible, however, to point to tendencies within Old Testament wisdom that anticipate apocalyptic thinking. Since none of these tendencies focuses on Jerusalem or the temple, a simple list of the more important ones must suffice: (1) a concern with wisdom and dream interpretation; (2) interest in creation, its orderliness, and ultimately the hiddenness of that orderliness; and (3) development in Job and Ecclesiastes in particular of the awareness that people do not always receive just retribution in this life.

69. Katrina J. A. Larkin (*The Eschatology of Second Zechariah: A Study*

break. What eventually emerges is a new type of literature — the apocalypse — in the third century B.C.E. with the Heavenly Luminaries (*1 [Ethiopic] Enoch* 72–82) and the Book of the Watchers (*1 Enoch* 1–36 in part or entirely) and in the second century B.C.E. with the Animal Apocalypse (*1 Enoch* 83–90) and Dan 7–12. Like postexilic prophecy, Jewish apocalypses also deal with the subjects of Jerusalem and the temple. The typology of apocalypses offered by the Apocalyptic Group of the Society of Biblical Literature Genres Project offers useful categories for pursuing these two subjects. That typology is based on two distinctions: (1) the presence or absence of an otherworldly journey, and (2) a review of history in contrast with cosmic or personal eschatology. Four types of apocalypse emerge within Judaism: (1) historical apocalypses with no otherworldly journey, (2) historical apocalypses with an otherworldly journey, (3) otherworldly journeys with cosmic and/or political eschatology, and (4) otherworldly journeys with personal eschatology.[70] The types that deal most extensively with Jerusalem and Judah are the first two, the historical apocalypses. Several were produced in association with the defamation of the temple by

---

of the Formation of a Mantological Wisdom Anthology [Kampen: Kok Pharos, 1994], 218–19) argues that Second Zechariah was a mantic anthology, whose eschatology also appears elsewhere in the Book of the Twelve in Joel 3–4; Amos 9:11–15; Obad 15–21; Mic 4:1–4, 6–8; 4:14–5:4 (Eng. 5:1–5); Hab 3:3–13; Zeph 3:14–20; Hag 2:20–23; Zech 8:20–23; Mal 3:19–24 (Eng. 4:1–6).

70. J. Collins, "Jewish Apocalypses," 21–44; A. Yarbro Collins, "Early Christian Apocalypses," 84–95. Cf. John J. Collins, *Daniel, with an Introduction to Apocalyptic Literature* (Forms of the Old Testament Literature 20; Grand Rapids: Eerdmans, 1984), 6–19. The development of a variety of types is further evidence of the vitality of apocalypticism. Differing hopes took on differing expressions.

Antiochus Epiphanes in 167–164 B.C.E. or with its destruction by Rome in 70 C.E.[71]

Historical Apocalypses with No Otherworldly Journey

It is appropriate to limit the investigation of this type of apocalypse to Dan 7–12 because the other three, the Animal Apocalypse (*1 Enoch* 83–90), the Apocalypse of Weeks (*1 Enoch* 93:1–14; 91:12–17), and *Jubilees* 23, make limited references to the future of Jerusalem. Daniel 7 concludes the Aramaic section of the book and does not explicitly mention Jerusalem or the temple. Even so, the persecution by Antiochus Epiphanes that centered there is discernible in the vision. That persecution is made explicit in 8:11–13, which speaks of the "transgression that makes desolate," that is, Antiochus's erection of an altar to Zeus in the temple in 167 B.C.E. In 8:14 an angel announces that the sanctuary would be given over to such sin for 2,300 "days and nights" (or 1,150 days). Then it would be restored "not by human hands," that is, by God (8:25). This number coincides approximately with the three-and-one-half years allotted to the "little horn" in 7:25 and became the focus of later recalculations: 1,290 days in 12:11, and 1,335 days in 12:12.

John J. Collins suggests that the number may not have been intended literally, but might have had primarily a psychological value to the faithful who were enduring persecution.[72] Lars Hartman argues, in fact, that timetables in apocalyptic literature

---

71. Issues such as the date and unity of the apocalypses are thoroughly reviewed in Michael E. Stone, "Apocalyptic Literature," in *Jewish Writings of the Second Temple Period* (ed. Michael E. Stone; Assen: Van Gorcum/ Philadelphia: Fortress, 1984), 394–427.

72. John J. Collins, *Daniel, First Maccabees, Second Maccabees* (Old Testament Message 16; Wilmington, Del.: Glazier, 1981), 115.

were aimed at the heart and hand, rather than the head.[73] Perhaps so, but another, not necessarily exclusive, explanation lies at hand. Robert R. Wilson argues that sometimes prophecy is fulfilled, but not up to the expectations of the author, his community, or subsequent readers.[74] In the Book of Daniel, then, the reconsecration of the temple may not have been seen as an isolated event, but as one ushering in the new age. In that case the date would have been revised in anticipation of the next event, the in-break of new age (see 12:13).[75]

Such a reading is entirely consistent with 11:31–35, the other place where the desolating transgression is mentioned. Daniel 11:34 speaks of a "little help" received by the victims of Antiochus, a phrase typically understood as a reference to the Maccabees. Apparently, the author(s) of 8:14 and 12:11–12 was (were) not satisfied with the state of affairs ushered in by the Maccabean revolt and urged the readers not to confuse what had happened with the kingdom of God: it had not yet come.

Daniel 9, which reinterprets the seventy years of exile predicted by Jeremiah (25:11–12; 29:10), is an example cited by Wilson in which a biblical author anticipated multiple fulfillment.[76] The rebuilding of the temple under Zerubbabel must

---

73. Lars Hartman, "The Function of Some So-called Timetables," *New Testament Studies* 22 (1976): 14.

74. Robert R. Wilson, "Unfulfilled Prophecy and the Development of the Prophetic Tradition," paper presented at the 1991 annual meeting of the Society of Biblical Literature in Kansas City. On the development of the figure of Daniel in Dan 8–9, see David Satran, "Daniel: Seer, Philosopher, Holy Man," in *Ideal Figures in Ancient Judaism* (ed. George W. E. Nickelsburg and John J. Collins; Society of Biblical Literature Septuagint and Cognate Studies 12; Chico, Calif.: Scholars Press, 1980), 36–37.

75. See Paul L. Redditt, "Calculating the 'Times': Daniel 12:5–13," *Perspectives in Religious Studies* 25 (Winter 1998): 373–79.

76. Wilson, "Unfulfilled Prophecy."

surely have seemed to many to be the fulfillment of Jeremiah's prophecy, though not with the full range of blessing portrayed in the Book of Consolation (Jer 30–31). By contrast Dan 9 says that the prediction that was fulfilled once after seventy years would be fulfilled again after seventy weeks of years.

These seventy weeks of years had both a punitive function "to finish the transgression, to put an end to sin, and to atone for iniquity" and a redemptive function "to bring in everlasting righteousness, to seal both vision and prophet, and to anoint a most holy place" (Dan 9:24). While "the transgression that makes desolate" was no doubt sinful, the view here seems wider: there was iniquity in Israel to atone for. The struggle over the office of high priest and the capitulation to Hellenism of some Jews, especially among the highest echelons, were very likely on the mind of the author(s) of Dan 7–12. In a world where kings desecrated God's altar, God himself would have to hold judgment. When all sin had ceased and been atoned for, then righteousness would prevail, prophecy would be fulfilled, and the temple would be reconsecrated.

The number seventy is used by other apocalypticists, who could speak of seventy generations of watchers (*1 Enoch* 10:12) and seventy shepherds to rule Israel (*1 Enoch* 89:59), and is not to be taken literally.[77] The first seven weeks in Dan 9 culminate with the completion of Zerubbabel's temple (9:25). The last week opens with the death of Onias III (9:26), is punctuated halfway by the desolating transgression (9:27), and would end

---

77. So Collins, *Daniel, First Maccabees, Second Maccabees*, 92–4. The concept of seventy weeks of years is probably a device for periodizing history in Dan 9. See Paul L. Redditt, *Daniel* (New Century Bible; Sheffield: Sheffield Academic Press, 1999), 158–63; and idem, "Daniel 9: Its Structure and Meaning," CBQ 62 (2000): 269–83.

after three-and-one-half weeks more, that is, not immediately, but not too much later either (9:26). The seventy weeks of years would, thus, open with the rebuilding of the sanctuary and end with its liberation from Syrian control. The new age, the age of God's everlasting kingdom, would then begin.

The same leave-it-to-God pacifism expressed in Isa 24–27 is expressed in Daniel too. Indeed, the attempt of the Maccabees to implement a political solution was brushed aside; human institutions were too much a part of the problem to be part of the solution. It is this strain of apocalyptic thinking that seems so futile to many modern interpreters, precisely because it offers no "solutions." Lou H. Silberman notes, however, that such thinking becomes the only viable way of thinking in certain circumstances, for example, life in a concentration camp.[78] Nor should one overlook the embryonic view of resurrection that surfaces in Dan 12:2, which promises that some who died (presumably martyrs) would be raised to new life.[79] As Christoph Münchow shows, in apocalyptic literature eschatological hope makes bearing the present possible, and proper ethical behavior is the bridge to the next eon.[80] Similarly, Ulrich Luck says 2 Esdras (=4 *Ezra*) broadened both the physical (natural) and temporal (historical) perspective to verify righteousness because life no longer seemed worthwhile without this broader perspective.[81]

---

78. Lou H. Silberman, "The Human Deed in a Time of Despair: The Ethics of Apocalyptic," in *Essays in Old Testament Ethics: J. Philip Hyatt, In Memoriam* (ed. James L. Crenshaw and John T. Willis; New York: Ktav, 1974), 198.

79. On the larger subject see John J. Collins, "Apocalyptic Eschatology as the Transcendence of Death," *CBQ* 36 (1974): 21–43.

80. This is the basic thrust of Christoph Münchow's *Ethik und Eschatologie* (Göttingen: Vandenhoeck & Ruprecht, 1981).

81. Ulrich Luck, "Das Weltverständnis in der jüdischen Apokalyptik," *Zeitschrift für Theologie und Kirche* (1976): 304.

Historical Apocalypses with an Otherworldly Journey

Second Esdras and the other two remaining historical apocalypses — the *Syriac Apocalypse of Baruch* and the *Apocalypse of
Abraham* — originated in the aftermath of the destruction of the
Second Temple and will be considered next.[82] All three apocalypses had to answer the question of how God could allow his
sanctuary to be defiled by heathen. One approach was to turn
to the past, to the destruction of Solomon's temple, and to the
explanation of that event in Scripture. In retrospect they could
speak of the sinfulness of Israel in the past (e.g., 2 Esd [=4 *Ezra*]
3:25–27; 2 [*Syriac*] *Baruch* 1). Then they could say that Israel of
the apocalypticists' day had sinned also and thus had borne the
punishment meted out by Rome (e.g., *Apocalypse of Abraham*
27:5–7).

That answer raised another question: Were the ancient Israelites or the contemporaries of the apocalypticists as sinful as
their conquerors? The question was not new. Isaiah 27:7–8 saw
the exile as the precursor to a more severe punishment of the
oppressors, while Deutero-Isaiah had understood Israel's punishment as double what it deserved and as redemptive for others.
Second (Syriac) Baruch 14–15 explained its severity as the result
of the control of this world by evil forces. Similarly, the angel
Uriel told Ezra that people must pass through suffering before
they can receive a reward (2 Esd [=4 *Ezra*] 7:14). Ezra himself, however, saw things differently. As Harrelson shows, Ezra
(despite the best arguments of his interpreting angel) identified

---

82. Scholars have long recognized a close relationship between 2 Esdras
(=4 *Ezra*) and 2 (*Syriac*) *Baruch,* often claiming that they reflect a rabbinic theology. The evidence, however, is not decisive. The *Apocalypse of
Abraham* is also very close. See Michael E. Stone, *Fourth Ezra* (Hermeneia;
Minneapolis: Fortress, 1990), 38–41.

himself with the sinners, for whom he expressed concern (4:38–43; 5:43–49; 7:47; 8:20–36).[83] Indeed, from the time of Moses on, those who had received the law had not kept it (9:29–37). In 10:7–14, 21–24, Ezra laid side by side the sorrow of the whole world over the loss of its inhabitants with the sorrow of Zion over her losses, and he called Zion the mother of the whole world (10:8). The restoration of the glorious mother would mean not only the restoration of Israel, but also the restoration of her other children: hence the necessity for a vast city (10:27, 55).

Apocalypses with Otherworldly Journeys with Cosmic and/or Political Eschatology

The third type of apocalypses features otherworldly journeys with cosmic and/or political eschatology. Of these apocalypses, *2 (Slavonic) Enoch* and the *Testament of Levi* do not mention Jerusalem or the temple and will be dealt with later. Two that do mention Jerusalem are *1 (Ethiopic) Enoch* 1–36 (Book of the Watchers) and *1 Enoch* 37–71 (Similitudes of Enoch). *First Enoch* 1–36 is a composite, within which *1 Enoch* 21–27 form a unit.[84] Starting from the far northwest (where he had gone in *1 Enoch* 17–19), Enoch journeys to Jerusalem, the center of the earth (26:1).[85] From the east side of the city a river flowed north (rather than south as in Ezek 47:1). In another direction (east? *1 Enoch* 28:1) and to the west of Jerusalem stood other mountains. The valleys between Jerusalem and the west moun-

---

83. Harrelson, "Ezra among the Wicked," 32–6.

84. George W. E. Nickelsburg (*Jewish Literature between the Bible and the Mishnah* [Philadelphia: Fortress, 1981], 48) divides the book into a number of sections of varying ages: *1 (Ethiopic) Enoch* 1–5, 6–11, 12–16, 17–19, 20–36. Within this last section, 21–27 describe one cosmic journey.

85. Ibid., 55.

tain were "deep and dry," that is, "accursed," so the accursed
peoples of the world would be gathered there for judgment.

In the Similitudes of Enoch, Jerusalem is less prominent. In
the second parable, however, Enoch learns that when the Elect
One (i.e., the Son of Man)[86] appears God will transform both
heaven and earth and cause the Elect One to dwell on earth
(45:4–5). While Jerusalem is not mentioned as his dwelling
place, no other place is conceivable. The coming of the Elect
One will be accompanied by the resurrection of the dead and
by the judgment (51:1–5). At the end of the parable Enoch
sees evil ones who lead people astray being cast into a crevice
in a valley (56:1–4). This scene is followed immediately by a
narrative of the coming of the Parthians and Medes, perhaps a
reference to their attack on Jerusalem in 40 B.C.E.[87] Jerusalem
("the city of my righteousness"), however, will survive when the
invaders become confused and attack each other (56:7). Then
people (Jews? Gentiles?) will be flown in chariots to Jerusalem,
where they will fall down and worship God (57:1–3).

Both of these passages express the hope that Jerusalem will
one day be the source of blessing and the bulwark against the
evil peoples that Ezekiel had predicted. Meanwhile, things will
go badly for the righteous. In this sin-filled world, wisdom could
find no home and returned to heaven (42:1). God's creation had

---

86. John J. Collins, "The Son of Man in Enoch," in *Ideal Figures in Ancient
Judaism* (ed. George W. E. Nickelsburg and John J. Collins; Society of Biblical
Literature Septuagint and Cognate Studies 12; Chico, Calif.: Scholars Press,
1980), 116. The Son of Man in Enoch "is conceived as a real being... [who]
symbolizes the destiny of the righteous community both in its present hiddenness and future manifestation. The application of the title to Enoch in 71:14
is secondary" (123).

87. *1 Enoch* 56:5 has been used to date the Similitudes. At least it provides
the terminus a quo.

become a world of injustice, the result of false wisdom, and will remain so until the new day.[88] Further, *1 Enoch* 27:4 taught that living righteously and showing mercy were the means to bridge the gap between the present and the future and to participate in that blessing.

Neither the city of Jerusalem nor the temple is mentioned in *1 Enoch* 72–82 (the Book of the Heavenly Luminaries).[89] What is advocated, however, is a solar calendar of 364 days in distinction from the shorter lunar calendar. Since God created the lights as signs, the differences constituted a problem. The "error" of the moon would be corrected in the new creation (72:1).[90] Such a calendar appears also in the *Book of Jubilees* and was followed by the covenanters at Qumran.[91] There is little question that the dispute over the calendar was one issue in a long-standing and bitter quarrel dividing the community that worshiped in Jerusalem. The author of the Book of the Heavenly Luminaries took sides in the controversy, grounding his calendrical calculations in God's unchangeable creation.

Apocalypses with Otherworldly Journeys with Personal Eschatology

The fourth type of apocalypse stems largely from the Diaspora and does not discuss the earthly Jerusalem. The exception might

---

88. Luck, "Das Weltverständnis in der jüdischen Apokalyptik," 297.

89. *1 (Ethiopic) Enoch* 72–82 was part of a longer text, fragments of which have survived at Qumran. The Book of the Heavenly Luminaries appears to reach well back into the third century B.C.E. See Nickelsburg, *Jewish Literature*, 47–8, 65 n. 4.

90. Davies, "Social World of Apocalyptic Writings," 265.

91. Geza Vermes, *The Dead Sea Scrolls in English* (Baltimore: Penguin, 1966), 43. On the eschatology of *Jubilees* 23, see Gene L. Davenport, *The Eschatology of the Book of Jubilees* (Studia Post-Biblica 20; Leiden: Brill, 1971), 32–46.

seem to be *3 (Greek) Baruch,* which opens with Baruch's weeping over the fall of Jerusalem. He is told at once (1:3): "Do not
concern yourself so much over the salvation of Jerusalem."[92] Apparently Baruch was concerned with how the proper relationship
between God and the people could be maintained without the
temple sacrifices. H. E. Gaylord Jr. answers that Baruch learned
that "there is a heavenly temple in which the prayers, virtues,
and good deeds are offered by Michael."[93] In short, *3 Baruch*
deals with the fall of Jerusalem by limiting its significance. That
the book speaks of sacrifice in heaven, identified as the prayers
or good deeds of the righteous in *3 Bar* 14, indicates that heaven
was conceived as a temple. Thus, the world could continue to
function in the absence of an earthly temple.[94] Neither do two
apocalypses with otherworldly journeys with cosmic and/or political eschatology written in the Diaspora discuss the earthly
Jerusalem: *2 (Slavonic) Enoch* and *Testament of Levi 2–5,* though
Testament of Levi 3 does speak of the "sweet savor" of bloodless,
rational sacrifices in heaven.[95]

Further, the type four apocalypses, *2 (Slavonic) Enoch, 3
(Greek) Baruch,* and the *Testament of Abraham,* exhibit a distinctly universalistic outlook.[96] Even so, in the *Testament of*

---

92. The translation is by H. E. Gaylord Jr. in *OTP* 1:663.

93. Ibid., 659.

94. See Martha Himmelfarb, *Ascent to Heaven in Jewish and Christian
Apocalypses* (New York: Oxford University Press, 1993), 34.

95. Ibid., 35, 42. Nor does the (Egyptian?) *Testament of Job* deal with Jerusalem or the nation, but concentrates on individual piety; see John J. Collins,
"Structure and Meaning in the Testament of Job," in *Society of Biblical Literature Seminar Papers* (1974): 1:39, 50. The provenance of the *Testament of Levi*
is debated. Howard C. Kee (in *OTP* 1:778) thinks the *Testaments of the Twelve
Patriarchs* arose in Syria or, perhaps, Egypt. E. P. Sanders ("Genre of Jewish
Palestinian Apocalypses," 451) lists them among Palestinian apocalypses.

96. John J. Collins, "The Genre Apocalypse in Hellenistic Judaism," in

Abraham the earthly temple is corrupt now, but will be restored in the last days. Meanwhile, heaven is the true sanctuary.[97] Also, it appears that the fragmentary *Apocalypse of Zephaniah* exhibits a similar universalism. Both Zephaniah (2:8–9) and a multitude of angels (11:1–6) intercede on behalf of the souls of all people in torment. Nevertheless, *Zephaniah* takes the "beautiful city" (idealized Jerusalem),[98] so prominent in his heavenly journey, as his model for heaven.

In summary, apocalypses in the Diaspora faced a new challenge concerning how to think about their belief system. Instead of looking back to the old temple or abandoning hope, they looked around at their fellow humans and looked up to God, their one source of salvation.

Jerusalem and the Temple in Related Literature

Literature containing apocalyptic imagery and/or eschatology is extensive and includes testaments, the *Sibylline Oracles,* and some sectarian texts from Qumran.[99] In the *Testaments of the Twelve Patriarchs* one finds mention of a new priesthood in *Testament of Levi* 18 and *Testament of Judah* 21, with the addition in the latter that the priesthood was superior to the earthly

---

Apocalypticism in the Mediterranean World and the Near East (ed. David Hellholm; Tübingen: Mohr, 1983), 547.

97. Himmelfarb, *Ascent to Heaven,* 66.

98. Ibid., 52.

99. On the dates and composition of these books see Nickelsburg, *Jewish Literature,* and the introductions to the books in *OTP.* See also Anitra Bingham Kolenkow and John J. Collins, "Testaments," in *Early Judaism and Its Modern Interpreters* (ed. Robert A. Kraft and George W. E. Nickelsburg; Philadelphia: Fortress/Atlanta: Scholars Press, 1986), 259–85.

kingdom.[100] *Testament of Judah* 24 speaks of a messiah, but not Jerusalem. The *Apocalypse of Daniel* 5:7–12 foresees a new Jerusalem no longer held in captivity because God was its salvation and dwelled in its midst. The *Sibylline Oracles* speak of Jews who fully honor the temple (3:575) and a future assault on the city that God will repel (3:657, 705). Additionally, in the end time the nations would go there to worship (3:715, 773–76). By contrast, *Sibylline Oracle* 4 can speak of the future destruction of Jerusalem (reflecting, no doubt, the events of 70 C.E.), the impiety of the last day, conflagration, resurrection, and judgment.[101]

When one turns to the Dead Sea Scrolls, one is confronted with numerous texts not harmonized into a systematic body of doctrines.[102] Moreover, many texts explicitly mentioning Jerusalem, Zion, or the temple are fragmentary, or they consist of only scriptural citations. Nevertheless, it is possible and necessary to examine a representative sampling to see how those texts portrayed the city and the sanctuary. Most scholars think that the Qumran covenanters constituted a peripheral group who had

---

100. On the issue of their relationship, see Anders Hultgård, "The Ideal 'Levite,' the Davidic Messiah and the Savior Priest in the Testaments of the Twelve Patriarchs," in *Ideal Figures in Ancient Judaism* (ed. George W. E. Nickelsburg and John J. Collins; Society of Biblical Literature Septuagint and Cognate Studies 12; Chico, Calif.: Scholars Press, 1980), 93–109.

101. The temple is mentioned again in *Sibylline Oracle* 5. The problem of distinguishing Jewish from Christian thinking in *Sibylline Oracles* 1, 2, and 5 has led to their exclusion from this study. On the temple in the *Sibylline Oracles,* see Marcel Simon, "Sur quelques aspects des Oracles Sibyllines juifs," in *Apocalypticism in the Mediterranean World and the Near East* (ed. David Hellholm; Tübingen: Mohr, 1983), 228–31.

102. Morton Smith, "What Is Implied by the Variety of Messianic Figures?" *JBL* 78 (1959): 66–72; John J. Collins, "Patterns of Eschatology at Qumran," in *Traditions in Transformation* (ed. Baruch Halpern and J. D. Levenson; Winona Lake, Ind.: Eisenbrauns, 1981), 372.

fled the pollution of the city of Jerusalem. Their enemies were the Hasmoneans, led at first by the Wicked Priest (Jonathan or Simon) and later by other equally guilty priests. Those enemies will meet their demise at the hands of the Kittim (Romans). The Wicked Priest himself had been opposed by the Teacher of Righteousness, who founded the community in the mid-second century. His successors looked toward the coming of God and the dawn of the new age.[103] As the War Scroll makes abundantly clear, they fully expected to participate in the war that ushered in that age.

One song, entitled "Apostrophe to Zion" by its translator J. A. Sanders, expressed their view of Zion. It opens with an expression of love for the city:

> I remember thee for blessing, O Zion;
> with all my might I have loved thee.
> May thy memory be blessed forever![104]

Present conditions in Jerusalem, however, were not right. The psalmist prayed for it to be purged from violence, falsehood, and evil, so the future would be pleasing to God.

The covenanters found widespread support for their views in the Hebrew Bible. In 4Q175 (Testimonia) 21–30, for example, they applied Joshua's curse against anyone who rebuilt Jericho (Josh 6:26) to the Hasmoneans for rebuilding Jerusalem. Similarly, in 4QpIsa[b] 5:11–14 they applied the woe in Isa 5:11 to the "Men of Scoffing who are in Jerusalem" (cf. the wicked priests

---

103. Nickelsburg, *Jewish Literature*, 122–3; Hengel, *Judaism and Hellenism*, 224–7; Vermes, *Dead Sea Scrolls in English*, 53–68.

104. J. A. Sanders, *The Psalms Scroll of Qumran Cave 11 (11QPs^a)* (Discoveries in the Judaean Desert 4; Oxford: Clarendon: 1965), 87.

in 1QpHab 9:4 and 12:7). These scoffers would be replaced by a messiah of Aaron and a messiah of Israel (4Q174 [Florilegium] 1:11–12). In the coming war the Sons of Light would emerge victorious over the Sons of Darkness and repossess Jerusalem. When that happy event should occur, the kings of the nations will serve Jerusalem and the oppressors will bow down and lick the dust off the feet of the righteous (1QM 12:13, 17; 19:5). The godly would then abide in the new Jerusalem, whose immense houses and broad streets are described in the fragment called "New Jerusalem" (5Q15).[105]

Conclusion

This survey focused on responses to the nonfulfillment of the hopes of Deutero-Isaiah and Ezekiel for Jerusalem and the temple, uncovering several protoapocalyptic and apocalyptic efforts to keep that hope viable. The protoapocalyptic texts Trito-Isaiah (56:1–8; 61:6) and Joel (3:1–4:21 [Eng. 2:28–3:21]) held out the hope for a more democratized cult to replace the hegemony of the Zadokite priesthood. Isaiah 24–27 probably had much the same idea in mind with its return to simpler times by means of a purged altar and a role for elders. Isaiah 65:17–25; 66:22–23; and 25:6–8 even depicted Jerusalem as a new paradise.

A second effort involved cognitive dissonance, in which eschatological hope was rewritten and even scaled down (Zech 11:4–17; 12:10–13:1). Even so, it was not abandoned, even

---

105. A picture of the new Jerusalem is found elsewhere in *1 (Ethiopic) Enoch* 90:29 and *2 (Syriac) Baruch* 4:4–5, which add the note that Abraham and Moses had seen it along with paradise.

though its fulfillment was postponed. A similar tactic was employed in the canonical apocalypse Daniel, with the idea of multiple fulfillment. The idea in Dan 8–9 was simply that God had promised more to Jeremiah for his city and people than the Maccabeans had accomplished. The call was for the faithful not to settle too cheaply.

A third effort at vitality can also be seen in Daniel. Given the conditions of this world, Daniel returned to the hope of Isa 24–27 that God himself would usher in the new day. On the other hand, the people at Qumran, every bit as convinced of the necessity for and the inevitability of the new Jerusalem, anticipated their own role in God's final battle against the nations.

Finally, the apocalypticists in the Diaspora made a fourth effort to keep alive their hopes for Jerusalem. They were prepared largely to abandon hope for an earthly Jerusalem (and a national restitution) in favor of a heavenly Jerusalem (and an individual or universal hope).

Along the way the apocalypticists saw the future Jerusalem functioning in several ways. First, the early and pervasive view was of Jerusalem as the navel or center of the earth (Ezek 48:15) or the mother of the earth (2 Esd [= 4 *Ezra*] 10:8). As such it was the source of God's blessing on Israel and even on Gentiles who came there to worship. Second, closely associated was the idea that Jerusalem would serve as the bulwark against the impious nations (e.g., Ezek 38–39; Joel 4 [Eng. 3]; 1 [*Ethiopic*] *Enoch* 28; 56–57). Third, Jerusalem sometimes served as the model city by which to judge all earthly cities. Fourth, by contrast contemporary Jerusalem could function as the stronghold of the impious (e.g., 4Q175 21–30; 4QpIsa[b] 5:11–14; 1QpHab 9:4; 12:7).

Apocalyptic literature is the product of peripheral groups or groups that perceive themselves to be relatively deprived. They are the product of faith under duress, a faith holding out when human grounds for hope were gone or seemed to be. As such they may continue even today to speak to persons who perceive themselves to be in situations beyond their control and to persons wanting to understand hope on the part of the hopeless.

– F I V E –

The Vitality of Wisdom in Second Temple Judaism during the Persian Period

– Leo G. Perdue –

The Diversity of Second Temple Judaism

Throughout the Second Temple period, including the time of Persian hegemony (539–332 B.C.E.), Judaism increasingly came to be characterized by significant religious and social diversity.[1] This heterogeneity was due in part to the different geographical, imperial, and national locations of Jewish communities in the major regions of the Eastern Mediterranean world. These communities existed not only in the Persian province of Yehud, but also in other important regions in what would later be called the Diaspora during the period of Hellenistic rule of Israel. Noteworthy were the international Jewish communities that flourished in Egypt, especially Alexandria, and in Babylon. These communities of the Diaspora, largely formed as the result of the conquest of the states of Israel and Judah and the

---

1. For a historical and social overview of the Persian period, see Jon L. Berquist, *Judaism in Persia's Shadow* (Minneapolis: Fortress, 1995). The primary "historical" texts are Ezra, Nehemiah, Haggai, Zech 1–8, 1 Esdras, and Josephus, *Antiquities* 11.

consequent exile of much of the leadership and upper class of their populations, significantly increased the variety and eventually stimulated the vitality of emerging postexilic Judaism in its diverse communities, both in Yehud and abroad.

The challenges of appropriating, adapting, or at times rejecting the sciences, religions, philosophies, and languages of other cultures and the efforts to gain the political tolerance, if not also direct support, of their governments were designed to allow Jews to practice their religion in predominantly non-Jewish sociopolitical environments. Some influential pagan writers in these predominantly non-Jewish countries eventually fostered in the late postexilic (Hellenistic) period anti-Semitic attitudes.[2] Jewish intellectuals, among them teachers and sages, created a significant body of literature that helped to shape the content and the contours of the varieties of Judaism in Palestine and the Diaspora and sought to maintain the integrity of their ancient traditions in the face of assimilation, fragmentation, and occasional incipient anti-Semitism.[3] This Jewish literature included, among many others, the wisdom texts of Prov 1–9 and the Book of Job in the Persian period, followed by the Testament of Qoheleth, the Wisdom of Jesus ben Sirah, and the Wisdom of Solomon during the time of significant Hellenistic influence.

---

2. Peter Dalbert, *Die Theologie der hellenistisch-jüdischen Missionsliteratur unter Ausschluss von Philo und Josephus* (Hamburg-Volksdorf: Reich, 1954); and W. D. Davies, "The Jewish State in the Hellenistic World," in *Peake's Commentary on the Bible* (ed. Matthew Black; London: Nelson, 1962), 686–92.

3. See Scott L. Harris, *Proverbs 1–9: A Study of Inner-Biblical Interpretation* (SBLDS 150; Atlanta: Scholars Press, 1995). Also see Dalbert, *Die Theologie der hellenistisch-jüdischen Missionsliteratur*; Martin Hengel, *Judaism and Hellenism* (trans. John Bowden; Philadelphia: Fortress, 1974), 107–254; and Michael Stone, ed., *Jewish Writings of the Second Temple Period* (Philadelphia: Fortress, 1984).

Wisdom and the Sages in the Persian Period: Social and Religious Movements

In the Persian colony of Yehud during the latter part of the sixth century B.C.E., the returning Jewish exiles from Babylonia (though not elsewhere) and the indigenous populations of Jews and mixed ethnic groups faced the challenges of restoring or reshaping what they could of the important social, political, and religious institutions that had largely collapsed during the Babylonian conquest and exile (586–539 B.C.E.) and, at the same time, of responding to the new opportunities and constraints of existing as a colony within this massive empire. The different responses to these challenges and opportunities took shape within a variety of Jewish social, political, and religious movements.

Significant tensions soon developed between the indigenous population living in Judah during the period of the Babylonian captivity and the returning exiles who comprised only a small portion of the descendants of the upper class of the royal family, priests, and other Jewish leaders deported to Babylon in 586. These returns, so it seems, occurred under governors appointed by the Persians (Ezra 2; Neh 7). Only a small number of the descendants of the first-generation exiles chose to return to Yehud (first under Sheshbazzar and then under Zerubbabel) to reclaim their families' properties (Ezra 1:2–4), to rebuild the temple (restored between 520 and 515 B.C.E.) that was to receive the stolen sacred vessels (6:3–5), and to resume what they contended was their rightful place in the rebuilding of Jewish society. In addition, two major reforms occurred in the fifth century B.C.E., under the leadership of Ezra and then Nehemiah. Eventually, the returnees had the better of the conflict largely because, due to their ready compliance and hereditary status, they enjoyed the support of the Persian authorities.[4]

Persian control was exerted over the colonies through the appointment of local governors who were to carry out as peacefully as possible the stated policies of the empire, collect its taxes, and maintain local political and social stability. Colonies were even allowed to establish and implement their own local customs, institutions, and religious expressions as long as peaceful submission to the empire was maintained. Political turmoil and revolution, however, were met with devastating imperial force. Local temples, including the one in Jerusalem, rebuilt to some extent by Persian support, aided the legitimation of the present imperial order and the collection of colonial taxes. The Persian rulers, who curried the favor of foreign gods for political if not also for religious reasons, were especially supportive of religious groups and institutions whose activities were carried out in the interest of the empire. Those that were not often fell victim to imperial destruction.[5]

In a useful heuristic analysis, though oversimplified, Paul Hanson argues that in general two major Jewish social and religious movements, often at odds with each other, took shape and gained momentum in the Persian colony of Yehud.[6] These movements, though splintering eventually into various identifiable sects (including especially the Pharisees, Sadducees, Zealots, and Essenes), were to continue through the Hellenistic period into

---

4. See J. Maxwell Miller and John H. Hayes, *A History of Ancient Israel and Judah* (Philadelphia: Westminster, 1986), 437–75.

5. Ibid., 443.

6. See my volume *Proverbs* (Interpretation; Louisville: Westminster John Knox, 2000).

the time of first-century imperial Rome.[7] One was the hiero-cratic movement headed by the Zadokite priests, who emerged from the dominant Aaronide priestly families and who for much of the Second Temple period controlled the high priesthood. The Zadokites held sway over the other Aaronide families, were in charge of the temple in Jerusalem, and sought out and usually achieved political alignments with governors appointed by the Persian rulers (e.g., Sheshbazzar and Zerubbabel, descendants of the Judean royal family), with centrist prophets who through their prophecies legitimated the current political order (e.g., Haggai and Zechariah), and with conservative sages and teach-ers who operated schools to educate scribes, lawyers, and other

---

7. Paul Hanson, *The Dawn of Apocalyptic* (Philadelphia: Fortress, 1975). For an application of Hanson's thesis to the first collection of Proverbs, see my essay "Wisdom Theology and Social History in Proverbs 1–9," in *Wisdom, You Are My Sister* (ed. Michael L. Barré; Catholic Biblical Quarterly Monograph 29; Washington, D.C.: Catholic Biblical Association, 1997), 78–101. Stephen Cook (*Prophecy and Apocalypticism: The Postexilic Social Setting* [Minneapolis: Fortress, 1995]) opposes the general thesis that apocalypticism was connected with marginality by arguing that apocalyptic arises from the Zadokite priests who were already in power; indeed, he contends that Ezek 38–39, Zech 1–8, and Joel are protoapocalyptic texts that originated among the centrist priests. In my opinion, one may well imagine that, in the early part of the Persian rule, the Aaronide priesthood, and especially the Zadokites who eventually came to control the high priesthood (which increasingly assumed some royal functions), gave an eschatological dimension to their theology of creation and providence. With the rebuilding of the temple, the refortification of Jerusalem, and the consolidation of local religious and political power under the Zadokites, it seems unlikely, however, that this priestly group would have looked to the future for redemption. Cook's thesis is not convincing when he attempts to separate apocalyptic from marginality. The future eschatology of apocalyptic theology in any period, whether postexilic Judaism or later, stems not from those in power and whose interest is served by maintaining the status quo but from those whose marginality will be removed by the upheaval of cosmic and social worlds that leads to a "new heaven and a new earth."

bureaucrats for governmental service and for shaping and interpreting the law for everyday life (the authors of Proverbs and Jesus ben Sirah). Originally, many of the leaders of this hierocratic movement were descendants of the exiles who chose to return to Yehud even though they had been born in Babylonian captivity or were quite young when taken into exile.

The "visionaries," to use Hanson's term, comprised the second social and religious movement in colonial Judaism during the Persian period and included early apocalypticists, peripheral prophets, Levitical families who were temple servants and singers, and critical sages. Though some of the early leaders of this movement may have come from among the exiles in Babylonian captivity, they tended to be less socially and religiously prominent than those in the hierocratic party and included members of the indigenous population not taken to Babylon. The visionaries largely became marginal in Yehud during the Second Temple period and enjoyed no political power, religious leadership of the temple, or social prominence.

One of the fundamental theological differences between these two movements resided in what might best be called their eschatologies or future stories. The hierocratic movement essentially operated with a realized eschatology, rooted in a social, yet pragmatic conservatism that saw, for example, the major features of the vision of the new exodus and new creation in Second Isaiah (Isa 40–55) as largely actualized in the early postexilic community in Jerusalem (see also Isa 41:25). Since Second Isaiah interprets Cyrus, the Persian emperor, as the messiah who was establishing a new cosmic kingdom under Yhwh's direction (Isa 45:1–7), the hierocratic movement could eventually interpret the failure to reestablish a Jewish monarchy under Zerubbabel or another descendant of David to be in accordance with divine providence.[8] Indeed, the families that came to claim the privilege of the high priesthood increasingly incorporated more and more of the symbolism as well as some of the political role of the former monarchy. The implications of this realized eschatology meant that the cosmic, social, and religious order that had come into place under Persian hegemony was to be sustained in several ways: through being loyal to the political order of foreign rule; through establishing the canonicity and authority of the Torah, which was read largely through the lens of the Priestly Code; through giving a dominant place to Jerusalem in Jewish religious and social life; through rebuilding the Jerusalem temple and reinstituting its cultic service presided over by the Zadokite priesthood; and through articulating a theology of creation and providence in which the orders of life in nature and in society were to be realized in the new Jerusalem and maintained through priestly ritual and moral behavior (see Ezra, Nehemiah, 1–2 Chronicles, the Priestly Code in the Torah, Haggai, and Zech 1–8).

The hierocratic movement received its economic support from the Persian government, from the sacrifices and tithes dedicated to the temple and its priesthood, and from the reclaiming of hereditary lands lost during the exile. Enjoying these political and economic advantages, the hierocratic movement continued to maintain social and religious power throughout the Persian and Hellenistic periods and, following the interlude of the Maccabees, well into Roman times until the fall of Jerusalem and the destruction of the temple in 70 c.e.

As mentioned, Second Temple Judaism also included another

---

8. See the royal attributes of the high priest in Exod 28–29, a Priestly text stemming most likely from the fifth century b.c.e.

social and religious movement, the visionaries, who were usually at odds with the hierocratic leaders. Taken as a whole these
groups comprised largely marginalized peoples who rarely enjoyed political, social, and religious power and status. Many of
these visionaries articulated a future story that imagined an impending act of God that would replace the existing political order
with a new one ruled over by a Davidic messiah and would re-
constitute the present temple service with legitimate priests who
would carry out proper rituals in the house of God purified of its
earlier desecration. This movement produced prophetic, apocalyptic, sapiential, and narrative literature, some of which would
eventually be included in the Hebrew and Greek canons.

Wisdom literature and the group of sages who produced it
flourished during the Persian period (539–332 B.C.E.), though
the origins of this social group and perhaps even its earliest literary and oral tradition may be traced back to the Solomonic
period (tenth century B.C.E.).[9] Indeed, most of the canonical
sapiential writings were written during this creative period of

---

9. Though there are more recent discussions, R. B. Y. Scott's careful
study traces wisdom back to the Solomonic court and is still, in my estima-
tion, a convincing argument: "Solomon and the Beginnings of Wisdom in
Israel," in *Wisdom in Israel and in the Ancient Near East: Presented to Professor
Harold Henry Rowley* (ed. Martin Noth and D. Winton Thomas; VTSup 3;
Leiden: Brill, 1955), 262–79. Scott, however, recognizes that much of the
literary tradition of Solomonic origins for wisdom as evidenced in 1 Kings
is "post-exilic in date and legendary in character" (279). The study by F. W.
Golka (*The Leopard's Spots: Biblical and African Wisdom in Proverbs* [Edin-
burgh: Clark, 1993]) is based on an ethnocultural analysis that attempts to
trace Israel's wisdom tradition to tribal, not royal, origins. In my judgment,
this study is unconvincing in both its methodology (ethnoculturalism) and
its conclusions. There may have been no Solomonic "Enlightenment," to use
von Rad's unfortunate term, but to negate the extant biblical evidence with
no evidence at all, outside of tribal folklore from recent African sources, lacks
credibility.

Persian rule: the first collection in Proverbs (Prov 1–9), the Book of Job (at least much of the poetry), and, during the transition from Persian to early Greek dominion, the Testament of Qoheleth. These books came to be included among the Writings of the Hebrew canon. The deuterocanonical texts of Sirach (Jesus ben Sirah), composed in Jerusalem during the early years of the Seleucid rule of Judah (ca. 190 B.C.E.), and the Wisdom of Solomon, deriving from Alexandria of Egypt in the first century B.C.E., were eventually included in the larger Greek canon. In addition to writing their own texts, the sages served as redactors who edited some of the other canonical literature, thus leaving their distinctive stamp of language and thought on certain nonsapiential texts (e.g., wisdom psalms, including perhaps Ps 1, 19, 34, 37, 49, 73, 111, 112, 119, 127, 128; the prophetic books of Amos, Isaiah, and Jeremiah; the Joseph Narrative; and Deuteronomy).

The sages became actively involved in the efforts to shape the social and religious character of Judaism during the Second Temple period and used their literary and editorial work, as well as their oral instruction, to this end. Through its theological and moral teachings, sapiential literature was designed either to help to create and then legitimate the evolving social world of Second Temple Judaism or to question and at times even subvert the existing political and religious order.

A close examination of wisdom literature and other texts that give evidence of sapiential editing makes it clear that two distinct groups of sages came into conflict during this period: conservative sages who were aligned with the hierocratic movement headed by the Zadokite priests (Prov 1–9; Sirach) and critical teachers who questioned and on occasion rejected the ideological underpinnings of the hierocratic movement (Job,

Qoheleth, and Agur [Prov 30]). This latter group, also marginalized, was socially compatible with the visionaries; that is, they too were on the periphery of power and influence in postexilic Judaism. The critical sages did not, however, anticipate a new cataclysmic act of God that would end the current, corrupt, social and religious order and bring about a new one. It may be, as Gerhard von Rad suggests, that these sages' disillusionment with the current corruption of world and social order came eventually to evoke the hopes and dreams of apocalyptic seers.[10]

Conservative Wisdom: Proverbs 1–9

The dating of the different collections assembled by scribal redactors to form the Book of Proverbs is difficult to establish.[11] Many scholars assume that the final editing of Proverbs occurred during the Persian period.[12] It is also likely that the initial collection of Prov 1–9 ("the Proverbs of Solomon son of David, king of Israel") was redacted and perhaps even largely composed during this same period. The reasoning behind this latter position includes a variety of considerations. In contradistinction to the

10. Gerhard von Rad, *Old Testament Theology* (trans. D. M. G. Stalker; New York: Harper & Row, 1962–65), 2:303–8.

11. For a review of opinions, see R. N. Whybray, *The Book of Proverbs: A Survey of Modern Study* (Leiden: Brill, 1995), 150–57. Whybray himself (*The Composition of the Book of Proverbs* [JSOTSup 168; Sheffield: JSOT Press, 1994]) thinks the book was put together over an extensive period of time and doubts that we have firm evidence for dating any collection of the book. For the view that Prov 1–9 originated in the monarchic period, see Bernhard Lang, *Wisdom and the Book of Proverbs: An Israelite Goddess Redefined* (New York: Pilgrim, 1986).

12. See Rolf Schäfer, *Die Poesie der Weisen: Dichotomie als Grundstruktur der Lehr- und Weisheitsgedichte in Proverbien 1–9* (Wissenschaftliche Monographien zum Alten und Neuen Testament 77; Neukirchen-Vluyn: Neukirchener Verlag, 1999), 268–69.

other collections, this one consists primarily of instructions and didactic poems, which give evidence of a significant intellectual capacity and achievement comparable to the Second Temple books of Job and Qoheleth. In addition, the personification of wisdom as a metaphor for the teachings of the sapiential tradition is found in other late texts (cf. Job 28; Sir 24; Wis 10–19). Likewise, the most significant literary parallels to Proverbs derive from texts of the sixth century and later (Deuteronomy and the Deuteronomic History, Jeremiah, the Joseph Narrative, Second Isaiah, and Malachi). Furthermore, this collection exhibits greater theological sophistication and more intentional association with Yahwistic religion than is the case with the others in Proverbs, indicating that substantial time had passed to allow for the integration of a more international wisdom into Israelite religion. For instance, the concern with the strange woman in this collection, now serving in part as a metaphor for non-Jewish culture and religion and not simply adultery and prostitution, demonstrates that the wisdom tradition is in transition from its more tolerant and self-acknowledged international stance to a more Israelite or Jewish outlook (cf. the frequent references to YHWH and the admonition to offer gifts, including firstfruits, to YHWH in Prov 3:9–10).[13] However, there is still no evidence in this initial collection of the nationalization of wisdom, evidenced by the incorporation of the traditions of salvation history (e.g., the exodus from Egypt, the law and covenant at Sinai, the temple, and Jerusalem as the city of God) that is present in the writings of Ben Sirah (early second century B.C.E.) and the Wisdom of Solomon (first century B.C.E.). Consequently, placing

---

13. For a detailed study of the strange woman, see Claudia Camp, *Wise, Strange and Holy: The Strange Woman and the Making of the Bible* (Sheffield: Sheffield Academic Press, 2000).

Prov 1–9 in the fifth century B.C.E., after the return from exile but prior to Ezra and Nehemiah, appears to be the best option for dating this collection.

School Settings and Social Roles

It is likely that many sages during the early Second Temple period who lived and worked in the city of Jerusalem aligned themselves with the Zadokite families that controlled the high priesthood throughout much of the Second Temple period and with the Aaronides who functioned as the temple priests.[14] Together, they formed what increasingly became the leadership of the hierocratic movement. These wise men, and perhaps wise women, were the sages who taught in the schools connected with the temple and local civil government and who helped to shape the intellectual and ethical formation of Second Temple Judaism.[15] The students they educated became scribes who worked for the religious and state authorities. Temple scribes

---

14. See James L. Crenshaw, "The Sage in Proverbs," in *The Sage in Israel and the Ancient Near East* (ed. John G. Gammie and Leo G. Perdue; Winona Lake, Ind.: Eisenbrauns, 1990), 208–10; and G. I. Davies, "Were There Schools in Ancient Israel?" in *Wisdom in Ancient Israel* (ed. John Day et al.; Cambridge: Cambridge University Press, 1995), 199–211; D. W. Jamieson-Drake, *Scribes and Schools in Monarchic Judah: A Socio-Archaeological Approach* (Sheffield: JSOT Press, 1991); Bernhard Lang, "Schule und Unterricht im alten Israel," in *La sagesse de l'ancien Israël* (ed. M. Gilbert; Bibliotheca ephemeridum theologicarum lovaniensium 51; Gembloux: Duculot, 1979), 186–201; and André Lemaire, *Les écoles et la formation de la Bible das l'ancien Israël* (Göttingen: Vandenhoeck & Ruprecht, 1981); idem, "The Sage in School and Temple," in *The Sage in Israel and the Ancient Near East* (ed. John G. Gammie and Leo G. Perdue; Winona Lake, Ind.: Eisenbrauns, 1990), 165–81.

15. For Israelite education in general, see James L. Crenshaw, *Education in Ancient Israel* (Anchor Bible Reference Library; New York: Doubleday, 1998).

aided the priests in interpreting the Torah in civil and religious matters and in translating and interpreting Hebrew for a population increasingly accustomed to Aramaic, the lingua franca of the Persian period. In addition, these temple scribes would have been involved in the administration and business operations of the temple and in legitimating the role of the ruling priesthood and the place of the temple in Jewish life. Scribal households may have served as guilds to educate children to enter into governmental service (1 Chr 2:55). Other sages may have been educated in provincial schools operated by the local government. The teachers in these settings also would have sought to undergird the political and social order of colonial Yehud as an integral part of the Persian Empire.

Creation Theology and Moral Discourse

The sages of ancient Israel and early Judaism articulated a theology of creation that integrated two traditions: the creation and sustenance of the world and the creation and providential guidance of humanity.[16] This means that moral discourse in the literature of the sages is grounded in creation theology. It is also evident that the creation theology of the sages in Prov 1–9 was used to authenticate the existing political, social, and religious order of the colony of Yehud within the Persian Empire. This first collection is neither radical nor subversive in content, for it seeks to form the character of students studying to become temple and civil scribes. By incorporating within their behavior the virtues of wisdom, students could expect to experience the blessings of life: longevity, status, joy, good family, prosperity, and success in their professions. These virtues include religious piety ("the fear

---

16. See my *Wisdom and Creation* (Nashville: Abingdon, 1994).

of the LORD") and cultic observance, trust in YHWH the God of righteousness and life, the pursuit and incorporation of wisdom through study and discipline, obedience to the teachings of the sages, charity toward others, hard work, the avoidance of the strange woman (who personifies evil, foreign religion and culture, and prostitution), truthful speech, faithfulness to one's spouse, and honesty.

Proverbs 3:13–20

The first important text that articulates creation theology is found in the poem located in Prov 3:13–20.[17] This text consists of three strophes: the joy of discovering wisdom (3:13–15), the portrayal of wisdom as a goddess who dispenses blessings (3:16–18), and God's use of wisdom in creating the cosmos (3:19–20). The poem is an *'ashre* ("happy" = "contentment, joy, well-being, and blessing") psalm (cf. Ps 32, 119) that begins with an extended "happy" saying (Prov 3:13–15) that sets the tone for the entire poem: the one who finds wisdom is "happy," for wisdom is far more valuable than treasures (cf. Ps 19:11 [Eng. 19:10]; Prov 8:19).[18]

For the second time in this initial collection (see Prov 1:20–33), wisdom (*khokhmah*) is personified as a goddess in the second strophe.[19] Here she is an ancient Near Eastern fertility goddess

17. Ibid., 80–84.

18. See my *Wisdom and Cult* (SBLDS 30; Missoula, Mont.: Scholars Press, 1977), 299–312; Otto Plöger, *Sprüche Salomos (Proverbia)* (Biblischer Kommentar: Alten Testament 17; Neukirchen-Vluyn: Neukirchener Verlag, 1981–84), 36; and Arndt Meinhold, "Gott und Mensch in Proverbien 3," *VT* 37 (1987): 468–77. According to Meinhold, Prov 3 argues that those who exhibit the proper attitude and behavior toward God and their fellow humans live in harmony with creation.

19. For an overview of wisdom as a deity, see Judith Hadley, "Wisdom and

who offers to her followers long life (3:2; 22:4), wealth (14:24), and honor (8:18; cf. 1 Kgs 3:3–14).[20] Tendering to her followers life in her right hand and riches and honor in her left, those who embrace her are called "happy" (Prov 3:18 = 3:13).[21] Wisdom is also portrayed as the tree of life (cf. 11:30; 13:12; 15:4), a common symbol for fertility goddesses, including the Canaanite goddess Asherah.[22] This metaphor of the fertility goddess indicates that wisdom is not only an intellectual exercise and a body of knowledge for understanding the world and making one's way successfully in life through the implementation of moral virtues. In addition, the pursuit and cultivation of wisdom is likened to the passionate quest to find and embrace a desirable woman. Wisdom is thus the object of human longing, discovery, and love.

---

the Goddess," in *Wisdom in Ancient Israel* (ed. John Day et al.; Cambridge: Cambridge University Press, 1995), 234–43. Bernhard Lang's lengthy study (*Wisdom and the Book of Proverbs: An Israelite Goddess Redefined* [New York: Pilgrim, 1986]) continues to be the standard reference on this topic.

20. Christa Bauer-Kayatz (*Studien zu Proverbien 1–9* [Wissenschaftliche Monographien zum Alten und Neuen Testament 22; Neukirchen-Vluyn: Neukirchener Verlag, 1966]) compares wisdom to *ma'at*, the Egyptian word for justice, truth, and order, who is personified as the divine daughter of the sun god Re.

21. Kayatz (ibid., 105) notes a large number of examples of the goddess Ma'at holding a symbol of life in one hand and a scepter symbolizing wealth and honor in the other. Also see W. F. Albright, "The Goddess of Life and Wisdom," *American Journal of Semitic Languages* 36 (1919–20): 258–94.

22. See Ralph Marcus, "The Tree of Life in Proverbs," *JBL* 62 (1942): 118–20; Ivan Engnell, " 'Knowledge' and 'Life' in the Creation Story," in *Wisdom in Israel and in the Ancient Near East: Presented to Professor Harold Henry Rowley* (ed. Martin Noth and D. Winton Thomas; VTSup 3; Leiden: Brill, 1955), 103–19; and G. Widengren, *Sakrales Königtum im Alten Testament und im Judentum* (Stuttgart: Kohlhammer, 1955). The tree-of-life image in Proverbs is associated with wisdom, the "fruit" of the righteous, "fulfilled desire," and a "gentle tongue."

Finally, in strophe three, which serves as the climax for the entire poem, Yhwh creates the heavens and the earth through this
wisdom made accessible to the pious who pursue her. Wisdom,
sought by schoolboys and possibly schoolgirls in their studies and
by old sages who realize that knowledge and moral perfection
are never complete, is the ordering principle of life and reality used by God in creating and sustaining the cosmos (cf. Ps
104:24; 136:5; Jer 10:12; 51:15). Two metaphors are used for
divine creation in this strophe: God is the architect who lays a
firm foundation for the cosmos (cf. Job 38:4–7; Ps 104:5), while
wisdom is the skill, plan, and knowledge at work in this building
activity. God is also the dragon slayer who divides (*baqa'*) the
"deep" (*tehomot*) or primeval ocean.[23] *Tehom* ("deep" or "cosmic
ocean"; Gen 1:2; 7:11; Job 38:16, 30; Prov 8:24, 27–28) may
be linguistically related to the Akkadian name for the chaos
monster, Tiamat. In any event, *tehom* or *tehomot* (a plural of
majesty?) in the Hebrew Bible refers on occasion to the chaos
monster defeated by Yhwh (Ps 74:12–15; cf. Gen 49:25; Deut
33:13; Ps 77:17 [Eng. 77:16]; Hab 3:8–10).

Proverbs 8

Proverbs 8 is also devoted to Woman Wisdom and comprises five
related parts: the introduction of Woman Wisdom (8:1–3), the
poem on Woman Wisdom as peripatetic teacher who issues her
invitation to the simple (8:4–11), the poem portraying Wisdom
ruling providentially over creation (8:12–21), Wisdom's origins
prior to creation (8:22–31), and the instruction of life issued by

---

23. Compare Marduk's splitting in half Tiamat in the Babylonian *Enuma
Elish* (E. A. Speiser in *ANET* 67).

Woman Wisdom to those who follow her (8:32–36).[24] What is clear in this chapter is that the metaphor of Woman Wisdom represents the sapiential tradition that provides insight into the nature of human life, the cosmic order, and the character of God. Sapiential teaching, then, once incorporated within human life and allowed to shape the character and behavior of the wise, enables the God-fearing and faithful sages to live in harmony with the creator and the life-sustaining creation.[25]

In the introduction and initial poem (8:1–11), Woman Wisdom as teacher travels to a city in order to invite the unlearned to become her students that they might find knowledge and discover insight. This suggests that wisdom instruction more than likely occurred primarily in urban settings and not in rural households. Metaphorically construed, it is wisdom in the city that becomes the link between heaven and earth where humans, guided by divine instruction, act to sustain the social and cosmic order and to experience the blessings of the creation. Wisdom teaches at the city gates, the normal place for human traffic and social activities, including the administration of law and the carrying out of at least some formal education. This image con-

---

24. See M. Gilbert, "Le discours de la sagesse en Proverbes 8," in *La sagesse de l'ancien testament* (ed. M. Gilbert; Bibliotheca ephemeridum theologicarum lovaniensium 51; Gembloux: Duculot, 1981), 202–18; and Patrick Skehan, "Structures in Poems on Wisdom: Proverbs 8 and Sirach 24," *CBQ* 41 (1979): 365–79. Another well-crafted poem on Woman Wisdom is found in Prov 1:20–33, on which see Phyllis Trible, "Wisdom Builds a Poem: The Architecture of Proverbs 1:20–33," *JBL* 94 (1975): 509–18; and Roland Murphy, "Wisdom's Song: Proverbs 1:20–33," *CBQ* 48 (1986): 456–60.

25. For a detailed study of sapiential character formation and the role of wisdom's discourse in shaping human virtue, see William P. Brown, *Character in Crisis* (Grand Rapids: Eerdmans, 1996). God as creator and order are the two related, prominent features of wisdom theology; see Lennart Boström, *The God of the Sages* (Stockholm: Almqvist & Wiksell, 1990).

nects the sapiential tradition to judicial matters that regulated Israelite and Jewish society.[26] Cosmic wisdom, which orders creation and sustains all life, is thus taught and administered legally in the city gates. Politically speaking, this metaphorical system of theological wisdom is one of the traditions that undergirds the imperial reign of Persia over the colony of Yehud.

Wisdom's discourse changes in the second poem (8:12–21), for now she, like a divine queen of heaven, engages in self-adulation.[27] It is here that providence becomes her fundamental activity and includes, among other things, the choosing of kings and nobles to govern with justice. The counsel (*'etsah*) that she gives to all rulers and governors of the world leads to their conceiving well-thought-out plans that will lead to success and life.[28] Through wise and righteous rule, the nations will live in concert with divine will and cosmic order. Conservative wisdom articulates a paradigm of order that permeates and links cosmology, society, and human nature. *Tsedeq* is the cosmic righteous order embodied in the social and political institutions of Yehud (8:15–16; cf. 25:5; 31:9), while *tsedaqah* refers to the behavior of those who follow the dictates of wisdom (10:2; 11:4, 6, 19). The *tsaddiq* is one who lives in harmony with cosmic and social order

---

26. For the sages, justice and its embodiment in law were not static. Rather justice, given expression in institutions of jurisprudence, is a divine act that is continually produced. Subsequently, human actions that are just are to actualize this dynamic power of divine justice in communal life. See Jacques Ellul, *Die theologische Begründung des Rechtes* (Beiträge zur Evangelischen Theologie 10; Munich: Kaiser, 1948), 56–89.

27. In Egyptian literature, the goddess Isis also sings praises to herself; Hans Conzelmann, "The Mother of Wisdom," in *The Future of Our Religious Past* (ed. James M. Robinson; New York: Harper & Row, 1971), 230–43.

28. P. A. H. de Boer, "The Counsellor," in *Wisdom in Israel and in the Ancient Near East*, 42–71.

and actualizes it in the formation of character and in human behavior (10:3, 16, 21, 24).[29]

In a world of colonialism where Yehud is a tiny province barely noticed in the massive Persian Empire, this didactic hymn undergirds the teaching that kings, even foreign ones, rule by divine decree (cf. Isa 44:28; 45:1–8) and governors appointed by these foreign kings enjoy divine selection. There remains, however, the responsibility of ruling and governing in justice. In wisdom thinking, justice is the creative force permeating society and cosmos and is to be strengthened by righteous rule and wise behavior. In the Persian colony of Yehud, this would indicate that Persian rulers and their provincial governors rule with divine legitimation, although they are to govern with justice. Yet the embrace of wisdom and the reception of her blessings are not limited only to royalty and their appointees. Rather, all who love wisdom will find her and rejoice in her passion. Her requited love culminates in dispensing her gifts of wealth and honor to all her lovers.[30]

In both the second and third poems, the value of wisdom is said to exceed that of wealth and prosperity. Placed in the social context of the Persian Empire, these poems teach students to pursue wisdom and virtue, not riches. This would suggest that, while students are promised that prosperity is a derivative of sapiential living (cf. 1 Kgs 3:3–15), the obtaining of wisdom that leads to well-being and harmony with God, nature, and humanity is far more valuable. Ideologically construed, this suggests that moral formation that leads to the undergirding and

---

29. Leo G. Perdue, "Cosmology and the Social Order in the Wisdom Tradition," in *The Sage in Israel and the Ancient Near East*, 458–59.

30. See Roland Murphy, "Wisdom and Eros in Prov. 1–9," CBQ 50 (1988): 600–603.

sustaining of the present social order is the prerequisite to the likely obtaining of status, honor, and wealth.

The subsequent poem is also a hymn of self-praise by Woman Wisdom (8:22–31), only here she portrays herself as the off-spring of God who is the first of God's creation and thus witness to the mighty acts of the creator in bringing the cosmos into being.[31] Once more YHWH is portrayed as the divine architect who carefully orders and gives stability to the cosmos, and he is the divine ruler or judge whose decree restrains the threat of the primeval deep from inundating creation. In addition, YHWH is the divine parent who both fathers (*qanah*; 8:22)[32] and gives

---

31. See Jean Noel Aletti, "Proverbes 8:22–31: étude et structure," *Biblica* 57 (1976): 25–37; Mitchell Dahood, "Proverbs 8,22–31: Translation and Commentary," *CBQ* 30 (1968): 512–21; George M. Landes, "Creation Tradition in Proverbs 8:22–31 and Genesis 1," *A Light unto My Path: Old Testament Studies in Honor of Jacob M. Myers* (ed. Howard N. Bream, Ralph D. Heim, and Carey A. Moore; Gettysburg Theological Studies 4; Philadelphia: Temple University Press, 1974), 279–93; R. B. Y. Scott, "Wisdom in Creation: The '*Amon* of Proverbs viii 30," *VT* 10 (1960): 213–23; Bruce Vawter, "Prov. 8:22: Wisdom and Creation," *JBL* 99 (1980): 205–16; R. N. Whybray, "Proverbs viii,22–31 and Its Supposed Prototypes," *VT* 15 (1965): 504–14; and Gale A. Yee, "An Analysis of Prov. 8:22–31 according to Style and Structure," *Zeitschrift für die alttestamentliche Wissenschaft* 94 (1982): 58–66. For ancient Near Eastern parallels, see H. Donner, "Die religionsgeschichtlichen Ursprünge von Prov. Sal. 8,22–31," *Zeitschrift für ägyptische Sprache und Altertumskunde* 82 (1957): 8–18; Kayatz, *Studien zu Proverbien 1–9*; Walther Eichrodt, *Theology of the Old Testament* (trans. J. A. Baker; Old Testament Library; Philadelphia: Westminster, 1961), 2:80–81; Othmar Keel, *Die Weisheit Spielt vor Gott* (Göttingen: Vandenhoeck & Ruprecht, 1974); Burton Mack, "Wisdom Myth and Mytho-Logy," *Interpretation* 24 (1970): 46–60; and Helmer Ringgren, *Word and Wisdom* (Lund: Ohlssons, 1947). For a discussion of the birth of gods and goddesses (theogonies) in Egyptian mythology, see Viktor Notter, *Biblischer Schöpfungsbericht und ägyptische Schöpfungsmythen* (Stuttgarter Bibelstudien 68; Stuttgart: KBW, 1974), 21–22.

32. The verb *qanah* may mean "to acquire or obtain," as in the sense of

birth (*khul*; 8:24–25) to Wisdom.[33] Due to her role as the child of God who is both the delight of her divine parent and the young child who rejoices over the world of human dwelling, Wisdom becomes the mediator between God and humanity, between heaven and earth.

In the concluding protrepsis (8:32–36), Wisdom — the first-born of creation, the witness and child of God present at the foundation of the earth, and queen whose providence guides the course of history, rulers, and nations — now issues again her invitation to obey her teaching. Once more she assumes the role of the teacher who offers life to those who follow her instruction, for her teaching offers them life-giving knowledge of God and the cosmos.

Wisdom has now become the goddess of life who builds her palace and initiates her cult (9:1–6). She sends forth her maidens to invite the unlearned to come and partake of her feast that

---

acquiring wisdom (Prov 1:5; 4:5, 7), or "to purchase," as in buying a male Hebrew slave (Exod 21:2). This is the meaning given by Vawter, "Prov. 8:22: Wisdom and Creation." In several texts, the verb means "to create," as in God creating heaven and earth (Gen 14:19, 22) or human beings (Ps 139:13). In the case of creating, the specific nuance is that of procreating, as in Deut 32:6 where God created or fathered Israel. "Create" fits the sense of the entire text, especially since the verb *khul* ("to writhe in birth pains") is used in Prov 8:24–25. See Paul Humbert, " *'Qana* en hebreu biblique," in *Festschrift Alfred Bertholet* (ed. W. Baumgartner et al.; Tübingen: Mohr-Siebeck, 1950), 259–66. For *qnh* as an epithet of God as creator, see the inscription *qn 'arts* ("creator of the earth") found on the Western Hill in Jerusalem and the Phoenician inscription of Karatepe, *el qoneh aretz* ("El, creator of the earth").

33. The verb *khul* reflects the activity of writhing in birth pains (Deut 32:18; Job 39:1; Ps 29:9; 51:7 [Eng. 51:5]; 90:2). The verb in Prov 8:24–25 is passive, "I was brought forth" or "I was given birth," with the one who bears not specifically named. It seems, however, from the context that wisdom as the child (*'amon*; 8:30) of God is created, i.e., fathered and given birth by YHWH.

leads to life. The seven-pillared house she constructs likely has cosmic connotations and suggests her role in the creation of a well-ordered world (see Sir 24 and Wis 6–9). In issuing her invitation, she becomes the embodiment of the sapiential tradition that offers life to its followers. By contrast, the strange woman in 9:13–18 personifies the various elements of folly that lead to death: foolishness, pagan culture and religion, and immorality. This opposition between wisdom and folly makes sense especially in a diverse sociocultural context in which Judaism seeks in a variety of ways to maintain its identity.

Seen in its social context, Prov 1–9 is a conservative tradition that seeks through its moral teaching and theology of creation to legitimate the existing political order of Yehud's identity as a colony within the Persian Empire. It is God, through wisdom, who appoints rulers and establishes their nations, while still demanding of them justice. Accepting Wisdom's invitation to enter her schools and learn her teachings stands at the heart of the obedient life that not only secures the order of the cosmos but also procures well-being and life and holds out the promise of status, honor, and prosperity to students who, in becoming sages, enter into the sociopolitical reality of colonial Yehud.

Subversive Wisdom: The Book of Job

The critical wisdom tradition emerging during the Babylonian exile and the Persian period is represented primarily by the poetic Book of Job, comprising texts also likely produced by teachers as school literature. The intellectuals who created this literature directly confronted the conservative sages who, prior to the exile, were composed of the scribal class active in governmental circles of the royal state and in the administrative affairs of the temple in Jerusalem. Later, after the exile, the successors of these sages worked in the government and temple of the Persian colony of Yehud. These sages used their teachings in traditional ways to support the political and religious control that, in the postexilic period, came to be wielded by the hierocratic movement and thus the prevailing social order that defined Yehud's role as a submissive and compliant colony in the Persian Empire.

Social Setting and Social Roles

Not all sages were educated in the temple school and civil academy of the Second Temple. While Prov 1–9 in all probability arose within the setting of either a temple school or civil academy that would be inclined to support the conservative Zadokites, the Book of Job, at least the poetry, would more likely have arisen within the context of a family guild of scribes, living and active either in Judah or Babylon during the Babylonian exile or in the colony of Yehud shortly following the return to Jerusalem after the Persian conquest.

The poetic dialogues are normally assigned either to the time of the Babylonian exile (587–539 B.C.E.)[34] or to the Persian period (539–332 B.C.E.).[35] Favoring the former date is Ezekiel's mention of Job (Ezek 14:14–20), the close relationship of Job 3 to Jer 20:14–18, some literary affinity to Deutero-Isaiah, and the plausible requirement that some catastrophe of major proportions must have evoked the radical theology of the dialogues that strongly question the justice of God. The dating of the

---

34. Samuel Terrien, "Job," in *The Interpreter's Bible* (ed. George A. Buttrick et al.; New York: Abingdon, 1954), 3:884–92.

35. Georg Fohrer, *Introduction to the Old Testament* (Nashville: Abingdon, 1968), 330; and A. de Wilde, *Das Buch Hiob* (Oudtestamentische Studiën 22; Leiden: Brill, 1981), 52.

poetry to the early Persian period is also based largely on circum-
stantial evidence: the representation of Job as an Edomite could
be a countermeasure to the exclusivity of Ezra's reform, while
the mentioning of "kings, counselors, and princes" (Job 3:14–
15) may reflect the political hierarchy of the Persian Empire
(see Ezra 7:28; 8:25; Esth 1:3–4). In either case, one may in-
fer from these dialogues that the Babylonian holocaust followed
by the enormous difficulties encountered in attempting to piece
together once more a Jewish nation in a conquered homeland
posed dramatic challenges to traditional faith and the moral life.
The poetry is one response to these crises that threatened the
survival of even a small, faithful remnant.

The household setting for the Book of Job is set forth as the
social world of the characters in both the narrative tale and the
later poetic additions. The prologue (1:1–2:13) presents Job as
an extremely wealthy farmer who is the senior male of a large
extended family that included seven sons whose houses typically
may have been connected or at least within the same compound,
whose eldest son presided over family feasts and appears to have
been the major heir apparent, and whose three daughters (presumably unmarried) appear to have continued to live at home
with their father. As the senior male, Job has the customary
responsibility for performing family cultic observances, in this
case, ensuring the ritual purity of the household, the offering of
burnt offerings for each member of the immediate family, and
presumably a prayer that, coupled with the offerings, was for the
forgiveness of sins.[36]

This social setting changes for Job in the poetic additions,

---

36. Leo G. Perdue et al., *Families in Ancient Israel* (Louisville: Westminster
John Knox, 1997).

but only in the sense that the catastrophes that led to Job's loss of wealth and family have led to the dissolution of his household. Only his wife remains, and they are in great poverty. In his remembrances of his earlier life in the soliloquy of Job 29–30, Job recalls both the loss of his household and his status in the community. Before disaster struck, Job recollects the respect accorded him even by the great ones of society as he came to offer judgment and justice as a judge who redeemed the poor, widow, and orphan and was champion to the resident alien. Indeed, his oath of innocence in Job 31 is presented in the form of a legal brief that one would expect only from a sage educated in judicial processes.

Of course, one may object that the social world of the story and dialogues of the Book of Job, retrojected into the distant past, is not necessarily equated with that of the sages who constructed this piece of didactic literature. It is probable, however, that even literary characters would reflect the social roles present in Israelite and Jewish society at the time the text was composed. That Job is a wealthy farmer and a sage who, prior to his catastrophic experiences, likely occasioned by the ravages of exile and the loss of the household, had been a highly respected judge, teacher, and counselor in his community should be taken seriously as an important context for the social setting of wisdom and the social roles and functions of the sages who produced this tradition.

It is plausible to assume that the poet who wrote the dialogues, with the exception of the later speeches of Elihu in Job 32–37, joined those sages who were critical of conservative wisdom and sought to subvert the political and religious order emerging in the early Persian period. Through the protests of Job the sage, the author of the poetry thus radically impugns the justice and integrity of God, openly denies that righteousness is a pervasive world order to be integrated into social life, and scoffs at the teaching of retributive justice as the instrument of divine providence in the world. In contrast to Woman Wisdom who chooses the rulers and governors of the earth to rule righteously over their kingdoms, Job presents God as the one who brings chaos to world order, denies life-giving counsel to counselors, turns the wisdom of judges into foolishness, removes kings from their thrones, strips priests naked, defeats the armies of mighty warriors, takes away skillful speech and discernment from the elders of village clans, and pours contempt on princes and governors. Nations rise and fall at his whim, and their peoples grope in darkness, denied the understanding that gives them guidance (12:13–25).

The order of the Persian Empire, along with the political and religious leadership of the little colony of Yehud, enjoys no divine protection from a wise and beneficent God. Even a repentant Job does not return to uphold the conservative social and religious position of his contemporary sages who wrote Prov 1–9. While God as divine warrior restrains chaos from overwhelming creation, this dark force is not eliminated from the face of the earth or even from afflicting the righteous. Suffering, including that of the righteous, is endemic to human existence. The moral life may aid in restraining the destructive power of chaos, but its power is great and cannot be completely vitiated.

The question is whether any of the critical sages, including those who shaped the poetry of Job, offered a competing social vision to rival that of the hierocratic party. Did they in some fashion find the alternative reality of the future stories of the visionaries appealing and thus join in their efforts not only to tear down but also to build and to plant? The answer appears to be no. While these radical sages made use of creation theology to countermand the rosy depiction of a just world that undergirded the political and religious dominance of Persia, its appointed governors, and its obsequious Zadokite priests, they struggled at attempting to propose an alternative vision. The question, then, is whether the dialogues attempt to set forth a subversive future story into which a struggling Jewish colony may live.

It is true, of course, that the sharp edge of the poetic dialogues came to be dulled by the additions of the poem on wisdom (Job 28) and the Elihu speeches (Job 32–37) and by the redactional process that incorporated not only these somewhat moderating pieces but also framed the radical poetry within a conservatively construed narrative folk tale. Those who transformed the poetic dialogues by these literary activities were among the conservative sages responsible for Prov 1–9 and, much later, Sirach.

Creation Theology and Moral Discourse in the Poetic Dialogues: The Quest for Future Vision

Once more sages, in this case the authors of the poetry of Job, draw on the rich traditions of creation theology for social purposes, only now, not to sustain an existing political and religious order, but rather to respond to its dissolution or, in a more proactive way, to undermine it.[37] The dialogues do not primarily seek to answer the question of innocent suffering, but rather to determine the character of God as creator and just sustainer of the world. Human suffering evokes this larger question of divine nature.

---

37. Perdue, "Cosmology and the Social Order," 469–70.

The Opening Soliloquy (Job 3)

The Joban poet draws heavily from the creation traditions of cosmology and anthropology in Job's opening soliloquy.[38] Echoing formal features of the lament, though without any references to God, this initial speech is filled with images of dark despair and utter hopelessness. What Job desires is not deliverance but, rather, a return to oblivion, not only for himself but also for the entire creation. Through the power of the spoken word, shaped in the forms of lament and curse, Job seeks to obliterate all existence.[39] In cursing existence — his own and that of creation — Job directly challenges and seeks to negate the order of the cosmos formed by the spoken word and the blessing that enable procreation to continue among all living creatures, including human beings (cf. Gen 2:1–3).[40] Job curses the day of his birth and the night of his conception, and he attempts to enlist the potent black magic of pagan priests to awaken the dark powers of Yam and Leviathan to destroy his own life and all of creation.[41] It is hardly coincidental that this turn toward the forbidden black arts of pagan religion underscores Job's move away either from the traditional temple religion of an exilic temple cult continuing to worship on the ruins of Jerusalem's sacred mount or from an early postexilic community's rebuilt temple and restored priestly order. The hierocratic undergirding of the

---

38. See my essay "Job's Assault on Creation," *Hebrew Annual Review* 10 (1987): 295–315.

39. Dermont Cox, "The Desire for Oblivion in Job 3," *Studi Biblici Franciscani* 23 (1973): 37–49; and idem, *The Triumph of Impotence* (Analecta Gregoriana 212; Rome: Gregorian University Press, 1978).

40. See Michael Fishbane, "Jeremiah iv 23–26 and Job iii 3–13: A Recovered Use of the Creation Pattern," *VT* 21 (1971): 151–62.

41. Cf. Yhwh's battle against Leviathan in Isa 27:1; Job 40:25–41:26 (Eng. 41:1–34); Ps 74:12–17; 104:25–26.

social world of colonial Yehud in the Persian period would be undermined by this metaphorical system of a collapse into chaos and the descent into the underworld, both for Job and even the great kings of the earth. If the poet is writing in Babylon during the exile, then we are unclear as to the nature of this community's worship. But even in this exilic context, Job's soliloquy would have shaken the foundations of any kind of traditional piety, even that practiced in a foreign land.

Job also draws on the anthropological tradition to speak of his conception and birth.[42] God as the one who causes a woman to conceive, who shapes the fetus in the womb, who is present and even assists in the birthing process, and who nurtures the newborn throughout life — taken together these images are commonly occurring depictions of creation in the Hebrew Bible (Jer 1:4–10; Job 10:8–13; Ps 139:13–18). A new birth is a time for celebration (see 1 Sam 1–2; Luke 1:46–55), but for Job, his own birth is a time for cursing. Night and Day, the personified temporal times of conception and birth, are cursed with sterility so that they are no longer capable of producing life. Instead, they are to be devoured by the monster Leviathan. In Job 3:11–19, Job's wish that he had died in the womb or as a still birth is a direct assault on the teaching that portrays God as the Lord of the womb (see Ps 22:10–11 [Eng. 22:9–10]; 139:13–16).

Job 10

Job 10:1–17 is fashioned in the form an accusatory lament in which the protagonist seeks not redemption but, rather, the in-

---

42. Leo G. Perdue, "Metaphorical Theology in the Book of Job: Theological Anthropology in the First Cycle of Job's Speeches (Job 3, Job 4–5 and Job 6–7)," in *The Book of Job* (ed. W. A. M. Beuken; Louvain: Louvain University Press, 1994), 129–56.

dictment of God. Continuing to exacerbate his assault on divine justice, Job accuses God of creating him, and presumably all humanity, for the purpose not of nurture but of destruction. While reminding God of human weakness and the brevity of life, Job does not expect his words to touch a compassionate chord in a potentially merciful savior. Job seeks not redemption but a respite from divine assaults that would allow him to die in peace. True, God is his creator in the womb, but not his redeemer. Instead, God has become Job's tormentor who is bringing him to destruction.

In spite of the allure of death, throughout the dialogues with his friends, Job chooses to launch an all-out assault on creation and seeks to expose God as a wicked tyrant, not a caring giver of life who shapes life in the womb, and to collapse the cosmos, as well as the sociopolitical structure grounded in its order, by the power of curse. This sage has witnessed the loss of his own faith and now with an angry voice seeks to undermine the theological meaning of traditional creation theology so as to subvert the social and religious order that it sustains.

The YHWH Speeches (Job 38:1–42:6)

In the climax of the book, the poet portrays YHWH as the Storm God who confronts the mortal who challenges his rule of the cosmos and the world of human dwelling.[43] The purpose of these speeches is to humble Job into submission so that he will then praise, not accuse, the creator of heaven and earth and its creatures.

---

43. Horst Dietrich Preuss, "Jahwes Antwort an Hiob und die sogenannte Hiobliteratur des alten Vorderen Orients," in *Beiträge zur alttestamentlichen Theologie* (ed. Herbert Donner et al.; Göttingen: Vandenhoeck & Ruprecht, 1977), 338.

Following his response to Job's challenge in 38:2–3, YHWH issues a series of impossible questions about the nature of heaven and earth and its creatures that he alone can answer, for he is their creator. In 38:4–11, YHWH depicts himself first as the divine architect who planned and built the foundations of the earth. He then becomes the nurturing parent who cares not for human beings but, rather, for the newborn Prince Yam, whose chaotic waters of destruction are constrained by bars, doors, and especially the power of divine decree.

Still addressing questions to Job, YHWH speaks of the light of morning and dawn (38:12–15), the divine instrument for removing the wicked from the face of the earth. In 38:19–38, the various components of the heavens are mentioned before which Job can only stand in wonderment. Striking is YHWH's statement that he causes it to rain on the desert that is devoid of human life (see Gen 2:4b–7). In a semiarid climate, such "waste" (from a human perspective) of a precious resource could only underscore one of the emphases of these two speeches: humanity is not at the center of creation.[44]

In Job 38:39–40:2, YHWH's first speech turns to the nonhuman creatures brought into being and sustained by divine providence. As the "Lord of the creatures," YHWH provides them with the food, instincts, and reproductive capacities to endure through the generations. Save for the horse, whose prowess in military engagements is underscored, these animals are wild creatures who dwell in regions uninhabited by human beings. These beasts neither fear nor allow themselves to be controlled by humans (contra Gen 9:1–17). This initial speech concludes

---

44. Matitiahu Tsevat, "The Meaning of the Book of Job," *Hebrew Union College Annual* 37 (1966): 73–106.

with an inclusio in which YHWH challenges his human opponent to respond (Job 40:1–2). Otherwise, the man must admit that he is unable to rule over creation. Job, overwhelmed by YHWH's wisdom and the awesome display of power, is struck silent (40:3–5). Humans like himself are not at the center of creation, while God takes care even of wild beasts in a world alien to human life.

In his second speech (40:6–41:26 [Eng. 40:6–41:34]), the Lord of creation offers his sovereign throne to Job on one condition: that he defeat the dreaded monsters of land (Behemoth = "mighty creature") and sea (Leviathan, a dragon of the deep) who represent not fearsome creatures (e.g., the hippopotamus and the crocodile) but, rather, the forces of chaos. These embodiments of chaos, especially Leviathan, while tamed by the great power of the Divine Warrior, still threaten the order of creation and all of divinely created and sustained life. They must continue to be subdued and restrained by the power of the creator. YHWH adds that it is not necessary to be condemned by Job for this mortal to justify himself (40:8). The combination of divine power and justice (40:8–9) intimates that these are the divine attributes responsible both for the origins and the sustaining of creation. This passing reference to divine justice suggests that YHWH's power, so evident in the creation and rule of the cosmos, is shaped by the features of godly justice that in wisdom literature is understood as the beneficent order of creation, society, and sapiential behavior that undergirds and sustains all of life and brings all of its dimensions into harmony.

Job's response to YHWH's challenge to engage these awesome monsters is one of meek renunciation of his earlier accusations against divine justice and the recognition, not of his own unworthiness, but rather of his own integrity and value. Job praises a deity who uses his power to create and sustain life, a deity, who, while not omnipotent, to this point, has continued to prevail. In his doxology of praise, Job pledges then that he will join Yʜwʜ in the continuing efforts to defeat the monsters of chaos and to maintain life-giving order in the universe. The Book of Job, then, is about power and its proper use, both by God and by human creatures.

The Book of Job, placed within the sociopolitical context of the collapse of the Judean state and the exile of its leaders in the Babylonian captivity, offers the following response to Jewish social groups, which are in formation as a result of social, political, and economic collapse, and which desire to reshape the future of Judaism in a Persian colony. In its social and political employment, power is not only constrained but also configured and directed by the features of justice, which is understood as the essential characteristic of Yʜwʜ that orders creation and may be embodied in human and social life. The unlicensed use of power, to enhance self-interest or the interests of a religious, social, or political group, leads not only to injustice and the diminishment of and tyranny over life in all of its manifestations, but also to the distortion of life-giving orders that ultimately leads to the unleashing of the forces of destruction, mythical representations construed in Job by the great monsters of the land and sea (Behemoth and Leviathan) and politically embodied in the wicked and the proud who seek through the misuse of power to promote their own interests.

In socioeconomic terms, the character Job represents the intellectual class of scribes who either remained in their Judean homeland in the Babylonian Empire or were teachers in the familial guilds of scribal families in the very early period of Persian rule. In either sociopolitical setting, these sages created a character, Job, to represent the misplaced righteous, pious leader of Jewish society who had attempted to use his wealth, influence, wisdom, and power for justice and goodness in the final stages of the life of the state of Judah and the new beginnings of Jewish life. This epitome of the pious, righteous leader sought to teach his family the ideals of Judahite religious tradition and to lift the poor from their misery and to support them in a just society (Job 1; 29). Job was the epitome of the righteous Jew, but in the emerging new order of Jewish life as first a Babylonian and then a Persian imperial colony, he became the embodiment of the displaced Jewish aristocrat whose teachings of a just and righteous God had fallen into disrepute. Job's own precipitous downfall led not only to his loss of status in the early formation of the new order but also to the degradation of poverty and his ostracism from social life. The honored aristocrat, renown for his justice and integrity, had become the object of ridicule by even the dregs of society (Job 29–31). In the crisis of Jewish life precipitated by the Babylonian exile, or in the confusion and dislocation of the early Persian period, a fallen, though indignant Job, cried out in anger against what he concluded must have been an unjust and capricious deity whose abuse of power led to the downfall of even the most righteous of faithful men and women.

Yet the subversive sages, opposed to the tyranny of imperial rule, were not content to settle for casting angry insults uttered by a misplaced aristocrat against an unjust God. Rather, through the voice of God in the whirlwind they defended the order of creation and divine justice, choosing to present a deity who, while possessing great power, must still continue to fight and then prevail against the forces of chaos in all of their malevolent incarnations, including political ones in imperial dress. In his final response (42:1–6), the outcries of Job turn into a doxology of praise of the God who fights against injustice and a pledge to join in the battle against the Behemoths and Leviathans in their cosmic and human form. The scribal creators of Job, then, are sages, probably teachers in familial guilds, opposed to those who misuse their influence and recast the tenor of their religious ideology to support an unjust empire that oppresses the poor and weak and that shapes a colonial Jewish religion and society based not on justice but rather on sycophancy toward foreign imperial rule that, when opposed, becomes ruthless and brutal in its suppression.

Conclusion

It may be that the Book of Qoheleth was composed during the transition from Persian to Greek rule. If so, the often-noted skepticism of this wisdom testament (i.e., first-person instruction), placed in the mouth of a long-dead Solomon who issues his instruction from the grave, came during a time of great disillusionment. The new day of Hellenistic rule, which replaced an increasingly oppressive Persian hegemony over its colonies, did not eventuate in the emerging apocalyptic dreams of liberation and restoration for Jews both in Yehud and the Diaspora. This did not mean that critical sages like Qoheleth abandoned creation theology and a firm belief in providence. But they did express a theology of oppression grounded in a static reality of an unchanging creation and an enigmatic, capricious rule of a hidden deity.[45] It was only with the merging of Jewish salvation

---

45. See my essay "Revelation and the Problem of the Hidden God in Second Temple Wisdom Literature," in *Shall Not the Judge of All the Earth Do What Is Right? Studies on the Nature of God in Tribute to James L. Crenshaw*

history and a teleological creation that the conservative sages reemerged to legitimate and sustain a social and religious order, expressed in the realized eschatology of the theocracy of Jerusalem (Jesus ben Sirah) and the unrealized hopes for a new exodus from Egyptian pogroms (Wisdom of Solomon).

(ed. David Penchansky and Paul L. Redditt; Winona Lake, Ind.: Eisenbrauns, 2000), 201–22.

– S I X –

Joyful Worship in
Second Temple Judaism

– John C. Endres –

What did Jews say and do in the rebuilt Jerusalem temple when they gathered for public worship? What roles did ordinary Israelites play? Were there professional mediators — priests and Levites — who helped them? If so, how did they conduct themselves? In other words, how did Jews worship and how did they experience their worship in the centuries after the return from exile in Babylon? Put differently, we are probing what they did and what spirituality of worship emerges.

Resources for Study of Worship

If you want to answer questions like these, many of the standard works on Israelite worship will not satisfy your curiosity, since they put little focus on the postexilic era. Important studies by Hans-Joachim Kraus and H. H. Rowley basically concern pre-exilic Israel,[1] and even the excellent study of worship by Walter

1. Hans-Joachim Kraus, *Worship in Israel: A Cultic History of the Old Testament* (trans. Geoffrey Buswell; Richmond: John Knox, 1966). His brief discussion of postexilic Jewish worship (229–36) concerns the Chronicler's view of issues such as the Passover during the time of Hezekiah/Josiah as

Harrelson, whose interests and passion inspired my concern for this topic, does not focus on this era.[2] Several factors may contribute to this lack of concern. First, a disparaging view of two major texts usually attributed to that time, the Priestly tradition in the Pentateuch and the Books of Chronicles, perdures in some circles. Both texts view Israelite worship through the lens of priestly groups, often compared negatively with the religion of the prophets. Second, many are put off by the long genealogies and lists of cultic regulations in these texts. Third, some theological principles do not match the sensibilities of many religious people today, for example, the principle of retribution in Chronicles[3] and the necessity of sacrifice to allay the power of sin in the Priestly Code. Fourth, a tendency among some Israeli and Jewish scholars to date the Priestly Code quite early makes this tradition more representative of monarchic than of postexilic reality.[4]

---

reflection of tension between Jerusalem and the Samaritans. H. H. Rowley (*Worship in Ancient Israel: Its Forms and Meaning* [London: SPCK, 1967]) occasionally surveys later evidence, e.g., the transformation of preexilic cultic prophets into postexilic Levites (170–75).

2. Walter Harrelson, *From Fertility Cult to Worship* (Garden City: Doubleday, 1969). He disagrees with the post-Wellhausen view of "radical decline in worship," and although he admits certain problems of the era he asserts that "the message of Israel's earlier spokesmen had not been lost" (132).

3. Richard D. Nelson, *Raising up a Faithful Priest: Community and Priesthood in Biblical Theology* (Louisville: Westminster John Knox, 1993), 132.

4. The foundations of this movement are found in Yehezkel Kaufmann, *History of the Religion of Ancient Israel* [Hebrew] (4 vols.; Tel Aviv: Bialik Institute-Dvir, 1937–56); abridged and translated as *The Religion of Israel: From Its Beginnings to the Babylonian Exile* (trans. Moshe Greenberg; Chicago: University of Chicago Press, 1960). A contemporary statement of this position is found in the writings of Jacob Milgrom; cf. *Leviticus 1–16* (AB 3; Garden City: Doubleday, 1991), esp. 3–13.

The Books of Chronicles

The Books of Chronicles, however, have a penchant for describing public ceremonies from a liturgical perspective.[5] To the careful reader they offer an intriguing resource for study of postexilic worship. The Chronicler reworked the Deuteronomic History to offer a postexilic Judean understanding of Israel's history. He added many comments and stories to the text he found in Samuel and Kings, and these additions may be considered "interpretive contributions." There emerges from this rewriting a new vision of the monarchy, the temple and land, and its public worship, usually located at the Jerusalem temple. Within these descriptions we can discover how people worshiped — the methods, moods, rituals, words revealed in the text — in light of their worldview and self-understanding. I describe this interpretive process in Chronicles as a "homiletic spirituality," a way of life that the Chronicler "preaches" by his fresh retelling of Israel's historical tradition.[6]

Although these worship narratives describe events from the era of the monarchy, they are not usually considered reliable indicators of preexilic worship because of the rewriting evident in them. Many studies have focused on the historical reliability of Chronicles and found it wanting. Others examine the Chronicler's retelling of Israel's history for evidence of a Priestly or Levitical bias of the author or as an indicator of the composer's social location. Sara Japhet's study of Chronicles, however, evinces more interest in theological and ideological

---

5. Sara Japhet, *I and II Chronicles: A Commentary* (Old Testament Library; Louisville: Westminster John Knox, 1993), 38–40, where she offers a sketch of public/liturgical ceremonies in Chronicles.

6. John C. Endres, *Temple, Monarchy and Word of God* (Message of Biblical Spirituality; Wilmington, Del.: Glazier, 1988), 19–20, 30–31.

concerns, allowing the book to provide a lens into the spiritual world of Jewish worship in the era when it was composed,
probably the late Persian era, around 400 B.C.E.[7] Indeed, his
description of old liturgical celebrations may well resemble the
worship of his contemporaries in subtle but significant ways.[8] I
also presuppose that the Chronicler viewed Israel's history from
a thoroughly liturgical perspective, so the public liturgies help
him to disseminate his view of Israel's life.[9] I therefore suggest
that Chronicles provides access to the milieu of worship in Second Temple Judaism, and I will show how study of this book
may reveal some major concerns in worship.[10] Though the Book

7. Sara Japhet, *The Ideology of the Books of Chronicles and Its Place in Biblical Thought* (Beiträge zur Erforschung des Alten Testaments und des antiken
Judentum 9; Frankfurt: Lang, 1989). These concerns emerge continually in
her commentary, *I and II Chronicles.*

8. Japhet, *I and II Chronicles*, 40: "The prevalence of the 'ceremonial'
component in the Chronicler's work may very well reflect his historical setting, in which public ceremonies may have occupied an important place in
the community's life."

9. William Riley, *King and Cultus in Chronicles: Worship and the Reinterpretation of History* (JSOTSup 160; Sheffield: JSOT Press, 1993), 193–94:
"The Davidic nation in the period of the Chronicler has become essentially
a liturgical nation existing among the nations with the providence secured by
their covenant relationship with Yahweh and by fidelity to that cultus which
was divinely initiated through the actions of the Davidic kings."

10. John Kleinig's study fills in parts of the lost picture by focusing on
choral music as an essential aspect of worship in the Chronicler's view; *The
Lord's Song: The Basis, Function and Significance of Choral Music in Chronicles* (JSOTSup 156; Sheffield: Sheffield Academic Press, 1993). While some
scholars have commented on the surprising role of choral music in Chronicles, more have investigated the roles assigned to the singers, especially in
terms of power and status (i.e., Levitical studies). Kleinig investigates the
most minor clues to the content, role, and function of sacred music in this
book and offers some delightful insights into the puzzling question of the
role of music and song in the postexilic temple. One of his more important contributions is a careful study of the correspondence between choral
music and the sacrifices offered in the Jerusalem temple. Kleinig is inspired

of Chronicles does not illustrate preexilic worship, it may offer significant help for the postexilic era.

The Book of Psalms

Another possible source for the practice and spirituality of worship is the Book of Psalms. In this century, following the form-critical studies of Hermann Gunkel and Sigmund Mowinckel, scholars have long held that the Psalms derive from and were shaped in the worship settings in Israel's life. Most Jews and Christians, accustomed to Psalms and other scriptural texts in contemporary worship, could comprehend by analogy how certain psalms might have played an important role in temple worship, just as they do later in synagogue and church.[11] Although use of the Psalms to generate a picture of Second Temple worship has proven difficult because they are notoriously difficult to date, we recognize that the Chronicler knew and loved the Psalms because he inserted psalm texts into some worship narratives. Finally, some psalms have superscriptions that ap-

---

by certain aspects of ritual theory developed by Victor Turner to investigate the meaning of particular aspects of ritual, the relation of action and verbal performance, the relationship between the structure of a ritual (with all its elements) and its meaning in culture. His study asks important questions, e.g., why are sacrifice and music paralleled in Chronicles? and what might be the meaning of this pairing?

11. For the use of the Book of Psalms in the Second Temple, see William Holladay, *The Psalms through Three Thousand Years: Prayerbook of a Cloud of Witnesses* (Minneapolis: Fortress, 1993), 55–66. Holladay searches for clues in the books of Haggai, Zechariah, Ezra, and Nehemiah as indicators of psalm use in early postexilic Israel. He also "dates" some psalms to the postexilic era by tracing influences (vocabulary and motifs) from prophetic texts, but especially from Jeremiah (Ps 31; 40:2–12; 51; 55:2–19; 69; 135; 148). He couples this with the linguistic studies of Avi Hurvitz on Ps 103, 117, 119, 124, 125, and 145 to establish postexilic language and diction. He also discusses reinterpretation of preexilic psalms when prayed in a postexilic context.

pear to function like liturgical or historical titles; regardless of their historical reliability, they offer some clues to the ongoing life of the Psalms in Judaism. Each of these resources — Chronicles, Psalms, and psalm superscriptions — can contribute to our picture of worship in Second Temple Judaism.

In this essay I will view Israel's worship by looking at three great liturgies: David's installation of the ark in Jerusalem (1 Chr 13–16), Solomon's temple dedication (2 Chr 5–7), and fasting in time of war (2 Chr 20). To discern the viewpoint of Chronicles — to determine what the Chronicler added, deleted, and changed in his major source and thus to identify his interpretation of the earlier tradition — I compare the text of Chronicles with Samuel-Kings. Where appropriate, reflection on psalm texts can enrich our view of the author's theology and spirituality. These comparisons are most easily made by reading the texts together, in synoptic fashion.[12]

David and the Ark (1 Chronicles 13–16)

After nine chapters of genealogies (1 Chr 1–9) the Chronicler starts to narrate Israel's story in midstream with the story of the death of Saul and his sons in the battle at Mount Gilboa. Omitting the long story of Saul's election and his demise (1 Sam 9–30) and also the divided kingdom after his death (2 Sam 2–4), the Chronicler features David's enthronement in Hebron and his capture of Zion, his capital city (1 Chr 11:1–9). There follows a long report on the personnel in David's army, naming

---

12. See the synoptic version of John Endres, William Millar, and John Barclay Burns, eds., *Chronicles and Its Synoptic Parallels in Samuel, Kings, and Related Biblical Texts* (Collegeville, Minn.: Liturgical Press, 1998).

the warriors who joined him at various stages, in Hebron and Ziklag (11:10–12:41 [Eng. 11:10–12:40]). But after capturing Jerusalem, David brought the ark into his capital and provided for worship in its presence. Here is an outline of events and texts in both Chronicles and Samuel.

	1 Chronicles	2 Samuel	Other Texts
David's proposal for the ark	13:1–4		
David goes to bring the ark	13:5–14	6:1–11	
Hiram's recognition of David	14:1–2	5:11–12	
David's children in Jerusalem	14:3–7	5:13–16	
David defeats the Philistines	14:8–17	5:17–25	
The ark brought to Jerusalem	15:1–16:6	6:12–19a	
David's psalm	16:7–36		various psalm texts
Levites appointed for the ark	16:37–43	6:19b–23	

Moving the Ark to Obed-Edom

David's decision to move the ark begins in a novel fashion in Chronicles: David consults with his leaders and then with all the "congregation of Israel," proposing transferal of the ark to Jerusalem. The word *congregation* alerts us to the worship milieu, for Chronicles uses this term in liturgical accounts.[13] The remaining text derives from Samuel, but the Chronicler refashioned it in two ways. First, he changed the order of events from Samuel so that David's decision about the ark stands first, showing us that David's fortune revolves around his care for the ark. Second, the Chronicler detected evidence of liturgical dancing, music, and song in the Samuel account: "Now David and all Israel were dancing before God *with all their strength, with songs*

---

13. Simon J. De Vries, *1 and 2 Chronicles* (Forms of the Old Testament Literature 11; Grand Rapids: Eerdmans, 1989), 136.

and with lyres and harps and timbrels, cymbals and trumpets"
(1 Chr 13:8).[14]

The text in italic derives from the Qumran version of
2 Samuel (not in the Masoretic Text); it reminds us that song
and music enliven the procession that David is leading (1 Chr
13:5–8). Here the Chronicler finds warrant for including liturgical song and choral music, and later he will add a "score" for
the ceremony in Jerusalem, the song of thanksgiving (16:8–36).
Chronicles thus transforms the ark's populist military escort in
Samuel to a full-fledged liturgical procession of "all Israel" to the
great city of Jerusalem. Perhaps in Second Temple times Jews recalled and celebrated the ark's entry with liturgical procession.
Still, David's first attempt to bring the ark to Jerusalem ended in
disaster: Uzzah tried to prevent the ark from falling off the cart,
but when he touched it he was struck dead for his offense. One
may raise the question why this happened, but the Chronicler
will not provide the answer at once.

Instead we learn that David's concern for the ark paved the
way for his prosperity in other spheres of life: his fame and Hi-
ram's recognition, the steady increase of his offspring, and his
military prowess. These motifs appear in 1 Chr 14, which neatly
follows David's initial measures to honor the ark. The causal
connection is only implicit, but the reordering of events probably
suggests a rhetorical strategy of the Chronicler.

Bringing the Ark to Jerusalem

Finally the historian returns to the story of David and the ark:
"[David] established a place for the ark of God and pitched a

---

14. Unless otherwise noted, quotations from Samuel, Kings, and Chronicles are taken from Endres, Millar, and Burns, *Chronicles and Its Synoptic
Parallels*. Quotations from other Bible books are from the NRSV.

tent for it. David said that no one except the Levites should carry the ark of God; for Yʜwʜ had chosen them to carry the ark of Yʜwʜ and to minister to him forever" (1 Chr 15:1b–2). David now realized God's strictures for this project, that Levites must carry the ark, so he was able to begin anew after he organized the priests and the Levites for worship. We may recognize the movement as a liturgical procession with the ark: when the Chronicler says that David "assembled all Israel" (15:3) he uses the same Hebrew root in the cultic term *congregation*. David appears vested in a white linen robe (15:27) appropriate for priest and Levites. God now approves the Levites' ministry: "Since God helped the Levites who were bearing the ark... they sacrificed seven bulls and seven rams" (15:26). The exuberant parade of David's era has become a grand liturgical procession replete with vested ark-bearers and choirs of singers, most of them Levites. As before, they are singing and dancing with gusto (13:8; 15:28), and here we learn an important characteristic of public liturgy in Chronicles: they moved "with rejoicing" (15:25).[15] In fact, this sense of joy so permeates the ceremonies in Chronicles that we may rightly characterize it as "joyful worship."[16]

Levites and Priests

For the Chronicler, the Levites were the sacred persons responsible for significant aspects of worship in the Jerusalem temple;

---

15. Cf. Japhet, *Ideology of Chronicles,* 253; Nelson, *Raising up a Faithful Priest,* 139.

16. The verb *rejoice* is found in 1 Chr 16:10, 31; 29:9; 2 Chr 15:15; 20:27; 23:21; 24:10; 29:36; 30:25. The adjective *joyful* is found in 2 Chr 7:10; 23:13. And the noun *joy* is found in 1 Chr 12:41 (Eng. 12:40); 15:16, 25; 29:9, 17, 22; 2 Chr 20:27; 23:18; 29:30; 30:21, 23, 26. Most uses of these words for *joy* occur in descriptions of great ceremonies and liturgies.

presumably he was thinking of Jerusalem in the Persian era.[17] As in Deut 10:8, only Levites were authorized to carry the ark in procession (1 Chr 15:2). Right worship depends on ministry by right persons following correct rituals. Then to specify the proper persons to carry the ark, the Chronicler adds a roster list of the Levites (15:4–10). Finally he describes their obedience to the proper prescriptions for their role as ark-bearers: "So the priests and the Levites consecrated themselves to bring up the ark" (15:14) — probably by bathing and abstention from sexual relations. Not only had Moses commanded that they carry the ark (15:15), but David had organized the Levites who were musicians and singers (15:16–22) and porters (15:23). Only the trumpets were not to be played by the Levites, but rather by priests (15:24). Perhaps this listing of choral musicians (15:16–24) reflects temple arrangements from the Chronicler's own time;[18] if so, the Chronicler was developing a sense of historical identity for various Levitical groups of his own day. Linking Levitical service, music, and song with David provided sound basis for their role in the postexilic temple.

Levites and priests also receive careful listing by genealogical groups in Chronicles. Scholars have sought — perhaps in

---

17. An excellent presentation of the roles of the Levites, especially in the composition and use of the Psalms, is Raymond Jacques Tournay, *Seeing and Hearing God with the Psalms: The Prophetic Liturgy of the Second Temple in Jerusalem* (trans. J. Edward Crowley; JSOTSup 118; Sheffield: Sheffield Academic Press, 1991), esp. part 1: "Levitical Singers, Cultic Prophets," 34–68. Part of his thesis is that many psalms traditionally dated to the monarchic era actually derive from the postexilic era, when the Levites were most active.

18. So argues H. G. M. Williamson, *1 and 2 Chronicles* (New Century Bible; Grand Rapids: Eerdmans, 1982), 122. De Vries (*1 and 2 Chronicles*, 145) states: "It is altogether fitting that the very singers of his own time should be symbolically and typologically present to participate in this first stage toward the development and perfection of the temple cult."

vain — to sort out the ideology and reality behind these group-ings, but some of the names in these lists prove intriguing for anyone familiar with the Psalms and their superscriptions. For example, we hear in 1 Chr 15:17 of Heman (Ps 88), Asaph (Ps 50, 73–83; 1 Chr 6:24 [Eng. 6:39]; 2 Chr 29:30), and Ethan (Ps 89). At the conclusion of this episode, additional familiar Levitical names appear: Asaph in 1 Chr 16:37, and He-man and Jeduthun (Ps 39, 62, 77; 1 Chr 25:1, 3) in 1 Chr 16:41. Although Korah does not appear prominently in Chron-icles (1 Chr 9:19, 31; 12:7 [Eng. 12:6]; 2 Chr 20:19) there are twelve psalms with this name in the title: Ps 42–49, 84, 85, 87, 88. These "sons of Korah" were undoubtedly a guild of Levitical temple singers that may have composed or collected and handed on the Korah collection in the Psalter. Hints like these sug-gest why the Chronicler emphasized liturgical song and music; they also raise tantalizing questions about relationships with the Psalms and the place of the Psalms in the worship of the Second Temple.

What were the roles and duties of these Levites? Besides carrying the ark, they had an important choral and musical min-istry: "[David] appointed before the ark of YHWH some of the Levites to serve, to invoke (*lehazkir*), to give thanks (*lehodot*), and to praise (*lehallel*) YHWH God of Israel" (1 Chr 16:4).

They sang different kinds of songs: songs of thanksgiving and of praise and songs invoking God. One could easily envision different kinds of songs that are well known from the Psalter: thanksgiving and praise, corresponding to thanksgiving psalms and hymns. Form-critical study of the Psalms resonates nicely with these, and one scholar suggests a convenient categoriza-tion: "to invoke through the Psalms of lament, to thank as in the thanksgiving Psalms, and to praise the Lord as in many

of the hymns of the Psalter."[19] Connecting the first, "to invoke," with laments or psalms of petition provides continuing
debate.[20]

Liturgical Patterns

The liturgy before the ark begins with song: "On that day,
then, David first ordained the singing of thanksgiving (*lehodot*)
to Yʜwʜ by Asaph and his kindred" (1 Chr 16:7, my translation). In 16:4 the Chronicler introduced the types of song (and
prayer) entrusted to Levitical choirs, but here we learn the type
of hymnody used on this particular occasion: thanksgiving. De-
scriptive words like "singing thanksgiving" may correspond to
ritual actions. Some relate the verb *lehazkir* ("to invoke" = "for
remembrance")[21] to a meal offering called the *'azkarah*,[22] but I
prefer the notion of invoking that connects it with psalms of
petition or lament. For example, *lehazkir* appears in the super-

---

19. Williamson, *1 and 2 Chronicles*, 127.

20. Some commentators oppose Williamson's connection of the lament
psalms with the verb *lehazkir* ("to invoke"). Taking his lead from earlier commentators, Roddy Braun (*1 Chronicles* [Word Biblical Commentary 14; Waco:
Word, 1986], 182, 185), e.g., translates this verb "to commemorate" and comments that Williamson is "probably being too precise to attach each word to a
type of Psalm" (192). Kleinig (*Lord's Song*, 35 n. 3) charges that "without giving any reason for his judgment, Williamson . . . *limits* [emphasis added] this
to invocation through psalms of lament, which is to be distinguished from
'thanking' through psalms of thanksgiving and 'praising' through hymns."

21. *The Revised Psalms of the New American Bible* (New York: Catholic
Book Publishing, 1991), ad loc., translates the superscriptions this way. The
ɴʀsᴠ translates these superscriptions as "for the memorial offering."

22. Milgrom (*Leviticus 1–16*, 177, 181–82) and Herbert J. Levine (*Sing
unto God a New Song: A Contemporary Reading of the Psalms* [Bloomington:
Indiana University Press, 1995], 10–11) describe it as a "token portion." Each
of them understands "remembrance" here as an indication that the portion
actually sacrificed represents the whole, a *pars pro toto*.

scriptions for the laments in Ps 38 and Ps 70,[23] and it is also found in other exilic or postexilic contexts of intercession or lamentation.[24] Another clue to a ritual meaning for *lehazkir* comes from a Priestly text, Num 10:1–10. When the Israelites were about to march from Sinai to Transjordan, God ordered Moses to make two silver trumpets (Num 10:1) that the priests would sound for their festivals, "joyous occasions" (10:10). Whenever Israel was attacked in their land by an aggressor the priests were to "sound an alarm with the trumpets, so that you may be remembered before the LORD your God and be saved from your enemies" (10:9). Being "remembered" by God leads to being "saved" by God, the primary goal of lament psalms. Priests blow the trumpets here as at other critical points in Israel's life: the installation of the ark (1 Chr 16:6, 42), the dedication of the temple (2 Chr 5:12–13), the rededication of altar and covenant under Asa (15:8–15), and the purification of temple in Hezekiah's time (29:27). Priests blow trumpets as instruments of prayer, especially prayer that leads to "saving" activity.

---

23. There the term is usually translated "for remembrance" (*Revised Psalms of the New American Bible*) or "to make memorial" (A. Cohen, *The Psalms: Hebrew Text, English Translation and Commentary* [Hindhead, Surrey: Soncino, 1945], 117). Cohen argues against a connection with lament psalms: "The meaning is not, as the older commentators supposed, to bring the plight of the sufferer to God's remembrance. The word is best understood in a technical sense. In connection with the meal-offering the priest was commanded to make *the memorial-part* (azkarah) *thereof smoke upon the altar* (Lev. ii.2); it is therefore possible that the term implies that the Psalm was chanted while that part of the sacrificial act took place. That it indicates a type of Temple-chanting is to be concluded from the statement: *And he appointed certain of the Levites to minister before the ark of the* LORD, *and to celebrate* (lehazkir) *and to thank and praise the* LORD (1 Chron. xvi.4)."

24. In these poems other forms of hiphil *zakhar* are used; see Isa 62:6; 63:7; Ps 71:16.

When David finally brought the ark into Jerusalem, there was
an elaborate liturgical celebration, including trumpets: "Benaiah
and Jahaziel were priests on the trumpets, continually before
the ark of the covenant of God.... With them — Heman and
Jeduthun — were trumpets and cymbals for playing, and instruments for the sacred song" (1 Chr 16:6, 42a). The Chronicler
added prayer texts to the ritual descriptions: a thanksgiving
song is presented as the Levites' choral text for the occasion
(16:8–36); it includes verses from several canonical psalms
(Ps 105:1–15; 96:1–13; 106:1, 47–48). Here the language of
"remembering" and "saving" by God also appears; when the
Chronicler cites Ps 105:1–15, the people of Israel are to remember God's actions for them (1 Chr 16:12, 15). In 1 Chr 16:15
the author altered the description of the psalmist, "[God] remembered his covenant forever" (Ps 105:8), to an order to the
congregation: "Remember his covenant forever." The assurance
of God's covenant fidelity has become a liturgical directive for
the congregation in the Chronicler's era; it now indicates "how
Israel was preserved among the nations."[25]

The Chronicler then quotes Ps 106:47 as a prayer of petition
that now hints at "tense relations between Israel and the hos-
tile nations":[26] "Say also, 'Save us, God of our salvation; gather
us and deliver us from the nations; to give thanks to your holy
name, to take pride in your praise'" (1 Chr 16:35). This plea
to God for deliverance and victory connects the prayer to a
realistic sociopolitical situation, Israel's subjugation to powerful

25. J. A. Loader, "Redaction and Function of the Chronistic 'Psalm of
David,'" in *Studies in the Chronicler* (ed. W. C. van Wyk; Ou-Testamentiese
Werkgemeenskap in Suider-Afrika 19; Potchefstroom: Pro Rege, 1977), 69–
75, 73.
26. Ibid., 72.

foreign nations.[27] The Chronicler's historical context calls for "a plea for deliverance," while the literary context in the David story suggests thanksgiving.[28] In a time of Persian control, this song exhorts the congregation to thank God for past acts of justice; it also alludes to their present need for saving (16:35). This strategy may remind us of the subversive function of many "spirituals" of the African-American song tradition: biblical traditions acceptable to white slave owners were crafted in music of lament (the blues). A lively religious faith cloaks the people's desires for powerful new saving acts from their God.

"Remembering" and "saving" thus bind together the two major aspects of David's psalm: thanking and praising God for all God has done for Israel. But David also urges God to save Israel — that they might have further reason to thank God! As in the Psalms, singing thanksgiving always presupposes strong prayer of petition or lament. Likewise, Levites trained to sing thanksgiving must also have been aware of the petitions and laments that lead to divine intervention. Not surprisingly, eleven of the twenty-six psalms attributed to Levites by their superscriptions are usually categorized as laments.[29] Finally, the theology of worship in this psalm seems more sophisticated than simple prayer and thanksgiving: praise for remembrance and salvation seems part of the theology of laments, which Chronicles inserts in its version of David's installation of the ark.

---

27. Cf. Nelson, *Raising up a Faithful Priest,* 131.

28. Trent C. Butler, "A Forgotten Passage from a Forgotten Era," *VT* 28 (1978): 145.

29. Heman (Ps 88); Jeduthun (Ps 39); Asaph (Ps 74, 77, 79, 80, 83); Korah (Ps 42/43, 44, 85). All of the Asaph psalms and two Korah psalms (44 and 85) are communal laments, which are even more appropriate to Levitical singing.

Solomon and the Temple (2 Chronicles 5–7)

After David made plans for worship and its ministers in the Jerusalem temple (1 Chr 23–29), Solomon succeeded him to the throne; but still there was no temple. Although God had promised "a sure house" (i.e., dynasty) to David (1 Chr 17) and David had won a series of military conflicts (1 Chr 18–20), the Chronicler does not focus on the future temple until the story of Ornan's threshing floor (1 Chr 21 // 2 Sam 24). David offered sacrifices and prayed there, and then God "answered him with fire from heaven on the altar of burnt offering" (1 Chr 21:26). Fire often signals a divine appearance, so this sign confirms David's choice of the site.[30] Finally, God quelled the pestilence that resulted from David's disobedient military census: he ordered the angel to return his sword to its sheath (21:27). This pattern — ritual action (sacrifice and prayer) resulting in the cessation of pestilence — comes from 2 Samuel, but Chronicles heightens God's acceptance of sacrifice with the fire from heaven — another theophanic experience.

Two Kinds of Worship at Gibeon and Jerusalem

The high place at Gibeon continued to operate at this time: "For the tabernacle of Yhwh that Moses had made in the desert and the altar of burnt offering were at that time in the high place at Gibeon" (1 Chr 21:29). So the people continued to offer sacrifices there, which may explain why Solomon could go there to sacrifice in a public liturgical event, with "all Israel" and "all the assembly." And since the tent of meeting from the desert era still resided at Gibeon (2 Chr 1:3b), Solomon was well advised to go there to "inquire" of God.

---

30. Williamson, *1 and 2 Chronicles*, 150.

Continuity of worship between Gibeon (tabernacle) and Jerusalem (ark) is evidenced in David's installation of the ark[31] in arranging the types of worship and the personnel required:

> Then David left Asaph and his kinsfolk there before the ark of the covenant of YHWH to minister on a daily basis (*tamid*) before the ark, as each day required, and Obed-edom and their sixty-eight kinsfolk; Obed-edom son of Jeduthun and Hosah as doorkeepers. He also left Zadok the priest and his kindred the priests before the tabernacle of YHWH in the high place which was at Gibeon, to offer up burnt offerings to YHWH on the altar of burnt offering, continually (*tamid*) in the morning and in the evening, according to all that was written in the Torah of YHWH that he commanded Israel. With them were Heman, Jeduthun, and the rest of those chosen — who were specified by [their] names to give thanks to YHWH "for his steadfast love lasts forever." With them, Heman and Jeduthun, were trumpets and cymbals for playing, and instruments for the sacred song, and the sons of Jeduthun were in charge of the door (1 Chr 16:37–42).

So David appointed Levites to attend to the ark in Jerusalem, and at Gibeon the priestly family of Zadok was left to officiate at the sacrificial offerings, along with the Levites Heman and Jeduthun, who were responsible for the music and song (and also for guarding the temple entrances). Worship at Gibeon combines sacrifice and song.

In Jerusalem, the choral ministry of the Asaphites was supposed to "coincide with the regular morning and evening

---

31. Cf. Nelson, *Raising up a Faithful Priest,* 134.

sacrifices at Gibeon."[32] The Hebrew word *tamid,* translated "on a daily basis" (16:37) and "continually" (16:40), also suggests that the times of sacrifice (morning and evening) at Gibeon were to be synchronized with the Levitical singing before the ark in Jerusalem.[33] This description reminds us of the Levites' duties set out by David: "They were to stand every morning to give thanks and to give praise to YHWH and likewise in the evening; and at every offering of burnt offerings to YHWH — at sabbaths and new moons and festivals — by number, according to custom concerning them, continually before YHWH (1 Chr 23:30–31)." Here the correspondence of song to sacrifice seems clear.[34] Chronicles devised a liturgical program of choral song (thanks and praise) synchronized with the offering of morning and evening sacrifices. Song and sacrifice are not yet joined together at Jerusalem (song without sacrifice), but Gibeon may reflect the pattern for Second Temple worship: song by Levites, with sacrifices offered at the same time by priests.[35]

Solomon Dedicates the Temple

After the temple was built and the proper articles and offerings had been installed, Solomon ordered the elders to bring the ark into the temple during the Festival of Tabernacles. While Solomon and the people were sacrificing sheep and oxen, the priests

---

32. Kleinig, *Lord's Song,* 108–9; he bases this conclusion on the formula "as each day required," which is related to *devar-yom beyomo* ("on each day what is proper to it"; NJPSV) in Lev 23:37, a text in the priestly liturgical/festival calendar.

33. Ibid., 74–75.

34. Ibid., 75.

35. Kleinig moves beyond "simultaneity" to "the synchronization of sacrifice and song" (ibid., 75–77) as the comprehensive view of worship in Chronicles.

installed the ark in the Holy of Holies. When they emerged, the Levites and priest trumpeters were raising sacred song of praise and thanks to God from a position east of the temple. Then the cloud filled the house and prevented the priests from continuing their ministry there.

When Solomon entered the liturgical scene, he greeted the people and addressed God, remembering God's choice of David, the site of the temple, and the assignment of its construction to himself, David's son (2 Chr 6:3–9). Then he moved to a bronze platform before the altar and assumed a position of prayer, kneeling with hands outstretched toward heaven (6:12–13). After this prayer, with its invitation to God to "rest" here, the fire and the cloud signified God's appearance and favor on the building and the worship being carried out here and on this occasion. All Israel sang a liturgical refrain while they worshiped. After this ceremony for the temple and the altar, Solomon dedicated the middle part of the court by making more burnt offerings and sacrifices.

When the Chronicler describes the ark's installation in the temple, he alters the account in Kings only slightly, but the changes illuminate liturgical developments. In Kings the priests carried the ark to the temple precincts, but Chronicles attributes it to the Levites (1 Kgs 8:3 // 2 Chr 5:4), since it was their role. On two points Chronicles agrees with Kings: (1) priests and Levites cooperated in transporting the tent of meeting and all the holy vessels (1 Kgs 8:4 // 2 Chr 5:5); and (2) priests bore the ark into the *devir,* the Holy of Holies (1 Kgs 8:6 // 2 Chr 5:7), which accords with Priestly directions in Num 4:5–20.

In Chronicles, the high point of this liturgy occurred when the priests left the temple:[36]

---

36. Japhet, *I and II Chronicles,* 579.

When the priests came out of the holy place, for all the
priests who were found [there] had consecrated themselves;
there was no keeping to divisions and the Levites who were
singers for all of them, Asaph, Heman, Jeduthun and their
sons and their brothers, were clothed in fine linen and with
cymbals and with harps and with lyres were standing east of
the altar; and with them were the priests, one hundred and
twenty of them sounding on the clarions. It happened, when
the clarion-players and the singers were as one, they made
themselves heard [with] one voice to give praise and to give
thanks to YHWH; and when they raised a sound with clarions
and with cymbals and with other instruments of music in
praise to YHWH: "For [he is] good, for his graciousness [is]
forever"; the house was filled with a cloud (2 Chr 5:11–13).

In many details this ceremony parallels the liturgy of David's
installation of the ark in 1 Chr 15–16:

- priests sanctified themselves before the ceremony (2 Chr
  5:11 // 1 Chr 15:14); here *all* the priests did so

- singers were Levites; same names for the special Levitical
  groups (2 Chr 5:12 // 1 Chr 16:37, 41; cf. 1 Chr 25:1–6;
  2 Chr 29:13)

- Levites, as well as priests, wore white linen vestments
  (2 Chr 5:12 // 1 Chr 15:27)

- musical instruments: cymbals, harps, and lyres (2 Chr
  5:12 // 1 Chr 15:16; cf. 25:1)

- 120 priests playing the trumpet (2 Chr 5:12 // the number
  of priests in 1 Chr 15 can be calculated as 120)[37]

---

37. Ibid., 580.

The Levites were standing east of the altar when the priests came out of the temple, so one could almost choreograph this part of this ceremony: from the west would be priests, 120 priests playing trumpets, then the Levites, and in the outer court the Israelites gathered to worship.

Chronicles describes the choral music, boasting that the trumpeters and singers played together in unison and all made themselves heard "as one voice." Trumpeters and singers join together to "praise and thank YHWH" while all the instruments produced songs of praise (2 Chr 5:13). Here are Levitical choirs and musicians positioned opposite the priests who were playing trumpets — all singing psalms of praise and thanksgiving to YHWH in complete unison. The refrain is familiar from the Psalter (e.g., Ps 100:5; 106:1; 107:1; 118:1, 29; 136:1) and from other liturgical ceremonies in Chronicles (1 Chr 16:34, 41; 2 Chr 7:3, 6; 20:21; see the texts on the following page).[38]

Both ceremonies utilize the same refrain and theophanic element of the cloud, representing God's glory. But they also differ. At Solomon's installation of the ark, Levitical choirs sang the hymn of praise, but when the temple was dedicated "all Israel" joined in the song while prostrating themselves and worshiping God physically (2 Chr 7:3). Finally, a heavenly fire descends on the burnt offerings (as when David offered sacrifice at Ornan's threshing floor; 1 Chr 21:26). As before, fire represents divine acceptance of Israel's worship and dedication of this place. Cecil B. DeMille would have loved this scene!

The temple dedication in Chronicles is quite similar to that in Kings; Solomon's gestures for blessing and praying basically

---

38. Cf. Raymond B. Dillard, *2 Chronicles* (Word Biblical Commentary 15; Waco: Word, 1987), 42.

Bringing the ark into the temple (2 Chronicles 5:13–14)	*Dedicating the temple* (2 Chronicles 7:1–3)
	When Solomon finished praying the fire came down from the heavens and it consumed the burnt offerings
[The Levites] raised a sound…in praise to YHWH: "For [he is] good, for his graciousness [is] forever"; the house was filled with a cloud, the house of YHWH; and the priests were not able to stand to minister in front of the cloud, for the glory of YHWH filled the house of God.	and the sacrifices. [*They*] *gave thanks to* YHWH, *"For* [*he is*] *good, for his graciousness* [*is*] *forever"* and the glory of YHWH filled the house. The priests were not able to come into the house of YHWH, since the glory of YHWH filled the house of YHWH. All the Israelites were looking on as the fire was coming down and the glory of YHWH [was] upon the house; and they bowed their faces to the ground upon the pavement and they worshiped.[39]

repeat those of the Chronicler's source. Spreading forth one's hands as a gesture of prayer is commonly recognized (1 Kgs 8:54; Ezra 9:5; Ps 44:21 [Eng. 44:20]). Solomon's prayer, focused on the house for God's name as a place of prayer, is little different than in Kings. Solomon begs God: "Give heed to the supplications of your servant and of your people Israel which they pray continually toward this place" (2 Chr 6:21). He repeats the prayers for God's intervention and pardon whenever Israel cries out to God. The lament-like tone of these prayers of peti-

---

39. The italic text is 2 Chr 7:3b transposed to the middle of 7:1.

tion complements the praise and thanksgiving of the Levitical choirs.

Chronicles omits the motif of God's election of Israel at the exodus (1 Kgs 8:51, 53), but incorporates parts of Ps 132 as the conclusion to Solomon's prayer. This psalm is a processional hymn that glorifies David's bringing of the ark to Jerusalem; it celebrates God's choice of the ark, of Jerusalem, and of David, so it was an appropriate song for the ark's entry into the new temple. In Ps 132 Israel begged God to accompany the ark into the temple (2 Chr 6:41) and then to care for the priests, the covenant partners, and the anointed ones (i.e., David and probably Solomon) (6:42). The verses from Ps 132 used in Chronicles fit the situation of Solomon's prayer quite nicely: David's son, Solomon, brings the ark to its new resting place — the temple — and then he asks God to be present here and to bless all the leaders.

Psalm 132 also appeals to God to restore the "rest from our enemies," perhaps in the Chronicler's day. Where the psalmist prayed that God's priests "be clothed with righteousness" (Ps 132:9), the Chronicler wrote: "may they be clothed with salvation" (2 Chr 6:41).[40] This public prayer combines psalmic praise, thanksgiving, and petition, reflecting a style of temple worship during the Chronicler's own era.[41] Begging God for justice may translate as an appeal for rescue from oppressive neighbors, a subtle but clear reference to hopes during the Persian era.

After Solomon's prayer Chronicles alters the ceremony in Kings where Solomon stood, turned toward the people, and

---

40. *Salvation* is related to the imperative "*save* us, O God of our *salvation*" at the end of David's psalm in 1 Chr 16:35, where God's intervention is demanded — perhaps from Persian domination.

41. Sara Japhet, *I and II Chronicles,* 601.

prayed a blessing prayer (1 Kgs 8:54–61). Chronicles, rather, records a visual theophany: fire descending from heaven onto the burnt offerings and sacrifices, signifying God's acceptance of the offerings, of this altar, and perhaps of the prayer. Then the cloud fills the temple and prevents the priests from entering it. This cloud of presence also implies divine approval of the temple: God truly responds to Solomon's invitation to come to this resting place.[42] When the Israelites had seen these symbols,[43] they bent their heads down, prostrated themselves on the ground in an act of worship, and sang the familiar refrain: "For good is he — for his steadfast love lasts forever."

The Chronicler's notion of liturgical worship also emerges from his editing of Ps 132. Where the psalmist appealed, "let your faithful shout for joy" (132:9b), Chronicles recasts it: "your loyal faithful ones, let them rejoice in good[ness]" (2 Chr 6:41b). As noted earlier, joy and rejoicing are recurring motifs in Chronicles, usually associated with the pageantry of public ceremonies, celebrations, and worship. "Goodness" is what God brings to Israel because of the covenant and its promise to David; at the end of this ceremony Solomon "sent the people to their tents rejoicing and with good hearts because of the good that YHWH had done for David and for Solomon and for Israel his people" (2 Chr 7:10). Israel rejoices because of God's goodness to them.

The liturgies of David and Solomon in these postexilic descriptions enrich our knowledge of worship in the late Persian era. Ritual accounts like these ought not be read as straightforward descriptions by observers; on the contrary, these accounts

---

42. Kleinig, *Lord's Song*, 167.

43. Each of these images of God's presence has its own religious history: fire in 1 Chr 21:26; Lev 9:24; and cloud in 2 Chr 5:14; 1 Kgs 8:10–11; Exod 40:35.

often acquire a prescriptive character for the congregation that receives such texts. Liturgical descriptions subtly prescribe the moods, contours, and ritual actions of worship in postexilic Israel.[44] They also serve a rhetorical function, encouraging people to rejoice in God's overwhelming goodness.

These ceremonial descriptions in 2 Chr 5–7 demonstrate the correspondence of the two types of worship — sacrifice and song — and also the two ministries responsible for them — priests and Levites. Here is a schema quite different from the way that many scholars interpret the cultus in the temple from the viewpoint of Priestly traditions. Beginning with Yehezkel Kaufmann, many scholars note that sacrificial rites do not contain or correlate with words, either prayer or song, so they occasionally speak of the temple as the "sanctuary of silence."[45] For his day, the Chronicler envisioned a new sense of temple worship, one including both sacrifice and song, where the words and motifs of the song suggest the theology and spirituality of the celebration.

Fasting and Holy War (2 Chronicles 20)

A third public worship service introduces us to liturgy in time of war, quite different from the situations of David and Solomon when Israel was at rest from its enemies. Although the Book of Kings recounts several events from Jehoshaphat's reign, this holy war narrative does not appear there, so this new composition

---

44. De Vries (*1 and 2 Chronicles*, 265) states: "[The Chronicler] means his description to be prescriptive; i.e., Israel's greatest joy ought ever to be to journey to the temple and take part in the sacred festivals. This is experientially the highest point of biblical piety."

45. Cf. Israel Knohl, *The Sanctuary of Silence: The Priestly Torah and the Holiness School* (Minneapolis: Fortress, 1995), 148–49.

comprises the Chronicler's theology and spirituality. The Judean king Jehoshaphat faced an attack from eastern peoples, particularly Ammonites and Moabites, whose land Israel had traversed en route to the promised land from Egypt. Although scholars have not reached consensus about the historical and sociological setting of this attack,[46] most agree that Jehoshaphat's religious response to the threat of war reflects the theological agenda of Chronicles. How should God's people react to the frightening news of enemies closing in, perhaps a few days' march from Jerusalem, at En Gedi? The description of this liturgical ceremony reflects religious sensibilities of the Chronicler's own era.

A Communal Fast

The king demonstrated genuine fear and determined to inquire of YHWH. Chronicles describes the ceremony carefully: "And he proclaimed a fast over all Judah. Judah gathered together to seek [help] from YHWH; also from all the towns of Judah they came to seek YHWH" (2 Chr 20:3b–4). Many consider fasting to be the generic description of the communal ceremony, its goal being to present their requests to YHWH. In postexilic Israel fasting seems to have characterized a kind of service that focused both on recognition of disaster and prayer to God in time of need.

---

46. Cf. Japhet, *I and II Chronicles*, 783–86; Philip R. Davies, "Defending the Boundaries of Israel in the Second Temple Period: 2 Chronicles 20 and the 'Salvation Army,'" in *Priests, Prophets and Scribes: Essays on the Formation and Heritage of Second Temple Judaism in Honour of Joseph Blenkinsopp* (ed. Eugene Ulrich et al.; JSOTSup 149; Sheffield: Sheffield Academic Press, 1992), 43–54; Ralph W. Klein, "Reflections on Historiography in the Account of Jehoshaphat," in *Pomegranates and Golden Bells: Studies in Biblical, Jewish, and Near Eastern Ritual, Law and Literature in Honor of Jacob Milgrom* (ed. David P. Wright, David Noel Freedman, and Avi Hurvitz; Winona Lake, Ind.: Eisenbrauns, 1995), 643–57, esp. 652–54.

They fasted and wept when they recalled the fate of Jerusalem: in Zechariah we hear that the people and the priests "fasted and lamented in the fifth month and in the seventh" (Zech 7:5). The holy city had been destroyed in the fifth month (2 Kgs 25:9), and in the seventh month Gedaliah had been assassinated (25:25),[47] so returnees from exile commemorated these tragic events. But fasting usually adds prayer or supplication to the weeping over disaster: in postexilic Isaiah's famous critique of fasting, he claims: "Such fasting as you do today / will not make your voice heard on high" (Isa 58:4b). Later, when news of Jerusalem's troubles reached Nehemiah in Susa, the Persian capital, he "sat down and wept, and mourned for days, fasting and praying before the God of heaven" (Neh 1:4), and a long prayer for the inhabitants of Jerusalem followed (Neh 1:5–11). Another narrative set in Persia views fasting with a comparable function: before Esther will approach the king to lift the death sentence against her Jewish people, she tells Mordecai: "Go, gather all the Jews to be found in Susa, and hold a fast on my behalf, and neither eat nor drink for three days, night or day. I and my maids will also fast as you do" (Esth 4:16). In a famous passage, the people of Nineveh fast after hearing Jonah's proclamation (Jonah 3:5, 7).

A familiar passage from Joel, another postexilic prophet, connects fasting and mourning with the time of tragedy,[48] possibly a locust plague:

---

47. David L. Petersen, *Haggai and Zechariah 1–8* (Old Testament Library; Philadelphia: Westminster, 1984), 285.

48. Hans Walter Wolff (*Joel and Amos* [trans. Waldemar Janzen, S. Dean McBride Jr., and Charles A. Muenchow; Hermeneia; Philadelphia: Fortress, 1977], 33) states: "The purpose of this assembly is the crying to Yahweh always associated with fasting."

Yet even now, says the LORD,
    return to me with all your heart,
with fasting, with weeping, and with mourning;
    rend your hearts and not your clothing.
Return to the LORD, your God,
    for he is gracious and merciful,
slow to anger, and abounding in steadfast love,
    and relents from punishing.
Who knows whether he will not turn and relent,
    and leave a blessing behind him, a grain offering and a
        drink offering
    for the LORD, your God?
Blow the trumpet in Zion;
    sanctify a fast;
call a solemn assembly (Joel 2:12–15).

During this assembly the priests and ministers cry to God in words reminiscent of some of the most insistent lament psalms:

Spare your people, O LORD,
    and do not make your heritage a mockery,
    a byword among the nations.
Why should it be said among the peoples,
    "Where is their God?" (2:17).

In response, God proclaims salvation for the people: fullness of crops, removal of their shame, defeat of the enemy, so that the people will praise God who remains present in their midst (2:18–27). This pattern of weeping, fasting, and prayer followed by an oracle of salvation from God and dramatic reversal also characterizes the narrative in 2 Chronicles.

A Communal Lament Liturgy

The postexilic laments envisage public liturgical ceremonies at times of intense need, and they demonstrate appropriate prayers along with their descriptions of the ritual. Here the king leads the assembly in the temple area, "in front of the new courtyard" where he proclaims a prayer to God (2 Chr 20:6–12):

> YHWH God of our ancestors, are you not the God in heaven? Do you not rule over all the kingdoms of the nations? In your hand [are] power and might so that none can withstand you. Did you not, our God, dispossess the inhabitants of this land from before your people Israel, and give it over to the offspring of Abraham your friend forever?...O our God, will you not give judgment against them? For we have no power (20:6–7, 12).

Although the king appears to question God, these are clearly rhetorical questions, which normally invite a resounding yes in response.[49] Next, he recalls the settlement in the land and Solomon's dedication of the temple for YHWH's name. This prayer recalls the pattern of Solomon's prayer at the temple dedication (esp. 2 Chr 6:28, 34; 7:14) — that whenever Israel suffers calamity they should come to this house of God and beg divine intervention. Jehoshaphat prays: "If disaster comes upon us, the sword of judgment or pestilence or famine, we will stand before this house and before you — for your name is in this house — and we will cry out to you out of our distress and you will hear and you will deliver" (20:9). This king certainly approaches the

---

49. Cf. Samuel E. Balentine, *Prayer in the Hebrew Bible: The Drama of Divine-Human Dialogue* (Overtures to Biblical Theology; Minneapolis: Fortress, 1993), 99.

temple correctly, going there to pray to God's name when Israel needs God's mercy. As one commentator suggests, "the conduct of the war is purely liturgical and is recorded in a way meant to support the theological agenda of the Chronicler."[50]

This royal prayer reminds God of two key facts from Israel's past: (1) it was God who transferred this land to Israel, pushing out its former inhabitants (2 Chr 20:7); and (2) Israel had responded to God by building this temple (20:8) and by obeying God — by not exercising their military option of destroying those peoples, the very ones now preparing to attack them (20:11). Ironically these foreigners act as if "they are repaying us" after we spared them! This complaint constitutes the center of Jehoshaphat's prayer. So he begs God to bring justice to this situation: defeat those who stand in the wrong, those poised to attack (20:12). As in psalms of lament, the speaker petitions God to restore peace, consisting of the just relationships already initiated by God's acts. Reminding God, making God mindful, functions both as part of the complaint and also as part of the king's persuasive rhetoric to God. Still, as noted above, the king has little doubt that God will act and intervene, so sure is he of God's power and greatness. Except for the near certainty of divine response, this prayer closely resembles the communal lament psalms, such as Ps 44, 74, 79 (which, incidentally, are attributed to Levitical groups: Asaph and Korah).

Jehoshaphat concludes on a humble note: "Will you not give judgment against them? For we have no power.... We do not know what we should do but our eyes are upon you" (2 Chr 20:12). His piety resembles that of David's farewell prayer in Chronicles (1 Chr 29:10–19, esp. v. 14): "But who am I, and

---

50. Klein, "Reflections on Historiography," 653.

what is my people ... for everything is from you." Israel's weakness and dependence provide a reason for the king's public prayer, and this expresses the deeper meaning of their fasting: "the strongest expression of human soul-searching and complete surrender to God."[51] As in laments, powerlessness also serves as motivation for God to act in their behalf.

In this liturgy the assembly was composed of "all Judahites," including their wives and children (2 Chr 20:13). This all-inclusive gathering also reflects other public ceremonies in postexilic times, especially in Ezra and Nehemiah.[52] Next a Levite named Jahaziel, from the house of Asaph, experienced the spirit of YHWH and proclaimed God's word for these people: "Do not be afraid, and do not be dismayed before this great horde, for the battle is not yours but God's" (20:15b). This speech is a salvation oracle, for that is what it proclaims: "Take your position: stand and see YHWH's deliverance of you, O Judah and Jerusalem" (20:17a). The war setting requires accurate translation of the word *yeshu'ah* as "deliverance," though it is often rendered "salvation" elsewhere. The same Hebrew root appeared in the prayers of David (1 Chr 16:35) and Solomon (2 Chr 6:41); such use of the word suggests a more concrete, less spiritual understanding of the word in each of these cases. Deliverance, God's response to Jehoshaphat in this case, and its appearance in other royal prayers, may help disclose deeper yearnings in the prayers composed by the Chronicler for people of his day. Royal prayers

---

51. Japhet, *I and II Chronicles*, 787.

52. After the return from exile, when they laid the foundations to rebuild the temple, there was a great liturgy in which "all the people" participated (Ezra 3:11). Three liturgies recounted in Nehemiah specifically mention women and children as well as men: the reading of the Torah (8:1–3), the covenant ceremony (10:29 [Eng. 10:28]), and the dedication of Nehemiah's wall (12:43). Each of these ceremonies is also characterized by joyful singing.

praising God never lose sight of the need for God's delivering and saving help. Conversely, even the prayers entreating God never veer from acclamation of God's power over all things. Recall how Jehoshaphat began his prayer: "Are you not God in heaven? Do you not rule over all the kingdoms of the nations?" (20:6). Praising God is never totally separate from invoking God's power to deliver.

Ritual description betrays the liturgical interests of the Chronicler. The king and the entire congregation bow down in worship of YHWH (2 Chr 20:18), and the Levitical choirs (both Korahites and Kohathites) stood up to praise YHWH the God of Israel "with a very loud voice" (20:19). Choirs usually praise God after the victory is won, but here the Levites seem certain of the outcome after hearing God's message. This apparent trust matches the king's certainty that God will act: "Trust in YHWH your God and you will be upheld" (20:20). Liturgical faith blossoms into faith on the battlefield, finally reaching a great crescendo when appointed singers parade in front of the army, singing: "Give thanks to YHWH for his loving-kindness lasts forever" (20:21). This favorite postexilic confession of faith helps to define the spirituality of the Levites who lead the way into God's battle.

When God's power completely overcomes the enemies of Judah, who should be surprised? The Judahites needed three days to despoil all the booty from the vanquished, so they named the place the Valley of Beracah, that is, the Valley of Blessing (2 Chr 20:26). This literary touch suggests that God's promise in Jahaziel's words has led to blessing for Judah. Similarly, God had hinted that such would be the divine response to public lament and fasting in Joel's day: "Who knows whether he will not turn and relent, / and leave a blessing behind him?" (Joel 2:14). The corresponding motifs in these two liturgical "fasts" play back and forth with a subtlety that just hints at both the ritual and the spirituality of public invocation of God's name in postexilic Israel. Finally, note how these events and this theology are intertwined with the actions and choral songs of Levites, which recalls for us their special ministry in the worship of the Second Temple.

Worship in the Chronicler's View

These three ceremonies provide an excellent sample of the Chronicler's view of liturgy and worship. Further study could examine other important narratives: David's enthronement (1 Chr 11:1–3; 12:39–41 [Eng. 12:38–40]), the registration of clergy and their divisions (23:2; 24:3–31), Solomon's enthronement (28:1–29:25), Hezekiah's purification of the temple (2 Chr 29), and the Passover celebrations of Hezekiah (2 Chr 30) and Josiah (2 Chr 35).[53] The picture would not differ much from what we have discovered. The sacrifices offered by the priests remain at center stage, most of the ceremonies feature choral music and song, the mood is festive (with great joy), and the participation is grand (all the people). Some views of worship from the preexilic era, for example, that priests sacrifice in silence and that psalms of praise were more congenial to the temple setting than those of lament and thanksgiving, are definitely altered. Rather, songs in Chronicles fashioned from canonical psalms demonstrate a clear role for the thanksgiving in public worship, and they also contain solid hints of the petitions directed toward their all-powerful God. The subtle hints about oppressors prob-

---

53. Cf. Japhet, *I and II Chronicles*, 39.

ably veils references to the view of Persian domination held by
Levites and priests.

In conclusion, we need not consider the role of priests and
the role of Levites in Chronicles as standing in great tension.
Perhaps they worked together with different specializations, each
responding to needs of the people who found in the temple a
center of God's creation and sense of order. One study of the
Psalms suggests this very process: "Though the people may have
brought their sacrifices to the priests, they brought their feelings
to the cultic prophets or nonpriestly Levites."[54] In subtle ways
the worship descriptions in Chronicles help to provide a realistic
social and religious setting for many of the psalms, not only
hymns of praise, but especially the communal laments connected
with Levitical groups. Finally, stereotypical views of postexilic
religion as dour, legalistic, and exclusivistic are challenged by
these joyful, grand, and inclusive celebrations of God's presence
and power. The Chronicler helps us to imagine worship with a
new song and in a new key.

---

54. Levine, *Sing unto God a New Song*, 55. He further notes: "Psalms supply
the explicit emotional links to ritual action that are only hinted at, if at all,
in the other biblical sources. The Psalms can then be seen as ritual utterance
parallel to the ritual offerings detailed in Leviticus and Numbers."

– S E V E N –

Sabbath and Synagogue

– Niels-Erik A. Andreasen –

More than thirty years ago H. H. Rowley made the following observation regarding Sabbath and synagogue: "In post-exilic days, if there had been no synagogues, it is difficult to see how [the Sabbath] could have survived, and it is significant that in our day impatience with the Sabbath as a day of rest is the accompaniment of the widespread abandonment of the Sabbath as a day of worship."[1]

In doing so, Rowley assumed that Sabbath and synagogue enjoyed a symbiotic relationship, not only following the destruction of the Second Temple in 70 c.e., but beginning already during postexilic times, perhaps in the form of "house synagogues" that provided a venue for regular Sabbath worship activities.[2] Admittedly, the evidence for those assumptions is limited, a fact that led Heather A. McKay to conclude that neither the Sabbath nor the synagogue can be associated by available evidence with regular and widespread communal worship activities until well into the common era.[3] McKay defined Sabbath and synagogue

---

1. H. H. Rowley, *Worship in Ancient Israel: Its Form and Meaning* (Philadelphia: Fortress, 1967), 241.

2. Ibid., 224, 241.

3. Heather A. McKay, *Sabbath and Synagogue: The Origin of Sabbath Wor-*

worship as communal prayers, hymns, or other religious rites conducted in a building or by a congregation on a regular basis during the hours of the Sabbath.[4] This clear and tightly argued analysis of the evidence does not consider the possibility that early Sabbath/synagogue communal worship may have centered around something else, such as the public reading and exposition of Scripture, perhaps accompanied by prayers and other types of devotions to holiness.[5]

This essay proposes that the Sabbath played an important role in shaping both the form and spirit of Israelite worship already in postexilic times, eventually in the form of the regular and somewhat familiar synagogue services, and that together the Sabbath and the emerging synagogue contributed much to the vitality of Israelite religion during that period and subsequently. Walter Harrelson (to whom I offer this essay) worked tirelessly to correct a common negative valuation of postexilic religion as mostly form without much spiritual content, depth, or ethical sensitivity and controlled by the newly codified Torah and the legalistic religious system of Judaism, "so beloved by Christians as their whipping boy."[6]

On the contrary, several important developments in postexilic

─────────────

ship in Ancient Israel (Religion in the Graeco-Roman World 122; Leiden: Brill, 1994), 245–51.

4. Ibid., 3–6.

5. Cf. Pieter W. Vander Horst, "Was the Synagogue a Place of Sabbath Worship before 70 c.e.?" and Lawrence H. Schiffman, "The Early History of Public Reading of the Torah," both in *Jews, Christians and Polytheists in the Ancient Synagogue* (ed. Steven Fine; New York: Routledge, 1999), 18–43, 44–56; Steven Fine, *This Holy Place: On the Sanctity of the Synagogue during the Greco-Roman Period* (Notre Dame: University of Notre Dame Press, 1997), 25–33.

6. Walter J. Harrelson, *From Fertility Cult to Worship* (Garden City: Doubleday, 1969), 130.

Israelite religion enabled it to invigorate both Jewish and Christian spiritual and religious life. These included (a) a new way for the community of faith to receive divine revelation, namely, through the Scripture then being collected and canonized; (b) a new means of extending the sanctity of the temple, priesthood, and cult to every member of the congregation, then scattered throughout the nations of the Near East, namely through a process of religious instruction; and (c) a new opportunity — apocalyptic vision — for believers to articulate their hope for God's eternal kingdom in ways that appreciated their present situation of oppression and displacement, their deeply felt religious and ethical obligations, and their international and even universal environment.[7]

The Sabbath and the emerging synagogue, which eventually formed a symbiotic relationship, provide natural foci for reflecting on the vitality of postexilic Israelite religion. First, they facilitated the communication and dissemination of God's revelation through the reading and study of Scripture in individual and congregational settings. Second, they enabled the sacred realm to penetrate every family, every home, every village of the community as they invited an encounter with God during the sacred hours at home and in the congregation of the faithful. Third, the association of Israel's hope with sacred time on the weekly day of rest infused hope itself with an intimate as well as cosmic dimension by connecting it with God's completed work of creation. Fourth, though commonplace to most western people in the form of Sunday and church, Sab-

---

7. Walter J. Harrelson drew attention to the three subjects of Torah, holiness, and eschatology during the postexilic period in his *Interpreting the Old Testament* (New York: Holt, Rinehart & Winston, 1964), 482–86, and returned to these themes in subsequent publications.

bath and synagogue are, in fact, unique religious institutions, both of which have left a remarkable imprint on economic and social structures in most of the world. In each case a new individual and universal dimension of postexilic Israelite religion was facilitated by Sabbath and synagogue. That in turn enabled Judaism — and eventually Christianity — to become effective world religions, which, in the final analysis, may represent the most vital contribution of Israelite religion during the period reviewed here.

Given the sparse textual evidence regarding the Sabbath and the synagogue, especially in the early postexilic period, their contributions to the vitality of Israelite religion must be teased out of a few texts, some of which introduce new and daring reflections upon the Sabbath. These reflections move us beyond the familiar commands to rest on the seventh day in imitation of the creator, to share this rest with those unable to secure it for themselves, and perhaps to do so in a corporate setting that opened the way for the synagogue to emerge. Rather, they anticipate a time when Sabbath and synagogue enjoyed a vibrant alliance of great importance for the form and function of Judaism and later Christianity. Thus, the Sabbath observance at home and in the synagogue that we recognize today sends its taproots down into the time of the Bible — all the way into postexilic Israelite religion. The last three texts in Isaiah that deal with the Sabbath (56:1–8; 58:13; 66:23) provide convenient starting points for introducing such new reflections upon the Sabbath.

Isaiah 56 and the Reinterpretation of the Torah

Isaiah 56 looks forward to the restored community of Israel following the Babylonian captivity. Despite existing legal instructions to the contrary (e.g., Deut 23:2–4 [Eng. 23:1–3]), foreigners and eunuchs were now to be included in the congregation of Israel. Eunuchs were to share the land with everyone else (Isa 56:4–5, 7), and foreigners would be invited to the house of God (the temple) in order to make it a house of prayer (*bettefilah*) for all peoples (56:7). The stated conditions for such inclusiveness were the admonitions to "keep my Sabbath" and "hold fast my covenant" (56:2, 4, 6).

Traditional interpretations have read this text as evidence of postexilic legalism and a doctrinaire Judaism that distinguished sharply and exclusively between Israel and other peoples and between the sacred and the common.[8] As an illustration of this, reference is sometimes made to Neh 8, 10, and 13 where Ezra the scribe reads the law of Moses to all the people (8:1–8) and reminds them of the Sabbath institution (8:14; 10:32, 34 [Eng. 10:31, 33]), followed by Nehemiah's enforcement of Sabbath observance in the city and by his mandate to the Levites to guard its gates (13:19–22).

But that misses what the prophetic text is saying; namely, that during this troubled period all peoples, including foreigners and eunuchs, no longer need to feel excluded from the congregation of Israel. Despite the stern words of the Torah, they now may belong to God's people and become true Israelites who observe the Sabbath and worship in God's house of prayer. This introduces the possibility of a new and genuinely inclusive

---

8. John L. McKenzie, *Second Isaiah* (AB 20; New York: Doubleday, 1968), 152; John D. Watts, *Isaiah 34–66* (Word Biblical Commentary 25; Waco: Word, 1987), 248; C. Westermann, *Das Buch Jesaja* (Das Alte Testament Deutsch 19; Göttingen: Vandenhoeck and Ruprecht, 1966), 248; R. N. Whybray, *Isaiah 40–66* (New Century Bible; Grand Rapids: Eerdmans, 1981), 197.

perspective on religion (Neh 8:8b). To achieve that goal, the prophetic text must actually break with past religious legislation and introduce a new interpretation of the law designed for a new time when the Torah would be collected, codified, canonized, studied, and made available to the common people. Rather than freezing instruction of the law into orthodoxy or legalism, this reexamination of the Torah and the dissemination of its instructions introduce daring new concepts of inclusiveness and acceptance.

Isaiah 56 opens by urging the hearers to do justice and righteousness (v. 1), which recalls the ethical demands of the prophets Amos (5:24) and Micah (6:8). This is followed by a blessing extended to just persons as in Ps 1, a wisdom psalm or song of instruction ("blessed is the one . . . "). In other words, we read of "marginal" members in the community, neither priests nor Levites, but common persons, even social outcasts, who need to learn the ways of God by doing justice and righteousness and who are eligible for the blessings of God that accrue to such individuals.

McKay correctly observes that, generally speaking, those Sabbath texts dealing with its observance by the common people focus on the instruction to refrain from performing one's daily work on this day (e.g., Exod 20:8–11; 31:12–17; 34:21; Deut 5:12–15), while those Sabbath texts dealing with worship and cultic duties are addressed to priests and Levites.[9] Isaiah 56, however, mentions neither work prohibitions on the seventh day nor temple liturgies and other rites during the sacred hours, but instead introduces the Sabbath as the day that gathers all true Israelites into the circle of God's people for prayer. It does

---

9. McKay, *Sabbath and Synagogue*, 41–42.

not specify what a person must do or not do in order to enter
the community of Israel, but indicates who a person must be in
order to belong, namely, a covenant member. Isaiah 56 follows
a chiastic structure between opening and closure:

opening: blessed are the just and righteous (1–2)
>   *at present...*
>   A the foreigner feels separate from God's people Israel (3a)
>   B the eunuch feels cut off from the future (3b)
>   *but with allegiance to the covenant and the Sabbath...*
>   B the eunuch will be given a future in God's house (4–5)
>   A the foreigner will join the congregation in God's house (6)
closing: God's house will become a house of prayer for all people (7–8)

The role played by the covenant in this context is both natural
and expected since it has always indicated membership in the
community of Israel (Gen 15; Exod 19:3–6; Josh 24; Jer 31).
But the presence of the Sabbath is puzzling. To be sure, Ezek
20:12, 20 (cf. Exod 31:12–17) identifies Sabbath observance as
a sign (mark) of Israel's covenant relationship with God. Here,
however, Sabbath and covenant stand parallel to each other,
not one as a sign of the other, but both providing access to
God's house for those who formerly were excluded from it. The
purpose of this access is to bring the marginalized into the joy of
membership in God's house of prayer evidently by giving them
the opportunity to worship on an equal footing with the entire
covenant community. Both covenant and Sabbath contribute to
that goal, for the covenant provides them with the legal right of
belonging and the Sabbath with the visible right of participation
and presence.

Isaiah 56 thus introduced a broadened interpretation of a familiar legal requirement, along with a public dissemination of Torah instructions whose codification and subsequent publication would make everyone accountable to them in a personal, equitable, and democratic way.

But thereby a new problem was introduced. The Torah originally called for a pure community that expelled nondesirables such as eunuchs and foreigners, a fact confirmed in Ezra 9 and Neh 13. Traditionally, Sabbath observance and covenant membership provided an important test case for distinguishing between a true Israelite and a foreigner, and yet Isa 56 now invites the latter to join the new community of worshipers. That required either outright rejection of the Torah, or a fresh interpretation of it, or at least a convincing explanation. This occurred when the prophet identified the two most powerful symbols of membership in the congregation of Israel — the invisible covenant relationship and the visible Sabbath observance — and extended invitations to both foreigners and eunuchs to participate in them. Observance of these institutions alone, without regard to an individual's heritage or circumstances, was then offered to all as a way of accessing the holy presence of God, here identified as the house of prayer for all peoples.

By means of this simple prophetic response to the Torah, postexilic Israelite religion and, later on, its younger Christian sibling were readied to become true world religions, responsive to changing times, locations, and circumstances. In this case, an invisible private assurance of divine acceptance and a visible public indication of divine acceptance through communal worship define the essential content and outer form of both religions. A new interpretation of the Sabbath made that possible, and the eventual establishment of the synagogue made it visible.

Isaiah 58 and a New Sense of Sanctity

To the casual reader, Isa 58:13 seems incongruous in its context, for it appears to introduce a strict religious requirement, Sabbath observance, in an otherwise compelling, almost contemporary call for high moral consciousness and broad ethical demands within the regular religious practice of fasting. Commentators have, therefore, repeatedly considered it a secondary addition.[10] This conclusion is unnecessary in context and even harmful to the text. In fact, on closer analysis, the chapter appears incomplete or fractured like a "torso" without 58:13–14.[11]

The chapter opens with a series of contrasts between self-centered religious expressions and ethically sensitive attitudes and conducts. These arise in a discussion over fasting, sackcloth, and ashes, undertaken by the worshiper for the purpose of making strong petitions that are nevertheless not heard by God (58:2–5). In their place, the prophet introduces three calls to genuine holiness in the form of ethical responsibilities toward the unfortunate. The first of these calls asks the religious observer to provide liberty to the slaves, food for the hungry, shelter for the homeless, and clothing for the naked (58:6–7). The second implores the worshiper to refrain from evil thoughts and words and oppressive actions toward others and instead to meet their needs and satisfy their desires (58:9b–10). The third introduces a kind of Sabbath keeping that directs religious observers' attention away from themselves and toward God (58:13).

These calls for genuine religion disclose a certain logical progression, whereas the resultant outcome remains very constant

---

10. Cf. McKenzie, *Second Isaiah,* 165; Westermann, *Das Buch Jesaja,* 271; Whybray, *Isaiah 40–66,* 212.

11. James Muilenburg, *The Book of Isaiah 40–66,* in *The Interpreter's Bible* (ed. George A. Buttrick et al.; Nashville: Abingdon, 1956), 5:677.

throughout, even though expressed with variations. Specifically, it promises the faithful observer that genuine religion leads to general well-being, such as the felt presence of the Lord and prosperity in the land (58:8–9a, 10–12, 14). The three appeals to practice genuine religion, on the other hand, show a distinctive progression of thought. First comes a call to consider the situation of the needy and to help them with acts of mercy (58:6–7). Next follows an appeal to the oppressors themselves to cease the oppression of others by thought, word, or action and to make restitution where warranted (58:9–10), all of which amounts to a changed attitude toward the needy. And, third, the passage turns to the Sabbath. At first sight this appears out of place, but on closer inspection it brings the entire chapter to a necessary and fitting conclusion.

The Sabbath reference begins by returning the reader to the opening discussion about genuine holiness and asking how one truly responds to the presence of God. The answer turns around the expression "your (own) pleasure" (*khefets*) in 58:3 and 58:13. That such a self-centered approach to worship will always render it unholy was established already in the case of Israel's daily worship (58:2) and fast days (58:3), and to the contemporary reader it is only natural that the prophet should criticize such self-centered religious practices as are portrayed here. Indeed, it resonates immediately with most Christian and Jewish understandings of biblical religion and ethics. Clearly, worship designed to direct the supplicant's attention to God cannot become self-serving and retain its integrity. To clinch this argument, the prophet turns to the Sabbath with its proscription of all work.

That complicates things a bit. At first blush, the Sabbath imposes yet another "hardship" on the observer by exacting a percentage tax on the worshiper's time with no apparent benefit accruing to the needy and suffering. Hence, the initial perception that this text does not fit its context of concern for the oppressed is perhaps understandable were it not that we have already come to expect new and daring readings of the law by this prophet. Moreover, we know from previous Sabbath laws and their interpretation that, evidently, nominal Sabbath observers did indeed consider ways to increase personal benefits, even during the day of rest, by placing additional hardships on servants. They did this, for example, by asking them to continue working during the day of rest (Exod 20:9–10; Deut 5:13–15), by granting an exception to the proscription of work during the busy harvest and sowing times (Exod 34:21), or by conceiving dishonest profit ventures during the sacred hours for urgent implementation following the Sabbath (Amos 8:5). It is precisely these apparently well-known efforts to stay observant while seeking personal benefits that Isa 58 deplores so much, and it is this criticism that connects the Sabbath reference to the opening sentiments of our chapter about worship that uses religion for personal profit.

To conclude his presentation of genuine religion, the prophet associates the day of rest with the delight and honor associated with observing it (58:13). The former term, *'oneg* ("exquisite delight"), expresses the pleasure that comes to people whose oppression is revoked and whose burdens are lifted, while the second, *mekhubbad* ("honorable"), refers to the respect one is called upon to show God, parents, and others worthy of it. Such honor gives structure to life, builds character, and infuses values into relationships. It makes the irresponsible person responsible and the oppressor a liberator. Understood this way, the Sabbath is not a burden to be carried, an opportunity to

be grasped, or an obligation to be fulfilled, but rather a liberating and character-building experience. That is to say, by turning
away from their own pleasure on that day, worshipers learn to
care for the needs of others. By finding pleasure and expressing
honor on the Sabbath, authentic worshipers take the second
step of changing their attitudes along with their actions. Such
a change in attitude is inspired by a more participatory and
immediate understanding of God's holy presence that, according to Ezekiel, had already symbolically left the temple, along
with its formal religious liturgies, and had settled among the
exiles and eunuchs (cf. Ezek 10–11). The Sabbath calls that to
attention here.

In both Haggai and Zechariah we find postexilic Judaism pre-
occupied with redefining sanctity in Judah and in Jerusalem,
which were being restored and yet reduced to a small province of world empires. Thus, the continuing sanctity of temple,
priests, high priest, people, and land itself were critical issues for
the new community (Hag 2:10–14; Zech 2:16 [Eng. 2:12]; 3:1–
5; 8:3). Meanwhile, the catastrophe of the Babylonian captivity
was explained in part as a punishment for the defilement of the
Sabbath (Jer 17:19–27; Ezek 20:12–13; 2 Chr 36:17–21) and of
the temple (Ezek 8; Jer 7). Not surprisingly, therefore, both the
Sabbath and later the synagogue were sought out as holding the
key to restoring and preserving sanctity in Israel. Eventually the
synagogue extended the temple sanctity into every community
and the Sabbath into every home once each week. The foundation for this new "democratic" or popular extension of holiness
into the life of every faithful worshiper, as introduced in Isa 56
and 58, prepared postexilic Israelite religion to become a world
religion that needed neither rabbi nor priest nor temple for its
sanctity and the felt presence of God, but that found its spiritual

nourishment in the life of every believing person and in the life of the worshiping community.

Isaiah 66 and Israel's Hope

According to rabbinic tradition, Isa 66:23 should be repeated after reading 66:24 in the synagogue so that the last words of the prophet would be words of comfort. Without that last difficult verse, the book would conclude with great peroration as follows: there will be a new creation like the first (66:22), and all people shall worship the creator in response, just as they did in the beginning (66:23). The last "embarrassing" verse (66:24) has perhaps received more detailed attention than it deserves, but in essence it simply says infelicitously that this new creation will be free of sin, which will be kept outside the holy city's walls and be subject to complete and visible destruction. While upsetting to our esthetic sensitivity, the description is vivid and unmistakably clear in its intention.

In the midst of this final prophetic vision of the world restored, the Sabbath appears, as does the new moon, to order the life of the inhabitants in that new world. A similar role is assigned to the Sabbath and new moon in the apocalyptic vision of a restored temple in Ezekiel (46:1–8). No other apocalyptic passage in Scripture makes overt reference to the Sabbath. However, we find the connection between it and the world to come in later Jewish and early Christian writing (e.g., *Jubilees* 2:17–33; *Life of Adam and Eve* 51:2; Heb 4:8–10).

It is not entirely surprising that the Sabbath should symbolize the world to come. Its association with creation as the culmination of God's creative work, the rest from labor that it affords, the promised presence of God during its holy hours, and per-

haps the concept of a world week — all led to the conclusion
that the Sabbath rest illustrates and anticipates the eternal rest
in the world made new. The world week, according to which the
present age of six thousand years will be followed by a thousand-
year messianic age preceding the eternal age to come, finds no
direct support in Scripture.[12] The millennium of Rev 20 is not
the last "day" of a world week, that is, the seven thousandth year
of earth's history, but rather preparation for the new creation
and the eternal world to come.

The notion, however, that the experience of rest and divine
presence on the Sabbath gives meaning to life in God's eternal
kingdom is found in Scripture (Heb 4:1–13), and it was a settled
idea among early Christian writers.[13] It remains theologically
significant for at least three reasons. First, it gives structure to
the meaning of eternal life by imparting to it a rhythm of time
and worship. Second, it anchors the eschatological hope in a
real-life sequence of work and rest. Third, it universalizes the
hope by disconnecting it from Mount Zion and associating it,
not with everlasting peace in Jerusalem, but with the eternal rest
for troubled people everywhere that is symbolized by the weekly
Sabbath rest. Hereby the concept of eternal life is characterized
as real life in a real world where people live and work, where
generations follow generations in a peaceful and fruitful land,
free of sin (Isa 66:24).

In this way, the Sabbath brought new and needed vitality to
the hope of postexilic Israelite religion. It was a vitality born of

---

12. 2 (Slavonic) Enoch 32–33 juxtaposes a reference to the Sabbath and
the seven-thousand-year world history. Cf. D. S. Russell, The Method and Message of Jewish Apocalyptic (Old Testament Library; Philadelphia: Westminster,
1964), 285–303.

13. Willy Rordorf, Sunday (Philadelphia: Westminster, 1968), 88–100.

reality. It imagines life in Jerusalem with old men and old women in the streets of Jerusalem, watching over the boys and girls crowding the streets of the city with their playing, presumably while their parents worked at home, in shop, or afield (Zech 8:3–5). With eternity anchored in real time, Israel could hope without flights of fancy into empty spaces by disembodied souls. Indeed, Israel cast its anchor of hope deep into a new reality that was free of evil, sin, and destruction but full of life, vitality, and responsibility for the welfare of young and old. This variety of hope in postexilic Israelite religion, a hope projected into the world to come, but complete with caring for life in all its forms and processes as we know them, is an invaluable religious heritage that invites further reflection in our time.

Sabbath and Synagogue

Having sketched some new and valuable contributions of the Sabbath to postexilic religion, I turn now to the difficult task of relating these to the question of the synagogue. Rowley's suggestion, mentioned earlier, that had it not been for the synagogue the Sabbath could not have survived in postexilic Judaism, is particularly interesting since Rowley had earlier allowed that there is "no tangible evidence in the Bible for the origin of the synagogue."[14] Indeed, the earliest direct evidence for the existence of something like a synagogue, identified as a place of prayer (*proseuchē*), comes from the reign of Ptolemy III in Egypt (third century B.C.E.) and not Babylon, as is proposed by those who associate the introduction of synagogues with the experience of the

---

14. Rowley, *Worship in Ancient Israel*, 222.

exiles removed from their Jerusalem temple.[15] This would support the traditional assumption that the synagogue originated in the Diaspora, but not necessarily as a substitute for or in the absence of the temple. Possibly the social and cultural insulation of dispersed Jews who settled in large cities or in isolated colonies surrounded by foreigners led to the eventual introduction of synagogues. Subsequent literary references to synagogues come from the Gospels, Josephus, Philo, and rabbinic sources in the early Christian era, by which time synagogues were located in Palestine.[16] Archeological discoveries attesting to the existence of synagogues at Masada and Herodion and at various sites in Galilee push that date back prior to the revolt in 70 c.e.[17] On the basis of the literary evidence it is generally concluded that the synagogue was a place of worship, a school, and possibly a venue for juridical and communal decisions.[18] Any additional evidence tracing the origin of the synagogue back into postexilic times and beyond is derived from certain earlier communal ac-

---

15. Lester L. Grabbe, "Synagogues in Pre-70 Palestine: A Reassessment," and J. Gwyn Griffeths, "Egypt and the Rise of the Synagogue," both in *Ancient Synagogues* (ed. Dan Urman and Paul V. M. Flesher; Leiden: Brill, 1995), 18–19, 3–16.

16. Cf. Matt 4:23; 13:54–58; Mark 1:21–22; 6:2; 12:39; Luke 4:14–15, 44; 7:5; John 18:20; Josephus, *Jewish War* 2.14.4–5 §§284–92; *Antiquities* 19.6.3 §§299–311. Philo (*On the Embassy to Gaius* 20.132) speaks of numerous synagogues in Alexandria. In a discussion of civil law, the Babylonian Talmud reports incidentally that 394 synagogues existed in Jerusalem (*Ketubbot* 105a). According to the Jerusalem Talmud, Vespasian attacked 480 Jerusalem synagogues (*Megillah* 3.1).

17. Archeological evidence of synagogues has been found at Masada, Herodion (in Judah), Migdal, Chorazim, Capernaum, and Gamla (in Galilee). See Paul V. M. Flesher, "Palestine Synagogues before 70 c.e.: A Review of the Evidence," in *Ancient Synagogues* (ed. Dan Urman and Paul V. M. Flesher; Leiden: Brill, 1995), 27–39.

18. See nn. 15–16 above.

tivities like those associated with the synagogue in subsequent times, such as public reading of the law (Neh 8:1–12) or communal gathering in the presence of a prophet for decision making (Ezek 20:1). But none of these gives any indication of being regular events as they would have to be in order to parallel later congregational practices in the synagogue.

Given this paucity of evidence regarding the early synagogues, one cannot with certainty cite a relationship between Sabbath and synagogue in postexilic Judaism. By focusing, however, upon the three characteristics of postexilic Israelite religion that generated so much of its vitality, one may surmise not only that the Sabbath participated in and contributed to that vitality, but also that the synagogue, when it fully emerged, tapped into these characteristics, made common cause with the Sabbath institution, and contributed to this vitality. Indeed, some will say, the synagogue secured the survival of postexilic Israelite religion in the form of Judaism and later Christianity as well.

The first characteristic of postexilic Israelite religion concerns the dissemination of the codified and canonized Scripture. During the postexilic period the Scripture, beginning with the Torah, was read in public for the purpose of enabling common people to understand it in the vernacular (Neh 8–9). It is not known when multiple copies of Scripture were available to individuals or groups, but whenever the law was read publicly it entered the public domain and became subject to public scrutiny and interpretation. Eventually "schools of interpretation," such as developed in the parties of Pharisees, Sadducees, and Essenes and in the published commentaries on Scripture, emerged. While the prophets, historians, and wisdom writers had long been quoting the law and commenting upon it in their own writings, following the exile it is intimated that prophecy would not continue as in the past and that the recorded and codified Scripture would eventually take the place of living prophets (cf. Zech 1:1–6), thereby putting the burden of reading and interpreting the sacred texts on the community of believers. That was a new development. Community access to and responsibility for religious texts, not unlike what happened during the Protestant reformation, does not occur without effort. It requires times and places such as a weekly day of rest and a "synagogue" for community meetings. Of course, any regular period spent by the community in the temple court or city square would accomplish the same, and such gatherings of common people may have inspired the formal establishment of the synagogue in the first place.[19] In time, however, the Sabbath and the synagogue found each other in a shared commitment to the task of reading and understanding the Scriptures (Luke 4:16–22) and thereby broke new and important ground in postexilic religion. Indeed, public reading and exposition of Scripture, rather than prayers, hymns, and liturgy, may well have characterized the earliest religious activities associated with the synagogue.

While we cannot be certain that this shared commitment to reading of Scripture began in early postexilic times, it may have. No matter when it happened the transformation of a sacred day without work into a day of reading and interpreting Scripture by the community in a common gathering place (house of prayer or synagogue) is surely remarkable. Moreover, when Sabbath and synagogue did find each other in a common commitment to the reading and interpretation of Scripture, something new happened of great importance, namely, regular access to the

19. Sidney B. Hoenig, "The Ancient City Square: The Forerunner of the Synagogue," in *Aufstieg und Niedergang der römischen Welt* (ed. H. Temporini and W. Haase; Berlin: de Gruyter, 1979), 2:9:1:448–76.

word and will of God by all members of the community.[20] That Jewish and Christian congregations now exist in every corner of the world testifies to the vitality that Sabbath and synagogue added to postexilic Israelite religion.

A second characteristic of postexilic Israelite religion was the new awareness of sanctity. Good reasons exist for concluding that throughout the Hebrew Scriptures the Sabbath was not understood merely as a day on which common work was proscribed, but also as a holy day. The presence of the Sabbath in the Decalogue (Exod 20:8–11; Deut 5:12–15), the Priestly instructions regarding it (Exod 31:12–17), its inclusion in the Holiness Code (Lev 19:2–3), its repeated mention along with the sacred days of new moon and annual feast in the prophets,[21] and Ezekiel's reference to the neglect of the Sabbath along with other sacred ordinances as a cause of Israel's failed salvation history (Ezek 20) — all indicate that in both preexilic and postexilic times the Sabbath was not viewed merely as a day without work but also as a holy day, and this not only for the temple personnel (as suggested by McKay),[22] but for ordinary Sabbath observers as well. Regrettably, we do not know how this sense of holiness on the Sabbath was practiced or expressed, but it

---

20. Lee I. Levine, "The Value and Origin of the Palestinian Synagogue," *JBL* 115 (1996): 432. See also A. Momigliano, *On Pagans, Jews, and Christians* (Middletown, Conn.: Wesleyan University Press, 1987), 89–91; A. I. Baumgarten, "The Torah as a Public Document in Judaism," *Studies in Religion* 181 (1985): 17–24.

21. Sabbath occurs fifteen times in the Hebrew Bible together with other holy times, e.g., new moon, assemblies, annual sacred times, appointed feasts, etc.: 2 Kgs 4:23; Amos 8:5; Hos 2:11 (Eng. 2:13); Isa 1:13; 66:23; Lam 2:6; Ezek 44:24; 45:17; 46:1, 3; 1 Chr 23:31; 2 Chr 2:3 (Eng. 2:4); 8:13; 31:3; Neh 10:34 (Eng. 10:33). These types of references continue into intertestamental literature.

22. McKay, *Sabbath and Synagogue*, 41–42.

stands to reason that if ordinary work was proscribed on the Sabbath, the sanctity of the Sabbath would be marked either at home or in a holy place (in distinction from the workplace), a conclusion confirmed by the report in Neh 13 that the governor of Jerusalem chased the people away from the public places of work and business (the gates) at the onset of the Sabbath. It is not clear from the texts to what degree the home (cf. Exod 16:29) or a place where God's presence was manifest (cf. 2 Kgs 4:23) attracted Sabbath observers most regularly at first. We know, however, that once the synagogue emerged, part of the Sabbath was spent there. While we do not know when this first happened or when it became a regular practice, in time it was firmly established. Hereby, the weekly Sabbath observance was broadened from a focus on the individual who refrained from work to, first, a focus on the family whose members stayed at home during part of the sacred hours and, second, to a focus on the entire community that gathered at a local place for Scripture reading, study, and prayer on the Sabbath. The likelihood that this began at some time during the postexilic period, perhaps most naturally in the Diaspora and later in Palestine, is considerable and once again gives evidence to the creativity and vitality of Israelite religion of that period. It enabled the religious community to survive intact without natural borders or political structures to hold it in place. If one wanted to invent a social and religious organizational structure designed to hold together the community, a better one could not be conceived. What is more, according to Isa 58, Sabbath observance invited the synagogue congregation to add ethical demands to its new sense of sanctity. By extending the principle of Sabbath observance from the practices of fasting and prayer to a concern for the welfare of others, the community called for a selfless attitude toward people in need of help and for the experience of joy that one receives from helping others.

The third characteristic of postexilic Israelite religion that must be highlighted is renewal of hope. Walter Harrelson defines Israelite worship as "an ordered response to the appearance of the Holy in the life of individuals and groups."[23] Following this definition, Harrelson proceeds to describe the ordering principles of Israel's times of worship (sacred times and places, attending priests, and ceremonies and liturgies) and concludes his study by affirming "that Israelite worship speaks of the God who comes."[24] The postexilic period was forced by circumstances to reexamine these ordering principles of worship, and the Sabbath along with the synagogue provided important focal points for such reexamination, something like the two centers of an ellipse.

These traditional ordering principles for worship were severely tested during the exile. The ancient Israelite calendar relating to the grain and fruit harvests and to the annual feasts and their accompanying historical commemorations celebrated at the temple was confronted by other calendars beginning in the spring when the high floods watered and fertilized the alluvial plains of Egypt and Babylon. The ensuing yearly cycle was associated with other annual feasts in honor of foreign gods and their temples. Sabbath and new moon, however, remained forever untouched by those changes. The Sabbath ran uninterruptedly throughout the year, wholly disconnected from the movements of the heavenly bodies and the seasons.

Although there is no direct evidence that the synagogue was invented to compensate for the lost temple during the exile and

---

23. Harrelson, *From Fertility Cult to Worship*, 19.
24. Ibid., 137.

in the Diaspora, we do know that the missing temple or access to the temple created a problem in postexilic Judaism. The urgent need to rebuild the temple in the Holy Land, along with the conviction that worship at local shrines had contributed to the captivity in the first place and had to be discontinued as a consequence of the Deuteronomic reform (2 Kgs 23), obviously created a problem in the Diaspora. It is perhaps telling that an alternate temple, albeit a bloodless one, was built in Elephantine in Egypt[25] and, more important, that the first indications of synagogues emerge shortly thereafter in the same general location. Thus, in due course, the synagogue did provide (alongside Sabbath) a second ordering principle, a replacement for the temple, as it were, where the worshipers found community and sought the presence of their God.

The other important aspect of Israelite worship, namely, that it responds to "God who comes," also calls for attention. This may well represent a particularly strong element in postexilic Israelite worship, namely, that worship must no longer be an act of "coming to God" either in the temple or at any other sacred place. Instead, worship now always involves "God's coming" to God's people — as God came to Abraham, to Moses at Sinai, into the temple, to the exiles, into the Second Temple, and will do so again at the end of the age.[26] Both Sabbath and

---

25. The Elephantine temple located in upper Egypt was destroyed and later rebuilt with reluctant encouragement from Jerusalem at the end of the fifth century B.C.E. The application for permission to rebuild came with the understanding that the temple services would comply with the instruction of Torah and no animal sacrifices would be presented. See H. L. Ginsberg in *ANET* 491–92.

26. I have explored this theme in "The Advent Hope in the Old Testament," in *The Advent Hope in Scripture and History* (ed. J. N. Olsen; Washington, D.C.: Review & Herald, 1987), 15–30.

synagogue reinforce this important spiritual insight into Israelite worship. They do so in particularly vibrant ways during the period under consideration when more than ever before many worshipers were prevented from coming to God, whether in the temple or at sacred times of harvest and commemoration, by geographical distances or due to other political obstacles. For all of them the sixth day, when all work was completed, invited faithful worshipers everywhere to wait for the sun to leave and for the Almighty to arrive. And into the synagogue they would then go to pray and to hear God's voice, encoded on the sacred scrolls. In this way, Israel's hope for the "one who comes" was renewed and affirmed for the individual at home and for the community in the synagogue once a week in a new and vibrant way, during the hours of the Sabbath.

– E I G H T –

The Vitality of Story
in Second Temple Judaism

– *Marti J. Steussy* –

The Importance of Story

Storytelling occurs in all human cultures. Its ubiquity suggests that despite our own culture's tendency to dismiss stories as "mere" entertainment, stories perform some important function in human existence.[1] Indeed, evidence is accumulating that narrative will even override memories of lived experience. A human-interest anecdote outweighs a thousand statistics, and a witness's memory of what her own eyes saw succumbs quickly to the "memory" of what she is told that she has seen.[2]

Second Temple Judaism has bequeathed to us an impressive heritage of stories — the massive histories of Torah and Chronicles, finely polished gems like Jonah and Susanna, and multistranded novellas like Tobit, Judith, and Esther. Some of these writings offer themselves as accounts of actual events, although probably none would satisfy modern criteria for historical

---

1. Wesley Kort, *Story, Text and Scripture: Literary Interests in Biblical Narrative* (University Park: Pennsylvania State University Press, 1988), esp. 8–13.
2. Daniel L. Schachter, ed., *Memory Distortion: How Minds, Brains, and Societies Reconstruct the Past* (Cambridge: Harvard University Press, 1995).

writing, while others seem to be more straightforward cases of historical fiction. All, however, shape their material in narrative form and use the techniques of storytelling to highlight meaning.

The vast majority of these Second Temple Jewish narratives are stories not only about events but about Scripture: they paraphrase, explain, or expand upon existing religious narratives. For example, Chronicles retells and renuances events recounted in Samuel and Kings, drawing upon either those books or earlier predecessors of them. Jonah, a short story presumably featuring the prophet mentioned in 2 Kgs 14:25, contains strong echoes of the Elijah/Elisha stories, Jeremiah, and Psalms. Susanna probes themes and characters from both Daniel and Jeremiah.[3] *Joseph and Aseneth,* a religious book not included in present Bibles, spins twenty-nine chapters out of the brief information in Gen 41 and Gen 46 that Joseph married the daughter of an Egyptian priest.[4]

Story and Identity in Second Temple Judaism

What role did these stories play in the life of the Jewish people that produced them, and why did the people so often weave their new stories from the loose threads of old ones? One key may lie in the identity-teaching function of stories. Before 587/586 B.C.E., Israelite/Judean identity had been a more-or-less simple matter of citizenship. But what did it mean to be a "Jew" when many lived in foreign lands and all lived under foreign

---

3. For a fuller discussion of intertextuality in Susanna, see Marti J. Steussy, *Gardens in Babylon: Narrative and Faith in the Greek Legends of Daniel* (SBLDS 141; Atlanta: Scholars Press, 1993), 146–54.

4. C. Burchard provides an English translation of the story, with comments, in OTP 2:177–47.

rule? What had this new Jewishness to do with the old Judah from which it took its name?

Second Temple Jews explored these questions via stories that connected new identity to the old. Not all these storytellers conceive of Jewish identity in the same way. In the Hebrew version of Esther, blood suffices to make a Jew Jewish, but Greek versions of Esther stress religious practices and especially prayer. Daniel stresses its hero's descent and religious practices but also validates him by modeling him on the "type" of Joseph. *Joseph and Aseneth* subordinates blood to religious identity entirely by showing, in the person of Joseph's wife, Aseneth, how someone who has no Israelite blood at all may become Jewish by embrace of the religion and its practices. In all three of these stories, continuity with the past is emphasized by linkages with figures and themes from earlier Scripture.

The Complexity of Story

However powerfully stories function in shaping perception and identity, they seldom do so simply. We must not reduce each story to a single straightforward "moral," but rather allow for multiple reflections within each story. Jonah illustrates this nicely. The story shows the inescapability of God's call (God will use a whale, if necessary, to point you in the right direction). It also shows God's protection (whales can save you from the raging sea). It debates the function of prophecy (is the prophet's job to predict the future or to get people to repent?). It comments on the faith potential of Gentiles (both the foreign sailors and the Ninevites prove more open than the Israelite prophet). It satirizes prophetic self-pity (like Elijah in 1 Kgs 19:4, Jonah responds to a victory by wanting to die). The nature of Jonah's psalm in Jonah 2 remains unclear: is it an exemplary prayer of repentance, or a spoof on the wordy piety of people who pray only in tight spots?

The relationship of Second Temple stories to existing religious writings gives them a special complexity. Each character, idea, historical incident, or verbatim quotation carried forward from earlier religious writings comes equipped with the nuances and meanings of prior usage. It then acquires overtones from the new story, overtones that neither harmonize completely with nor entirely damp out the original set. Scholars call this interplay of meanings "intertextuality." An example is the echoing between Benjaminite/Agagite conflict in Esther (Esther and Mordecai are Benjaminites; Haman is an Agagite) and that between the Benjaminite Saul and the Amalekite Agag in 1 Sam 15. If we read the Second Temple stories (or for that matter, the writings of the Second Testament) in isolation from their scriptural allusions, we miss out on a whole set of fascinating interactions.

A Case Study: Bel and the Dragon

The story of Bel and the Dragon offers an interesting opportunity to study the complex probing of identity in Second Temple stories. Roman Catholics, following the Greek version of the First Testament, traditionally regard Bel and the Dragon as the fourteenth chapter of Daniel. Protestants place it, along with other Additions to Daniel, in the Apocrypha. What makes Bel and the Dragon particularly interesting is the existence of two versions.[5] Comparison of the versions allows us to see how dif-

---

5. The two versions appear side by side in an English translation by Witton Davies in Robert H. Charles, ed., *The Apocrypha and Pseudepigrapha of the Old Testament* (Oxford: Clarendon, 1913), 1:658–64; and in Steussy, *Gardens in Babylon*, 57–61.

ferent situations and settings find reflection in subtle differences of storytelling.

The older of the two versions, usually referred to as the Old Greek, appears to have come from Alexandria in the late second century (135–120) B.C.E.[6] A later version traditionally bears the name of the second-century C.E. translator Theodotion, but was probably done considerably before Theodotion's time. It appears to date from not later than 30–50 C.E. and was probably done in northern Syria or Asia Minor.[7] The Theodotion version eventually displaced the Old Greek, and for Bel and the Dragon it underlies standard English translations such as the NRSV.

Bel and the Dragon contains three substories. Theodotion's telling locates the action in the court of Cyrus of Persia (the king who encouraged Judean exiles to return from Babylon to Jerusalem and rebuild the temple in the 500s B.C.E.). Daniel appears, as he does in the early chapters of the Hebrew/Aramaic version of Daniel, as an honored "companion of the king" (this may be an official title). The following retelling is based on my own translation.[8]

The Babylonians have an idol named Bel, around whom the first substory (which I refer to as "Bel") centers. The idol receives a daily ration of twelve barrels of fine flour, forty sheep, and six barrels of wine. The king worships it every day.

---

6. Steussy, *Gardens in Babylon*, 28–31.

7. Dominique Barthélemy, *Les devanciers d'Aquila* (VTSup 10; Leiden, Brill, 1963), 148–55; supported by Pierre Grelot, "Les versions grecques de Daniel," *Biblica* 47 (1966): 381–402; Klaus Koch, "Die Herkunft der Proto-Theodotion-Übersetzung des Danielbuches," *VT* 23 (1973): 362–65; Steussy, *Gardens in Babylon*, 32–37.

8. Steussy, *Gardens in Babylon*, 55–69. Quotations from both versions of Bel and the Dragon are my translations; other biblical material is quoted from the NRSV.

"Why don't you worship Bel?" the king asks Daniel.

"I don't revere idols made with hands, but rather the living God, Creator of heaven and earth, who has dominion over all flesh."

The king, in a comic demonstration of gullibility, responds, "You believe Bel's a living god, don't you? Haven't you seen how much he eats and drinks every day?"

Daniel laughs. "No way, Your Majesty! This is clay on the inside, bronze on the outside, and has not eaten or drunk, ever."

Angry, the king summons Bel's priests and lays down the rules of engagement: "If you don't tell me who eats up these supplies, you die — but if you show that Bel eats them up, Daniel dies, since he blasphemed against Bel."

"Let it be just as you've said," Daniel answers.

The king, Daniel, and the seventy priests of Bel go to the temple, where the priests invite the king himself to set out food and then lock and seal the room. Why are they so confident? The storyteller lets us in on their secret: "They knew they'd made a hidden entrance under the table, and they'd always come in through it and consume everything." Suspense increases — the priests have a way to make good on their boast that all the supplies will be gone in the morning!

While the king sets out the food as instructed, Daniel issues orders to his servants, who sprinkle the entire sanctuary with ashes. This done, the door is locked and sealed. During the night, as anticipated, the priests enter with their wives and children and consume all the food and drink.

Early the next day, the king comes to the temple and requests that Daniel inspect its seals. Daniel confirms that they are intact. The doors are opened. The king looks in and sees empty tables. "You're great, Bel! There's no trickery about you, not any!"

But again Daniel laughs. "Look at the ground and realize whose tracks these are!"

The king reports, "I see the tracks of men, women, and children!" Furious, he has the priests and their families arrested. After they confess and show him their hidden entrance, the king has them executed. He turns the idol over to Daniel, who destroys it and its temple.

The second, much briefer substory (which I call "The Serpent") proceeds similarly.

This time the Babylonians are worshiping a big serpent. "You *can't* say this isn't a living God," the king tells Daniel — "so worship it!"

Daniel answers, "I worship Lord my God, because *he* is a living god. But you give me permission, Your Majesty, and I'll kill the serpent — without sword or stick!"

The king gives permission. Daniel mixes pitch, fat, and hair into balls that he puts in the serpent's mouth. The serpent "ate them and blew up," says the narrative. "Look at these things you all have been revering!" Daniel tells the king.

But the Babylonians are not pleased to have their god destroyed, much less to have the king disrespecting national gods. Their displeasure drives the third story (which I call "The Lion Pit"). "Hand Daniel over to us," the people tell the king. "If you don't, we'll kill you and your family."

Under duress, the king hands over Daniel, who is consigned to a lion pit. The seven lions in the pit normally eat two humans and two sheep each day, but to encourage them to eat Daniel, those rations are withheld.

The scene shifts abruptly to Judah, where the prophet Habakkuk has just finished preparing stew and bread to take to reapers in the field. An angel tells him to take it "to Babylon, to the lions' pit, for Daniel."

The prophet protests, "Lord, I've never seen Babylon. I don't know the lion pit!" The angel lifts him by the hair and whooshes him to Babylon, where Habakkuk urges Daniel to receive the lunch.

Daniel, who can always be counted on for quotable lines, answers, "Yes, you remembered me, God! You don't forget people who love you." He eats, while the angel returns Habakkuk to his own place.

After this interlude, we skip to the seventh day, when the king comes to the pit to mourn for Daniel. (You will recall that the king sent Daniel to the pit only under duress.) Glancing into the pit, he is startled and joyful to see Daniel sitting there. This time, the king recognizes Daniel's God: "You are great, Lord, Daniel's God! There isn't any other than you!" Then the king pulls Daniel out of the pit and throws Daniel's enemies in, where they are gobbled instantly.

Plot Structure

We begin our study of these stories by listing the plot events presupposed by both versions. Not every event is actually mentioned in the text — presumably God prevented the lions from eating Daniel in the pit, but neither version explicitly says so.[9] At this level the versions are identical. The events of each substory (Bel, the Serpent, and the Lion Pit) form a V-shaped pattern, which scholars call a chiasm (or chiasmus). In turn, the content in each of these sections is also presented in a V-shaped pattern:

9. A later expansion lingers upon the lions in some detail; see Louis F. Hartman and Alexander A. Di Lella, *The Book of Daniel* (AB 23; Garden City: Doubleday, 1978), 22.

Bel   **Daniel's religion makes king curious/angry**
                    king tests priests and Daniel
                      Daniel makes secret preparations
                        priests make secret preparations
                        priests' preparations persuade king
                      Daniel's preparations persuade king
                    king punishes priests, rewards Daniel
The Serpent   **Daniel's religion angers king (implicit)**
                    king threatens Daniel's religion
                      Daniel/king test king's religion
                      Daniel discredits king's religion
                    king accepts Daniel's religion(?) (implicit)
The Lion Pit **Daniel's/king's religion angers people**
                    people frighten king
                      king gives Daniel to people
                        people try to kill Daniel (lions)
                          Lord saves Daniel from lions (implicit)
                        people try to starve Daniel (implicit)
                          Lord feeds Daniel (via angel via Habakkuk)
                      king recovers Daniel
                  king adopts Daniel's religion
                    Daniel/king punish people

Each substory begins when Jewish religious behavior provokes pagans (Daniel's behavior provokes the king in Bel and the Serpent, the king's perceived Jewishness provokes other subjects in the Lion's Pit). This theme reflects a real problem in Diaspora life: Jewish refusal to honor pagan deities often offended pagans, who thought it good manners to honor any god that came along. In the first two substories, confrontation leads to a test of pagan religion. In both of these confrontations, Daniel's own wit brings him triumph. The third segment tests the protective power of Daniel's God. Here triumph comes not through human cleverness but through divine intervention. This structure reinforces the message that pagan religion rests on human contrivance (and can therefore be debunked by merely human effort), while Judaism praises the acts of an actual and efficacious deity (who fends off would-be debunkers quite capably). The arrangement also reminds us that the most important figure in these stories is, finally, not Daniel but Daniel's God.

The use of dialogue in different segments underlines the contrast between the first two substories and the third. The third segment has less dialogue in both versions, and Daniel, so loquacious in the first two segments, says nothing in the Lion Pit sequence except that God has remembered him, as God typically remembers those who love God. When the chips are down, it is divine action and not human talk that saves the Jew.

Interplay with Other Scripture

In addition to its obvious ties with the Book of Daniel, which we shall explore later, the tripart story of Bel and the Dragon draws in the Prophet Habakkuk; in fact, the opening line of the Old Greek version says, "From the Prophecy of Habakkuk." (Given the tendency of Hellenistic writers to associate their work with more ancient authorities, one need not suppose that Habakkuk actually wrote the story.) The obtrusiveness of the lunch-delivery episode, which introduces different characters, a different setting, and a quite different style of divine action from that found in the rest of the chapter, suggests that it is probably a late addition to the sequence. That the two versions of Bel and the Dragon are much more similar in the Habakkuk portion than they are in the rest of their text supports this conclusion.[10] The incident is, however, part of both versions as we have them now, so we do need to ask how it contributes to the final story and what difference it makes that the lunch was delivered by Habakkuk (rather than by, say, a lunch-bearing stork).

Habakkuk, as we know him from the prophetic book bearing his name, appears to have prophesied toward the end of the Judean monarchy. This would make him roughly contemporary with, if a bit older than, Daniel, whose career begins early in Nebuchadnezzar's reign, according to Dan 1–2. This would make both prophets rather old by the time of Cyrus's accession, but we shouldn't lean too hard on dates since Jews in the Hellenistic era appear to have been rather unclear about the timing of events in the sixth century B.C.E. We see a general tendency to collapse time spans, treating events as closer together than they actually were (e.g., Jdt 4:3 and 2:1 place the consecration of the Second Temple prior to Jerusalem's fall to Nebuchadnezzar, although this mistake is so egregious it may be a deliberate signal of fictionality). For our purposes, the important thing is Habakkuk's association with Judah and the coming of the Babylonians.

What were Habakkuk's concerns? His book opens with an energetic complaint: "How long shall I cry for help, / and you will not listen? /...Destruction and violence are before me; /... justice never prevails" (1:2–4). Habakkuk does not specify whether the problem of unrighteousness is internal (Judean) or external, but we suspect the former, for God answers, "I am rousing the Chaldeans [Babylonians],... / to seize dwellings not

---

10. Carey A. Moore, *Daniel, Esther, and Jeremiah: The Additions* (AB 44; New York: Doubleday, 1977), 146–47.

their own" (1:5–11). This raises a new theological problem for the prophet: "Is [the Babylonian enemy] then to keep on emptying his net, / and destroying nations without mercy?" (1:12–17). The second chapter of Habakkuk's book responds that justice will be done — "if it seems to tarry, wait for it" (2:3) — and mocks the powerless idols of the Babylonians (2:18–19). The book closes with a psalm of praise to God as divine warrior (Hab 3).

The Habakkuk literature thus displays important points of contact with the Book of Daniel in general. It asks about God's role in handing over the Judeans to Babylon. It asks whether foreign oppression will be allowed to continue indefinitely and gives assurance that at an "appointed time" (Hab 2:3; Dan 8:19; 11:27, 29, 35) it will stop. In the meantime the righteous must live faithfully (Hab 2:4).

We can also see some specific connections between Habakkuk, especially in its Greek version, and Bel and the Dragon. Both mock idols[11] (and Hab 1:16 even introduces the motif of sacrifices and rich portions). Both affirm God's ultimate succor "for those who love him" (Bel 38). The Greek version of Habakkuk promises that "earth will be filled with knowledge of the glory of the LORD" (Hab 2:14): "[God] will be recognized when the years draw near," and even "[the foreign conqueror] will turn his spirit, and review, and make propitiation: 'this strength is my God's'" (Hab 1:11 Septuagint), all of which find at least partial fulfillment in the king's acclamation of Daniel's God in Bel 41. Meanwhile, Habakkuk predicts that "destruction will come

---

11. Wolfgang M. W. Roth explores the development of this theme in Second Temple literature in "For Life, He Appeals to Death (Wis 13:18): A Study of Old Testament Idol Parodies," CBQ 37 (1975): 21–47.

upon the ungodly" (Hab 1:9 Septuagint), as indeed it does in Bel 22 and 42.

Finally, Bel and the Dragon may be playing with and transforming images in the final verses of Habakkuk, which speak of praising God even when the fields yield no food (3:17–18). In Bel and the Dragon, Habakkuk's situation has changed; his field is yielding well enough that he must carry lunch to the reapers (another Second Temple passage, *Lives of the Prophets* 12:4–7, expands upon this incident),[12] but Daniel still hungers. Habakkuk closes with assurance that God will "set me upon the heights" (3:19 Septuagint), which may bear some relation to his airborne transport in the Daniel story and perhaps also the tradition, noted in the first verse of the Old Greek version of Bel, that Habakkuk was of priestly family.

These connections may strike the reader as rather distant; and indeed without the direct reference to Habakkuk in Bel and the Dragon, one would be tempted to dismiss them. But early Jewish expansions upon biblical texts often did play fast and loose with what we might regard as the facts of the case. For example, when *Sanhedrin* 93a expands upon Jer 29:23, the Israelite wives referred to by Jeremiah somehow become a daughter of the Babylonian king Nebuchadnezzar.

Another important intertextual symbol in Bel and the Dragon is Babylon, which enters the story loaded with significance from its appearances in the history of Judah and particularly in the prophetic writings. I have already observed how Babylon figures in Habakkuk's discussion with God. The city bears the same mixed nuances in other biblical books. Babylon is God's tool for punishment of a disobedient Judah (e.g., Jer 20:4–6

---

12. Translated by D. R. E. Hare in *OTP* 2:393.

[which mentions a false prophet going to Babylon]; 21:4–7). But the prophets are sure that Babylon will be punished in its turn (e.g., Jer 51). Jeremiah 51, one of many prophetic statements about Babylon's fall, is particularly interesting because it mentions a "serpent" (NRSV has "monster," but the Septuagint of this passage uses the same word as the Daniel story we are studying), lions, and Bel who must "disgorge what he has swallowed" (Jer 51:34, 38, 44)[13] — a striking link between the apocryphal chapter we have been discussing and the Book of Jeremiah.

Both of these kinds of passages, those in which Babylon is God's instrument for punishment and those in which it is doomed to destruction, view Babylon as an embodiment of evil and danger, a city/people inimical to Jewish survival. But Babylon has another significance, especially in Jeremiah. Jeremiah's vision of the figs (24:1–7) and his letter to the exiles (Jer 29) view Babylon as a place to which God has sent some good Judean people. Jeremiah counsels them to settle in, live faithfully, and even "seek the welfare of the city where I have sent you into exile, and pray to the LORD on its behalf, for in its welfare you will find your welfare" (29:7). Here Babylon has become a place in which Jews can prosper and in which Jewish and pagan welfare can coincide.

The Masoretic Book of Daniel similarly shows two sides of Babylon. In Dan 1–6, Babylon is a place in which Jews prosper (despite intermittent threats) and even bring prosperity to the

---

13. These connections were pointed out by Nehemiah Brüll, "Die Geschichte von Bel und dem Drachen," *Jahrbuch für jüdische Geschichte und Literatur* 8 (1887): 28–29. For an English-language discussion of this article, see Charles James Ball, *The Additions to Daniel* (Speaker's Commentary; London: Murray, 1888), 2:323–60.

city's rulers. Daniel 7–12, by contrast, depicts Babylon as one of a series of corrupt foreign empires destined for destruction (7:4–5 portrays it as a beast from the sea). Babylon continues to show two faces in Bel and the Dragon: does the city's paganism mean sure destruction for a faithful Jew, or may the Jew thrive there, perhaps even as the most honored of the king's companions?

The treatment of Babylon in Jeremiah, a book with multiple ties to the Daniel literature,[14] posed a special problem for ancient Jewish understanding of Daniel's personal status. Jeremiah 29 (the very chapter that encourages Jews in Babylon to "build houses and...plant gardens"; 29:5) vehemently repudiates those who claim to prophesy in Babylon (29:15–19). This must have caused discomfort to Jews who cherished the Daniel stories, for while the Book of Daniel itself never calls him a prophet, perhaps to avoid Jeremiah's censure, we know from the book's placement in the Greek Bible and comments like Matt 24:15 that many people did consider Daniel a prophet.

In light of this, it is surely significant that succor for Daniel comes from Judah by the hand of an authoritative Judean prophet. The rescue legitimates Daniel and his activity in Babylon. In a wider sense it reassures the Diaspora audience that Judah and "Babylon," which becomes symbolic for any foreign land, are not so very far apart. God can bridge the distance in an instant, and Judah remains capable of offering sustenance to her far-flung children.

The feeding also legitimates Daniel by its resonance with God's care for Elijah (1 Kgs 17:4–6, 16; 19:5–8). Habakkuk's

---

14. On ties between Jeremiah and the Daniel literature, see the Scripture indexes in John E. Goldingay, *Daniel* (Word Biblical Commentary 30; Dallas: Word, 1989); and Steussy, *Gardens in Babylon*, 147–54, 161–62.

unusual mode of transport provides a further connection to prophetic literature in its resemblance to Elijah's departure in a whirlwind (2 Kgs 2:11) and, even more strongly, the Prophet Ezekiel's trip to Babylon (Ezek 8:3).

Differences between the Versions

While the two versions of Bel and the Dragon are virtually identical in event structure, they vary noticeably in their exact wording — noticeably enough to suggest that they are independent tellings of the story, rather than one being a revision of the other. Systematic patterns of difference between them give each version its own characteristic emphases.

One of the most striking differences involves the relative strengths of the roles of the king and Daniel. We see this already in the opening verses (1–2) of each version:

Old Greek	Theodotion
From the prophecy of Habakkuk (Jeshua's son, from the tribe of Levi). There was a certain man, a priest, named Daniel (Abal's son), who was a companion of the king of Babylon.	King Astyages was gathered to his fathers, and Cyrus the Persian took over his kingdom. Daniel was a companion of the king, honored above all his friends.

Old Greek's title line places the entire story in the context of Jewish religious tradition; its opening verses give genealogical information about both Habakkuk and Daniel, but this version does not name the Babylonian king. Theodotion's opening locates the story with respect to the chronology of Gentile kings, of whom it names two, but it gives no information about Daniel's background or parentage.

The pattern of relatively greater prominence in the Old Greek for Daniel and relatively greater prominence in Theodotion for the king continues throughout the respective narratives. Old Greek mentions Daniel by name thirty-two times, Theodotion only twenty-six times. Almost half (49 percent) of the dialogue in Old Greek belongs to Daniel, while his words comprise less than one-third (32 percent) of Theodotion's dialogue. This means that in Old Greek Daniel far outtalks the king (who has about one-third of the dialogue in both versions) while in Theodotion the king speaks slightly more than Daniel.

Old Greek's tendency to adopt a Jewish frame of reference emerges again in the language used for God. Each version mentions God first in verse 4:

Old Greek	Theodotion
The king revered [Bel]. The king went every day and worshiped it; but Daniel prayed to Lord.	The king revered [Bel], and went every day to worship it; but Daniel worshiped his own God.

Old Greek's narrator names God from Daniel's Jewish viewpoint, using "Lord" as a proper noun. Theodotion's narrator speaks of God from the king's point of view as Daniel's God. In Theodotion, the narrator does not refer to God in Jewish fashion as Lord until partway into the Habakkuk episode (34).

Verse 5 of each version gives Daniel's response to the king's question, "Why don't you worship Bel?" Old Greek's powerful Daniel responds almost scornfully — playing to the sympathies of an already-convinced Jewish audience — while Theodotion's Daniel gives a more patient explanation accessible to Gentiles:

Old Greek	Theodotion
Daniel answered the king, "I revere none but the Lord God, Creator of heaven and earth."	He answered, "I don't revere idols made with hands, but rather the living God, Creator of heaven and earth, who has dominion over all flesh."

Old Greek's Daniel continues to play a more assertive role when he ups the ante on the king's proposal rather than simply accepting it (9: "Let's do it this way: if I don't show you that it's not Bel who eats them, I'll die, and my folk with me"). He supervises preparations for the test (11: "Your Majesty, you have seen for yourself that things are laid out. Let's have *you* seal the sanctuary doors, when it's locked"), while in Theodotion the Bel priests give directions and the king himself sets out the food. In Old Greek Daniel orders his own servants to clear the temple, while in Theodotion the Bel priests leave of their own accord. In Old Greek Daniel lets no one else observe the ash-strewing, while in Theodotion the king watches it. In Old Greek Daniel orders the closing and sealing of doors, while in Theodotion the king and Daniel do this together.

The next day, Old Greek's Daniel tells the priests and king to inspect the seals, while in Theodotion it is the king who tells Daniel to do it. Old Greek's Daniel is comfortable enough to "laugh uproariously" at the king's response to the empty tables, while Theodotion's Daniel simply "laughs" (this contradicts the usual pattern of more extravagant statement in Theodotion's version). Old Greek's Daniel names the priests' trickery in so many words (19) while Theodotion's explicit accusations of lying come from the priests against Daniel (12). In Old Greek Daniel shows the king the hidden doors, while in Theodotion the priests do. Theodotion's king is angry at the deception and destroys the priests, but Old Greek's king simply turns them over to Daniel, who does not destroy them — following his own plan (9b) rather than the king's (8).

In accordance with Daniel's more active role in Old Greek, its crowd gathers in verse 28 against Daniel, while in Theodotion's telling the crowd rallies against the king. In the Habakkuk episode, the Greek syntax of the angel's orders to Habakkuk stresses the person to whom the lunch goes (i.e., Daniel), while in Theodotion's telling the angel's syntax emphasizes the location (i.e., Babylon). Old Greek's narrator confirms Daniel's statement that Lord has remembered him (39: "so the Lord God remembered Daniel"), while Theodotion's does not. And in its final statement, Old Greek explicitly tells us that the evildoers were eaten up in front of Daniel, while Theodotion uses an ambiguous "him," which could refer to either Daniel or the king.

In short, Daniel is the "reference character" and a more active player than the king in Old Greek, while Theodotion uses the king as reference point and gives him a relatively more important role throughout.

The two versions also differ in their alignment of Daniel and the king vis-à-vis other character groups. In Old Greek Daniel and the king, the only two characters mentioned in the opening two verses, appear essentially allied against the priests and the crowd. But Theodotion's second verse, which mentions that Daniel is honored "above all his [Daniel's? the king's?] friends," gives early notice of a story in which Daniel will be pitted against rival advisers, with the king presiding over the conflict. Theodotion's king reveals his relatively greater distance from Daniel when he describes Daniel's statement about Bel as blasphemy (in Old Greek 9 the king more neutrally describes Daniel as having said that "[the provisions] aren't eaten by [Bel]"). We have noted that in Old Greek Daniel and the king supervise preparations in Bel's temple together; the narrator also tells us that Daniel's plan "seemed a good idea" to the king. In Theodotion, the priests direct preparations.

Even at the moment when the doors of the temple are opened and the king, seeing empty tables, acclaims Bel's faithfulness, his words in Old Greek are apparently directed to Daniel (for they refer to Bel in the third person: "Bel is great! There's no trickery in him!"), while in Theodotion the king speaks to Bel ("You're great, Bel! There's no trickery about you, not any!"). After Daniel reveals that this first impression is mistaken, the king and Daniel together ("they") locate the missing supplies in the priests' quarters in Old Greek, while in Theodotion (following the reading of pre-Hexaplaric manuscript 987)[15] it is the priests themselves who show their secret arrangements to the king.

A similar pattern emerges in the Serpent substory when the king responds to Daniel's request for permission to kill the snake (26):

Old Greek	*Theodotion*
The king agreed. "You've got it!"	And the king said, "I'm giving it to you."

Old Greek's phrasing shows "agreement" between the king and Daniel and makes Daniel the grammatical subject of the king's reply. Theodotion's king simply grants permission, and

---

15. Angelo Geissen, *Der Septuaginta-Text des Buches Daniel: Kap. 5–12, zusammen mit Susanna, Bel et Draco, sowie Esther Kap. 1,1a-2,15, nach dem Kölner Teil des Papyrus 967* (Papyrologische Texte und Abhandlungen 5; Bonn: Habelt, 1968).

he himself is the grammatical subject of his permission-granting statement.

One might expect, in light of Theodotion's relatively greater emphasis on the foreign court and its point of view, that Daniel's opponents (the Bel priests and the crowd) would have a more prominent role in Theodotion's telling. This is indeed the case. Not only do Babylonian priests direct preparations for the showdown in Bel's temple, call Daniel a liar, and show the king the hidden door themselves, but they get a significantly larger allotment (25 percent) of the dialogue in Theodotion's telling of the Bel episode than they do in Old Greek's (4 percent). In Theodotion we get a narratorial glimpse into their minds (31) and the crowd later protests the priests' fate (28). In the Lion Pit episode, Theodotion again gives Daniel's opponents (this time, the crowd) a larger share of the episode's dialogue (32 percent) than does Old Greek (14 percent).

Theodotion's telling has a more extravagant, less realistic style than Old Greek's. Theodotion has forty sheep where Old Greek has four (3), a big serpent (24), two sheep fed to the lions daily in addition to two humans (32), these rations withheld from the lions when Daniel is put in the pit (32), a more extensive description of the angelic airlift (36), Habakkuk shouting (37), Habakkuk returned to Judah instantly (39), the king shouting loudly (41), and evildoers eaten instantly (42). For all its emphasis on the court setting, Theodotion's characters show less respect for the king than do Old Greek's: Theodotion's Daniel laughs at the king's initial boast about Bel (7) and physically restrains the king from entering Bel's temple (19). In the Lion Pit substory, Theodotion's crowd threatens to kill the king and his family, while Old Greek's crowd simply complains about the king's religious attitudes (29).

Finally, Theodotion uses more developed theological language: it speaks of Daniel's God as "ruler of all flesh" (5) and the "living God" (5, 25) in contrast to the idol that is "made by human hands" (5). Old Greek's Daniel swears "by Lord the God of gods" (7) that he can prove Bel does not eat anything, while Theodotion records no such oath. Perhaps the oath seemed frivolous, or perhaps the phrase "God of gods" seemed too admissive of other gods. Theodotion's Daniel reaffirms his worship of the "living God" in the Serpent episode (25) while in Old Greek Daniel simply offers to kill the serpent.

Both versions of Bel and the Dragon may be classified as court legends, a type of story celebrating a particular ethnic group's successes in the rough-and-tumble of court life. W. Lee Humphreys proposes a further distinction between "court contests" (featuring relatively collegial competition for rewards) and "court conflicts" in which "one faction seeks the ruin of the other."[16] Bel and the Dragon (in both versions) leans distinctly toward the latter category, although it also incorporates elements of idol parody, literature that mocks pagan worship of images (or in the case of the snake, a mortal animal).[17] The versional differences noted above nudge Old Greek more toward idol parody while Theodotion retains stronger court legend features.[18]

---

16. W. Lee Humphreys, "A Life-Style for Diaspora: A Study of the Tales of Esther and Daniel," *JBL* 92 (1973): 211–23, quotation from 217.

17. Roth provides the classic description of the idol parody genre, but writers like Ball (*Additions to Daniel*, 346) and William H. Daubney (*The Three Additions to Daniel* [Cambridge: Deighton & Bell, 1906], 195) had already commented upon this thrust in Bel and the Dragon. In addition to the idol-parody element, Lawrence M. Wills finds elements of prophetic legend in Old Greek; see his *Jew in the Court of a Foreign King: Ancient Jewish Court Legends* (Harvard Dissertations in Religion; Minneapolis: Fortress, 1990), 129 n. 102.

18. Wills, *Jew in the Court of a Foreign King*, 129–37.

Differences between the versions become more striking when we relate them to political circumstances in the settings from which these versions likely come (Alexandria of the second century B.C.E. for Old Greek and Asia Minor or Syria in the first century C.E. for Theodotion).[19]

During the period from which our Old Greek version seems to stem, the Ptolemaic kings of Egypt were not well received by native Egyptians or by even the large Greek population of their capitol city, Alexandria.[20] One historian describes the Greek and Egyptian populations of this time and place as "addicted to over-excitement and rioting."[21] Jews, however, had enjoyed good relationships with the rulers since the city's founding,[22] and it was they who provided the king's primary political support. In 175–174 B.C.E., Jerusalem's high priest Onias III, deposed by the king who controlled Judea, took refuge in Egypt. His son Onias IV built a temple near Alexandria that continued to operate, according to Josephus, far into the first century C.E.[23] Thus

---

19. Steussy, *Gardens in Babylon,* 173–91.

20. Harald Hegermann, "The Diaspora in the Hellenistic Age," in *The Cambridge History of Judaism,* vol. 2: *The Hellenistic Age* (ed. W. D. Davies and Louis Finkelstein; Cambridge: Cambridge University Press, 1989), 143.

21. Michael Grant, *From Alexander to Cleopatra: The Hellenistic World* (New York: Macmillan, 1982; repr. 1990), 48.

22. Hegermann, "Diaspora in the Hellenistic Age," 121–22. Josephus alleges that they were granted full citizenship by Alexander himself (*Against Apion* 2.4 §35; *Jewish War* 2.18.7 §487). There had indeed been trouble around the accession of Ptolemy VIII Physcon (reigned 145–116 B.C.E., the period from which the Old Greek version dates) because the Jews supported his rival, Cleopatra II, but the tension was resolved by Physcon's marriage to Cleopatra and good relations between the sovereign and the Jewish community once again resumed (Hegermann, "Diaspora in the Hellenistic Age," 142–43, although he refers to Physcon as Ptolemy VII).

23. Michael E. Stone, *Scriptures, Sects and Visions: A Profile of Judaism from Ezra to the Jewish Revolts* (Philadelphia: Fortress, 1980), 79–80; Josephus, *Antiquities* 13.3.1–3 §§62–73; *Jewish War* 7.10.2–4 §§420–36.

Egypt's Seleucid kings had warm relationships not only with mercenary and mercantile Jews but also with priestly families.

Against this background, the political prominence, assertiveness, and alliance with the king that Old Greek ascribes to Daniel make perfect sense. Even the assignment of Daniel to a priestly family squares with the realities of Jewish life in late second-century Alexandria. The antagonism of the crowd and the distinction drawn between the "people of the land" and the king's cronies in Old Greek 30 ("the king, seeing the local crowd gathered against him, called for his companions") also square with the Egyptian situation.

At a quite different level, the trickery connected with Bel seems more plausible when we consider this description of procedures at one of Alexandria's better-known temples:

> In this temple of Sarapis, strange wonders could be seen. They included the sight of an iron statue of Ares propelled into the embrace of a lodestone Aphrodite by the combined action of magnets and invisible wires.... It was likewise in Alexandrian shrines that the principle of the siphon was applied to making water into wine; and when the congregation arrived in the temple, hidden hydraulic bellows ingeniously caused fanfares of trumpets to blare out, or the altar-fire to burst into a seemingly miraculous blaze. Moreover, the expansive force of hot air created by burnt offerings was utilized to throw open the temple doors and propel the image of its god forward, so that he came to meet and greet his devotees; and a variety of novel lighting effects included the internal illumination of statues so that light shone out of their eyes.[24]

---

24. Grant, *From Alexander to Cleopatra*, 230.

References such as Wis 15:18–19 and *Epistle of Aristeas* 138 suggest that veneration of live snakes was also practiced in Egypt at about this time.

Elsewhere in the Greek-influenced Mediterranean world, Jewish communities lacked the unique power wielded by the Alexandrian Jewish community. They were more likely to live as one among many ethnic groups in hellenized urban centers, and conflict between them and other ethnic groups was common.[25] Judaism's ethics and monotheism attracted many converts, especially in Asia Minor (which is one reason why Christianity later found this such a rich mission field), but insistence on customs like Sabbath observance (a problem especially in military service) and refusal to worship other gods could quickly create trouble, particularly in the context of cults that proclaimed the reigning ruler divine. Ephesus, a likely city of origin for the Theodotion translation of Daniel, seemed to have particular inclinations in this direction.[26] Theodotion's telling of Bel and the Dragon, with its strong court-legend features, accurately reflects the concerns of Jews in the "administrative and entrepreneurial class"[27] in this free-for-all milieu. Jews here would not be as familiar with the protocol of actual high court circles as were Jews in Alexandria (thus the less realistic, more fairy-tale flavor of the Theodotion version) and were forced to compete on a more equal footing (thus the relative diminution of Daniel's

25. S. Applebaum, "The Legal Status of the Jewish Communities in the Diaspora," in *The Jewish People in the First Century: Historical Geography, Political History, Social, Cultural and Religious Life and Institutions* (ed. S. Safrai and M. Stern; Compendia rerum iudaicarum ad Novum Testamentum 1; Philadelphia: Fortress, 1974), 1:453–54.

26. Helmut Koester, *Introduction to the New Testament* (Hermeneia: Foundations and Facets; Philadelphia: Fortress, 1982), 1:33–35, 369.

27. Wills, *Jew in the Court of a Foreign King*, 197.

role and enhancement of his opponents'). Intimate familiarity with things Jewish could not be assumed (hence the shift of reference from Daniel in Old Greek to the king's point of view in Theodotion, and from matters Jewish in Old Greek to matters Babylonian in Theodotion), yet conversion of pagans was a real possibility (thus Daniel's patient theological explanations to the king and the more highly developed theological vocabulary in Theodotion).

The Versions of Daniel

In general, a story's possible meanings emerge not only from the text and its social context, but also from its interaction with the literary context; readers will tend to notice emphases that relate the story to associated material. Bel and the Dragon's most obvious and important literary context is the Book of Daniel, to which the story was attached in Greek Bibles. How does Bel and the Dragon influence our reading of the rest of Daniel?

The Old Greek version of Daniel, as we know it from Papyrus 967,[28] arranges chapters in the following sequence (using the conventional chapter numbers of English translations): 1–4, 7–8, 5–6, 9–12, Bel, Susanna. This is, according to the dates given in this version, the chronological order. Between 3:23 and 3:24, Old Greek inserts a long poetic sequence not present in the traditional Hebrew/Aramaic text of Daniel. Protestant Bibles title this sequence "The Prayer of Azariah and the Song of the Three Young Men" and place it in the Apocrypha, among the Additions to Daniel.

---

28. Winfried Hamm, *Der Septuaginta-Text des Buches Daniel . . . nach dem Kölner Teil des Papyrus 967* (Papyrologische Texte und Abhandlungen 10 [on Dan 1–2] and 21 [on Dan 3–4]; Bonn: Habelt, 1969, 1977); and Geissen, *Der Septuaginta-Text des Buches Daniel.*

The Hebrew/Aramaic text of Daniel, which probably represents a stage of development later than the Old Greek, has only twelve chapters. They are arranged by genre, with legends comprising Dan 1–6 and apocalyptic visions appearing in Dan 7–12.

Theodotion's version of Daniel seems, in the core twelve chapters, to revise the Old Greek into something more like the Hebrew/Aramaic text. (It seems to be later than both.) It begins with Susanna (probably because Theodotion's version of Susanna presents Daniel as a precocious child), followed by Dan 1–12 (in the same order as the Hebrew/Aramaic text but including the extensive poetic additions in Dan 3), then closes with Bel and the Dragon. Thus, except for Bel and the Dragon, this version (like the Hebrew/Aramaic text) gives genre priority over chronology in chapter arrangement. (A chronological ordering using the dates given in this version is Susanna, 1–4, 7–8, 5–6, 9, 11–12, 10, Bel.)

All these books of Daniel contain two different types of worldview: that of the legends, echoing Jer 29's hope that "Babylon" can be a place of prosperity for good Jewish people; and that of the apocalyptic visions, portraying foreign empires as hopelessly corrupt and predicting their overthrow in terms even stronger than Jer 51. Both Greek versions, by the very act of including two additional legends and by beginning and *ending* with legends, shift the total impact of the book away from apocalyptic fervor toward exploration of the possibilities of life in "Babylon."

The legends themselves can be read with the accent on God's sovereignty[29] or on God's power to protect faithful individuals.

---

29. Danna Nolan Fewell expertly highlights this theme in Dan 1–6 in *Circle of Sovereignty: A Story of Stories in Daniel 1–6* (Bible and Literature Series; Sheffield: Almond, 1988).

The Hebrew/Aramaic version of Daniel leans toward a sovereignty accent because this common thread unites the legendary and apocalyptic sequences (remember that apocalyptic plays a more prominent role here than in the Greek versions). The Greek versions increasingly accent God's protection of the virtuous. This is due partly to the inclusion of Susanna (which involves no foreign sovereigns at all), partly to the poems in the Greek version of Dan 3 (which shift attention away from the king's point of view toward the faith and experience of the young men inside the furnace), and partly to the addition of Bel and the Dragon (where the Habakkuk episode serves the same function as the poems in Dan 3, directing our attention to the faith and experience of the persecuted Jew who is delivered). In sum, the additions affect the Book of Daniel by emphasizing God's protection of the faithful in an ongoing Diaspora life, rather than God's sovereignty over and ultimate overthrow of foreign kings, which is the central thrust of the Hebrew/Aramaic version.

Let us now turn the question around: how does the rest of Daniel influence our reading of Bel and the Dragon? It draws out the theme of God's sovereignty, especially since both Greek versions place Bel and the Dragon immediately after the apocalyptic visions of Dan 9–12. The legendary accent of both Greek Daniel books, however, inclines us to notice more how that sovereignty is expressed in protection of the righteous and less how it belittles the foreign gods. In other words, juxtaposition with the rest of Daniel accents the court-conflict features of Bel and the Dragon and draws attention away from idol-parody elements. These effects are stronger in Theodotion than in Old Greek, since the Theodotion versions of both Susanna and Bel and the Dragon deemphasize Jewish political power in favor of stress on God's protection of faithful Jews who lack special privilege and "pull." Even the Theodotion version presents an influential Daniel, but he engages in a more equal competition with the other courtiers than in Old Greek.

Finally, juxtaposition of Bel and the Dragon with the rest of Daniel underscores the chapter's resonance with additional Scriptures, particularly Jeremiah. We realize more acutely than ever the conflicting implications of "Babylon," its danger and its possibilities. To the Diaspora Jew, or even Jews living in Judea under foreign rule, these connections say, "This story is about you, and what the prophets' words mean for your life. Take heart: the foreign rulers whose whims you suffer, and the other peoples with whom you compete, remain subject to the sovereignty of God, who does not abandon those who love him."

Closing Reflections

Our study of Bel and the Dragon showed how the story's structure and its resonances with other Scripture encouraged Diaspora readers to embrace their Jewish identity. Such tales built confidence that the "living God" would look after the faithful amid the complexities of their conflicts with pagan competitors and pagan powers in the Hellenistic world. Subtle variations between the Old Greek and Theodotion versions show how storytellers finely shaped their tales to the particular nuances of their settings. We have no way of knowing how much of this nuancing was conscious and how much of it happened unawares in the course of many tellings and retellings, although I am inclined to suspect most of it was done unconsciously. The Old Greek version of Bel and the Dragon probes the tensions of a setting in which Jews held high courtly position and wielded considerable political power. The story urges them to assert their faith boldly. Theodotion's version, which at first glance tells "the same story" but differs from the Old Greek in many small ways, adapts itself to a more predominantly Gentile context, suggesting God's protection of faithful worshipers even when they are politically vulnerable.

The narratives we have inherited from Second Temple Judaism provide an important legacy with respect to both content and process. The content of these stories is interesting in its own right, especially when we realize how it is enhanced by the interplays between the stories and other Scripture. "Babylon" offers a multifaceted symbol of worldly culture that, today as in Hellenistic times, provides both opportunity and threat. Daniel, who so cleverly debunks false gods, could easily be a role model for persons who seek to challenge the unrealistic but oh-so-impressively marketed claims of consumerism or nationalism today; and Daniel, who is remembered by God even in the lion's pit, could be a sign of hope for those same persons when those who are accustomed to being ruled by consumerism and nationalism lash back.

We learn, however, from the process of these stories that the claiming and living of Scripture involves a process of ongoing storytelling. The religious literature we receive from the past is full of tensions and multiple possibilities. By taking those loose ends and weaving new stories around them, preachers and teachers help us clarify the multiple ways in which past faith can enlighten present. The Second Temple's stories offer both fabric for that weaving and a guide in the technique.

– N I N E –

The Book of Tobit
as a Window on the Hellenistic
Jewish Family

– Will Soll –

No volume on postexilic Judaism would be complete without some attention to the Jewish family. Family life is an important part of any culture. For postexilic Judaism, it may have had particular importance, since for most of the period, Jewish national sovereignty was an elusive dream; Jews increasingly lived as a minority among other nations. In these circumstances, family life became particularly important for the transmission and preservation of Jewish identity.[1]

Until recent years, discussion of the Jewish family in the Hellenistic period relied heavily on rabbinic material.[2] There has been a shift away from this as it has been increasingly recognized that these rabbinic sources derive from a later period and

---

1. See John M. G. Barclay, "The Family as Bearer of Religion in Judaism and Early Christianity," in *Constructing Early Christian Families* (ed. Halvor Moxnes; London: Routledge, 1997), 66–72.

2. S. Safrai, "Home and Family," in *The Jewish People in the First Century* (ed. S. Safrai and M. Stern; Compendia rerum iudaicarum ad Novum Testamentum 1; Fortress: Philadelphia, 1976), 2:722–833.

may not be as representative of the entire Jewish community as was frequently assumed. Attention has therefore shifted to primary evidence such as inscriptions on tombstones and legal documents. We have, for example, marriage contracts from Elephantine (ca. 400 B.C.E.)[3] and documents relating to marriage and divorce from the region of the Dead Sea (ca. 125 C.E.).[4] John J. Collins sums up the character of marriage that emerges from these documents as that of a legal contract, concerned primarily with property and money.[5]

This is an important corrective to the overly idealized view of marriage that might be found in the Bible and other religious documents of this period. At the same time, the picture that emerges from these documents is distorted, or at least limited, by their narrow focus and legal character. Collins points out that the legal documents need to be complemented by "narratives that illustrate the normal working out of relationships," but that unfortunately, "we have very few narratives of family life in this period, apart from Tobit."[6]

---

3. Emil Kraeling, *The Brooklyn Museum Aramaic Papyri: New Documents of the Fifth Century B.C. from the Jewish Colony at Elephantine* (New Haven: Yale University Press, 1953); Bezalel Porten, *Archives from Elephantine: The Life of a Jewish Military Colony* (Berkeley: University of California Press, 1968); H. L. Ginsberg in *ANET* 222–23, 548–59.

4. See Léonie J. Archer, *Her Price Is beyond Rubies* (JSOTSup 60; Sheffield: JSOT Press, 1990), 291–300; Naphtali Lewis, *The Documents from the Bar Kochba Period in the Cave of Letters* (Jerusalem: Israel Exploration Society, 1989); Y. Yadin, J. C. Greenfield, and A. Yardeni, "Babatha's *Ketubba*," *Israel Exploration Journal* 44 (1994): 75–101.

5. John J. Collins, "Marriage, Divorce and Family in Second Temple Judaism," in *Families in Ancient Israel* (by Leo J. Perdue et al.; Louisville: Westminster John Knox, 1997), 107–15, 148–49.

6. Ibid., 149.

So it is to Tobit, the narrative that most thoroughly depicts family life in the Hellenistic era, that we turn. Tobit portrays through narrative the texture of many aspects of family life, such as weddings, burials, meals, sleeping arrangements, arguments, admonitions, farewells, and reunions. In so doing, it may serve to complement the picture that emerges from the legal and halakhic sources.

While Tobit presumably reflects some actual customs and situations, it is a work of fiction and as such is subject to idealization, distortion, and selectivity. Take, for example, divorce. The aforementioned marriage contracts regard divorce as a routine, unexceptional development, yet the possibility of divorce is not mentioned in Tobit. Thus, even as we profit from the window that Tobit provides, we must allow that other sources may yield complementary or even contradictory results.

The full text of Tobit has come down to us in two Greek recensions — that represented by Codex Sinaiticus (=S) and that represented by codices Vaticanus and Alexandrinus (=BA) — though the original text was either Aramaic or Hebrew.[7] J. D. Thomas demonstrates that S is the earlier of the two recensions,[8] and his conclusions are vindicated by the Qumran material.[9] S is now generally regarded as the preferred recension; most translations, however, make some use of BA as well.[10]

---

7. See the discussion in Carey A. Moore, *Tobit* (AB 40A; New York: Doubleday, 1996), 53–60.

8. J. D. Thomas, "The Greek Text of Tobit," *JBL* 91 (1972): 463–71.

9. Joseph A. Fitzmyer, "The Aramaic and Hebrew Fragments of Tobit from Cave 4," *CBQ* 57 (1995): 655–75.

10. Especially to fill in the lacunas that occur in S at 4:7–19a and 13:6b–10a. The translations of Tobit employed in this essay are my own, and are from S unless otherwise noted. Quotations from other biblical texts are from the NRSV.

The Story of Tobit

Intelligent use of the Book of Tobit requires familiarity with its plot.[11] For those who are not familiar with it, the following summary may be helpful.

The Book of Tobit introduces us to a Jewish[12] household: father Tobit, mother Anna, and son Tobias. Though exiled in Nineveh in the days of the Assyrian Empire, they know how to combine piety with success in the Gentile world, until a wicked king, Sennacherib, ascends the throne. His misrule and persecution force the Tobit family into hard times. Sennacherib not only kills many Jews but also refuses to allow their corpses to be buried. In defiance of the royal will, Tobit sees to the burial of Jewish corpses. As a result, Tobit has to hide, and his property is confiscated (1:1–20).

After Sennacherib's death, Tobit's nephew Ahiqar intercedes for him with the next emperor and Tobit is allowed to return to Nineveh. But his troubles and those of the Jews are not over. During the Feast of Pentecost, Tobit comes upon another corpse, which he again buries. Exhausted and demoralized, he falls asleep in the courtyard. This becomes the occasion for yet

---

11. The plot summary I give here applies to both S and BA. I assume, with most scholars, that the book is fictional. Even if there was a "historical" Tobit, his connection with the protagonist of this book is purely nominal. One clear indicator of this is the dependence of Tobit on folktales that are "fairy tales" in the strict sense of the word; see W. Soll, "Misfortune and Exile in Tobit: The Juncture of a Fairy Tale Source and Deuteronomic Theology," *CBQ* 51 (1989): 209–31.

12. Because of their loyalty to Jerusalem (Tob 1:4–7; 5:14; 13:9–17), I refer to the Tobit family as Jewish, even though the narrative states that they come from the northern kingdom (1:2). The narrative in its present form was written for Jews who would identify with Tobit as one of their own.

another affliction when bird droppings fall in his eyes, forming cataracts that cause blindness (1:21–2:10).

Tobit prays for death, but he also recalls some money he left in trust with a relative[13] named Gabael in Rages, a city in Media. Should he not tell Tobias about this money before God grants his prayer? So Tobit dispatches his son to Media, but not before he provides him with lots of good advice (4:5–19) and a guide. The guide makes himself out to be Azariah, a relative from Tobit's tribe of Naphtali, but he is in reality the angel Raphael.

Raphael proves to be not only a good guide, but a healer[14] and a matchmaker as well. As healer, Raphael instructs Tobias to catch a large fish that has attacked him as he washes in the Tigris River and preserve its liver, heart, and gall for use in healing and exorcism (6:1–9). As a matchmaker, Raphael informs Tobias that in Media dwells a Jewish girl named Sarah, daughter of Raguel and Edna, who would make a fine wife for him, by virtue of her character, beauty, wealth, and her family's close relation to Tobias. Tobias has heard of her, and he has also heard something else: that she has already had seven husbands, each of whom was killed on their wedding night by a demon.[15] But Raphael reminds Tobias of his father's instruction to take a wife from his kinfolk and assures him that, by burning the fish heart and liver and by a prenuptial prayer the demon can be driven out (6:10–18).

When Tobias is introduced to Raguel and Edna, they are as

---

13. In S, Gabael refers to himself as Tobit's "cousin" (*anepsios*; 9:6).

14. The name Raphael means "God heals."

15. The reader of the Book of Tobit has already heard about this, for at the same time Tobit prayed for death, Sarah made a similar request as a result of the demon's persecution and the reproach it caused her (3:8–10). See Soll, "Misfortune and Exile in Tobit," 228.

delighted to learn that he is Tobit's son as they are grieved to hear of Tobit's blindness (7:1–9). A marriage contract between Tobias and Sarah is quickly sealed, whereupon the newlyweds go up to the bridal chamber. Raphael's remedy proves effective; the demon flees all the way to Egypt; and after prayer, both Tobias and Sarah sleep safely through the night (7:10–8:9a).

Meanwhile, Raguel gets up in the middle of the night and has his servants dig a grave for Tobias so that, if he died like the others, he can be buried without anyone knowing it (8:9b–14)! When a maidservant looks into the bridal chamber and reports that the couple is sleeping unharmed, Raguel is overjoyed, praises God, and orders his servants to fill in the grave before daybreak. At breakfast, he reaffirms Tobias as his own son and heir and swears to detain him for a fourteen-day feast in celebration of the wedding. While Tobias is thus detained, Raphael goes to Gabael to retrieve the money and invite him to the wedding feast (8:15–9:6).

After the fourteen days, Tobias entreats Raguel not to press his hospitality and to let him return to Tobit and Anna, who have become anxious about his return. Raphael and Tobias go on ahead of Sarah, so that Tobit's blindness may be healed by use of the preserved fish gall. The old man's first joy at seeing his son again with his own eyes is immediately increased, not only by Sarah's arrival but also by his ability to go out to meet her "in full vigor, with no one leading him," in front of all the people of Nineveh. A second wedding feast of seven days is held in honor of Tobias and Sarah, with Ahiqar and his nephew Nadab on hand.

When the time comes to pay "Azariah," he reveals himself to them as Raphael, an angel, who really neither ate nor drank anything; what they saw was a vision. Raphael explains that he was sent in answer to their prayers and exhorts them to continue in their piety (Tob 12). Tobit praises God and predicts a glorious future for restored Israel (Tob 13–14).

The Idea of the Family

Tobit deals with many matters that we commonly associate with family. Yet it is fair to ask what connection our idea of family has with any concept that would have been employed in Hellenistic Judaism.

The English word *family* can be used in many ways, but the picture it evokes most readily in the contemporary Western mind is that of the nuclear family: mother, father, and their children.[16] Even in our contemporary society, this definition is controversial, and when we are offered it, or anything else, as a definition of family in the course of current political debate, we want to know the corollary ideas and proposals to which the definition is linked.

This definition becomes even more problematic when we turn to Tobit. Our author simply had no word available that meant "nuclear family." This is not because husband-wife and parent-child were not of primary importance to him, as we shall see. These relationships, however, do not create an insular group, but realize their full importance within a larger network.

These difficulties of definition underscore James Casey's point that the family is "not necessarily defined by objective criteria

---

16. E.g., the first definition of "family" in the *American Heritage Dictionary* (3d ed., 1992) is "a fundamental social group . . . typically consisting of a man and woman and their offspring."

like property or descent, but by a certain idea of itself."[17] Rather than hold rigidly to a preconceived notion of the family and plunder Tobit for data that fit, it is more fruitful to begin by inquiring after the idea of the family that the book conveys.

The Family and Lineage

Family identity and connections in Tobit are fundamentally expressed through the language of lineage. This does not, however, constitute an objective criterion, since much of this language is fairly general, fictional, or metaphorical. Rather, lineage is used to create an idea of the family that informs not only particular family relations but the sense of Jewish existence in a Gentile world.

The importance of kin and ancestors is stressed from the outset. In 1:1, Tobit is provided with a genealogy and a tribe (*phylē*; the tribe is also designated *oikos* [lit., "house"] in 1:5). We are then told (1:3) that Tobit performed many charitable acts for his kinsmen (lit., *adelphoi*, "brothers") and his people (*ethnos* in the sense of "members of my family, my group").[18] Tobit marries "a member of[19] his own family (*patria*)" (1:9).

The family depicted in the first nine verses of the book is an interrelated combination of several layers, from immediate ancestors and the extended family of uncles, aunts, and cousins, to the clan, the tribe, and finally the nation. It is not always possible to separate these layers with linguistic or interpretive certainty;

---

17. James Casey, *The History of the Family* (New Perspectives on the Past; Oxford: Blackwell, 1989), 7.

18. Frank Zimmerman, *The Book of Tobit* (New York: Harper, 1958), 46.

19. Lit., "from the seed of"; the word *seed* also occurs in the genealogy in 1:1.

rather, the book tends to move toward as much integration and overlap as possible of these different senses of family.

The idea of family in Tobit also forms an important point of connection with the traditional literature of the people. Tobit urges his son to "marry a woman from the descendants of your ancestors...for we are descendants of the prophets"[20] (4:12). "Lineage" here becomes inseparable from a sense of the biblical text and its significance for the community. In particular, Tobit has the patriarchs of Genesis in view: "Remember, my son, that Noah, Abraham, Isaac, and Jacob, our ancestors of old, all took wives from among their kindred" (4:12).[21] Many commentators note that Gen 24 in particular, where Eleazar goes on a long trip to seek a wife for Isaac from among Abraham's folk, served as a literary model for Tobias's journey.

Another important literary connection is "The Story of Ahiqar," a popular wisdom tale that framed two collections of proverbs. The original text, probably from Syria, reflects a polytheistic Near Eastern religious background. The story circulated in Christian and Jewish circles; these versions, "to varying degrees, assimilated the polytheism of the original to a monotheistic viewpoint,"[22] replacing references to "the gods" with references to "God" or "the Lord." The author of Tobit doubtless had before him such a monotheized text. He then took the further step of making Ahiqar a Jewish hero, bringing him into Tobit's family as his nephew. The connection serves to locate Tobit more plausibly in the court affairs of Assyria and

---

20. The same expression also occurs in the New Testament in Acts 3:25.

21. The inclusion of Noah in this list is interesting since he is the ancestor of all humanity, and nothing is said in Genesis about the genealogy of his wife.

22. J. M. Lindenberger in *OTP* 2:486.

provides a contrast to the behavior of Tobias and Sarah in the person of Ahiqar's nephew, Nadab.[23]

"Are You Looking for a Tribe and a Family?"

One vignette from the book illustrates the importance of tribe and genealogy in everyday relations particularly well. It occurs when Tobias introduces Raphael to Tobit as a potential guide for the journey to Media:

> Then Tobit said to him, "My brother, of what family and from what tribe are you? Tell me, brother." He answered, "Why do you need to know my tribe?" And he said to him, "I should like to know of what tribe you are,[24] brother, and your name." He replied, "I am Azariah, the son of the great Hananiah, one of your relatives." Then Tobit said to him, "Welcome, and may God save you, brother. Do not be angry with me, brother, because I wished to learn your tribe and family.[25] It turns out that you are a kinsman of mine, of a good and noble lineage. For I used to know Hananiah and Nathan, the sons of the great Shemaiah; they used to go with me to Jerusalem and worshiped with me there, and were not led astray. Your kinfolk are good men, and you are of good stock. Hearty welcome!" (5:11–14).

In BA, Raphael's first answer to Tobit is even more caustic: "Are you looking for a tribe and a family or for a man whom

---

23. Nadab is called "Nadin" in the original Aramaic text of Ahiqar. For further reflection on the connection of Ahiqar and Tobit, see Lindenberger, ibid., 488–90; and J. C. Greenfield, "Ahiqar in the Book of Tobit," in *De la Tôrah au Messie: Mélanges Henri Cazelles* (ed. M. Carrez, J. Doré, and P. Grelot; Paris: Desclée, 1981), 329–36.

24. So BA; S has "truthfully whose you are."

25. "Your tribe and family" in BA; S has "the truth about your family."

you will pay to go with your son?" But in neither case are we supposed to believe that Tobit is being fussy or snobbish. Rather, the angel's question gives Tobit an opportunity to display his "family values," values that we can confidently ascribe to the author of the book as well. Raphael's question is not really a rebuke but a kind of test that Tobit passes.

This episode illustrates Casey's observation that in preindustrial societies caste serves the functions currently given to educational and professional credentials. This function of caste leads to a keen interest in genealogy: "Where a people lacks the organic unity of a modern society, men like to 'situate' an individual before doing business with him."[26]

Yet there is an irony in this scene with Raphael: the angel is lying through his apparent teeth. True, the deception is completely benign, but the genealogy he offers is still objectively worthless. Tobit is stretching the truth as well, either here or earlier in the book. His assertion that Raphael's alleged father and uncle used to go to worship with him to Jerusalem is at odds with his previous assertion that he alone went to Jerusalem whereas all the rest of his kindred worshiped the calf at Dan (1:5–6).

It is fair to conclude that in this exchange very little actual information is given about ancestors or events. The conversation is, however, still effective in "situating" (to use Casey's term) the two men with respect to each other. Both show that they speak the language of genealogy and therefore may plausibly claim to embody the values implied in being a person of "good family."

In real Hellenistic Jewish life, such an exchange would probably have provided more objective information, especially where

---

26. Casey, *History of the Family*, 22.

parents and grandparents were concerned. The more distant past and the broader family units may well, however, have been the subject of plausible invention. The genealogies of preindustrial societies fundamentally deal with values that are so important that if suitable ones cannot be discovered they must be invented. At bottom, the concept of lineage "means simply purity or honour. A pride in ancestors, and a reverence for them, were the ways in which that purity was maintained."[27] In such genealogical systems objective information would have been subordinated to the moral content of the idea of genealogy.[28]

Take, for example, the term *tribe* used so often in Tobit. While the earliest tribes were probably groups bound by common descent, by the time of the monarchy the term came to designate primarily people who lived in the same region. "Tribal" identity would seem to be unascertainable in the postexilic Diaspora. Yet we know that, for some, such claims were meaningful; Paul boasts proudly of being "a member of the tribe of Benjamin" (Phil 3:5).

There may have been others in the Jewish community who viewed the claim to belong to a tribe as affectation; their voices may be reflected in the sardonic response of Raphael, "Are you looking for a tribe and a family or for a man whom you will pay to go with your son?" The Book of Tobit, however, urges that such forms of identification be taken seriously, for they align

---

27. Ibid., 38.

28. Jews, of course, were by no means distinctive in their concern for genealogy. Sarah Pomeroy writes that some Greeks created fictitious genealogies in order, e.g., to share the reputation of a particularly famous practitioner of a trade; "Some Greek Families: Production and Reproduction," in *The Jewish Family in Antiquity* (ed. Shaye J. D. Cohen; Atlanta: Scholars Press, 1993), 163.

the individual with the group, with certain values, and with the sacred story.

Two Dutiful Only Children

The "children" in the Book of Tobit, Tobias and Sarah, are fully grown adults on the threshold of marriage. This does not signal an end or even a diminution of their roles as children; the role is rather one they have been in training for all their lives but can only now begin to play in earnest.

The command to honor father and mother is taken to refer primarily to adult children. After Tobit has prayed for death, he enjoins Tobias,

> My son, when I die, give me a proper burial. Honor your mother and do not abandon her all the days of her life. Do whatever pleases her, and do not grieve her spirit in any way. Remember, my son, that she went through many trials for your sake while you were in her womb. And when she dies, bury her beside me in the same grave (4:3–4).

The command applies equally to in-laws. When Tobias takes his leave of Raguel and Edna, he says, "I have been commanded by the Lord to honor you all the days of my life" (10:13).[29] Fortunately, the problem posed by "honoring" two sets of parents in different cities is resolved by the older age of Tobias's parents, to whom he gives proper burial in Nineveh before going to live with his in-laws in Ecbatana, treating them "with great respect in their old age" before burying them as well (14:13).

This serene view of filial obligations, a view that portrays them as posing no conflict whatever for those who have to carry

---

29. So the Latin version; the Greek is uncertain but probably has a similar sense.

them out, is characteristic of Tobit. It is not that the obligations themselves are remarkable; on the contrary, they are common in traditional societies. What is remarkable in Tobit is the degree to which they are internalized by Tobias and Sarah. While marriage is frankly presented in Tobit as a potential source of tensions (albeit ones that can be overcome; see below), there is no hint that Tobias and Sarah have the slightest bit of difficulty embracing their roles as adult children. These are ideal children who act exactly as their parents would have them.

Nowhere is this parento-centric perspective clearer than in the attitudes expressed toward the dilemma involving Sarah and the demon. It is plausible, though a bit comic, that Raguel's concern for himself as a parent intrudes even into his delight that the grave he dug will not be necessary, since Tobias has survived his wedding night. "Blessed are you," Raguel prays to God, "for you had mercy on two only children" (8:17). But even the "two only children" themselves share this view to a remarkable extent. When the reproach of Sarah's maidservant drives her to the brink of despair over her marital misfortunes, she refrains from suicide because it would bring further reproach on her father (3:10), and she laments, "I am my father's only child; / he has no other child to be his heir" (3:15). Finally, and most ludicrously, is Tobias's objection to marrying a woman whose husbands are killed by a demon on their wedding night, one that implies that he would be perfectly willing to face certain death in Sarah's bedchamber if only he had a brother: "So now, since I am the only son my father has, I am afraid that I may die and bring my father's and mother's life down to their grave, grieving for me — and they have no other son to bury them" (6:15).

The selfless resolve of Tobias and Sarah is never mitigated; it

is simply opposed by an equally extreme counterexample provided by the story of Ahiqar. On his deathbed, Tobit recounts
"what Nadab did to Ahiqar who reared him." This nephew, who
should have honored Ahiqar like a father, "went into the eternal
darkness, because he tried to kill Ahiqar" (14:10).

The deeds of Nadab correspond to what parents fear, just
as the deeds of Tobias and Sarah correspond to what parents
wish. Neither portrait has psychological depth. Yet, if the Book
of Tobit does not provide much insight into the ways that adult
children would have faced their obligations, it does give us insight into why parents held these obligations so dear. It is not
simply a matter of having someone to support them in their
old age and bury them when they are gone. Children renew
their parents by appropriating their parents' virtues and by giving them grandchildren who hold the promise of even further
renewal.

This continuation of identity is particularly emphasized in the
case of Tobit and Tobias. The names are virtually identical, the
former being a rarer, contracted form of the latter (cf. the names
Abram and Abraham in Genesis). To suggest, as Walther Eissfeldt does, that the hero of the original Tobit folktale "has split
into two characters, father and son," is to misunderstand both
the complexity of Tobit's debt to folktales and the purposive
identification of the two in the book.[30] When Tobias arrives at
the house of Raguel, the latter remarks to his wife Edna, "How
much the young man resembles my kinsman Tobit!" even before
he knows who Tobias is.

---

30. Walther Eissfeldt, *The Old Testament: An Introduction* (trans. P. R. Ack-
royd; New York: Harper & Row, 1965), 584. For a more detailed discussion
of Tobit's relation to the folktale tradition, see Soll, "Misfortune and Exile in
Tobit," 210–19.

Once Raguel learns Tobias's identity, he exclaims, "Blessings on you my child, son of a good and noble father." Raguel's words of recognition and blessing will be echoed and elaborated several days later at Tobias's wedding feast, when Gabael calls Tobias "good and noble," an indication that Tobias has come into his own. Yet this augments Tobit's status rather than detracting from it; Gabael proceeds to refer to Tobit as "good and noble, upright and generous." Gabael concludes his blessing by expressing the physical likeness Raguel had observed in even stronger terms: "Blessed be God, for I see in Tobias the very image of my cousin Tobit." The use of "image" recalls the language of the Priestly source in Genesis, which tells us that humanity is created in the divine image (Gen 1:27) and that Adam "became the father of a son in his likeness, according to his image" (5:3). This theology of the divine image becomes the basis of the likeness between humanity and God and also expresses the means through which humanity is renewed.[31]

"Inheriting" Sarah

We have already referred to Tobit's instructions to Tobias to take a wife from his kindred. That a Jewish father should tell this to his son is hardly a surprise, though Tobit's anxiety on the subject seems to indicate that at least some Jews in the Hellenistic Diaspora married Gentiles. What is surprising is the degree of close kinship advocated in the prospective wife, which is unparalleled in any other postexilic Jewish work. In this regard,

---

31. Ps 104:30 applies this same principle to animal species: "When you send forth your spirit, they are created; / and you renew the face of the ground." Context makes it clear that this renewal refers to the new "generation" of creatures.

the example of the patriarchs takes on a special importance for Tobit, since they married their cousins.

It is difficult to tell exactly what degree of relationship Tobit envisages in his instructions to Tobias. He tells him not to marry a foreign woman who is not of his father's tribe (*phylē*). And he says that Abraham, Isaac, and Jacob all took wives from their kindred (*adelphoi*) and that Tobias too should love his kindred (*adelphoi*). With the example of the patriarchs, a close degree of prior kinship between husband and wife is hinted at, though not directly advocated.

Yet the reader has been prepared for Tobit's discourse with the statement, at the end of the preceding chapter, that "it fell to Tobias to inherit [Sarah] before all others who desired to take her" (3:17). While we wince at the extent to which Sarah is referred to in proprietary terms, we should not miss the narrator's emphasis: Tobias has a right to her that usurps anyone else's. We learn from Raphael's later speech to Tobias that the latter's right to Sarah is based on closeness of kinship (6:12). This right is said to be so strong that Raguel cannot give Sarah to another without violating the law of Moses and incurring the death penalty (6:13).

Just how the author of Tobit arrives at these strictures is unclear, especially since none of the possibly relevant laws prescribes the death penalty. Frank Zimmermann attempts to derive the obligation from the law of "levirate marriage," whereby the brother of a man who dies without a son has an obligation to marry the wife who is left, and "the firstborn whom she bears shall succeed to the name of the deceased brother" (Deut 25:5–10).[32] This is the only case in biblical law where one individual

---

32. Zimmermann, *Book of Tobit*, 82–83.

is obligated to marry another by virtue of a kinship relationship. But if levirate law applied to Tobias, the question would be how closely he is related to one of Sarah's dead "husbands" rather than to Sarah or Raguel. Sarah is never described as a widow, and it may be questioned whether any of her marriages were consummated. Finally, the concern of levirate marriage to perpetuate the name of the dead husband is never invoked in Tobit.

More promising is the law in Num 36:8–9:

> Every daughter who possesses an inheritance in any tribe (*matteh*) of the Israelites shall marry one from the clan (*mishpakhah*) of her father's tribe, so that all Israelites may continue to possess their ancestral inheritance. No inheritance shall be transferred from one tribe to another; for each of the tribes of the Israelites shall retain its own inheritance.

This law closely parallels the situation in Tobit, especially if the author of Tobit took "clan" to refer to a specific group within the tribe and not as a way of referring to the tribe itself. Moreover, this law shares with Tobit a concern for the inheritance of a daughter. Sarah's status as an heiress is central to all of the discussions about whom she marries.

To appreciate the importance of Sarah's status we can compare Tobit with Gen 24, the quest for a wife for Isaac. In both cases, the finding of a suitable bride involves a long journey to a close relation (closer, in fact, than those who lived nearby). In both cases, a trusted servant plays a crucial role. And in both cases, the marriage is readily assented to without any kind of courtship and is settled with an exchange of property. But at this point a crucial difference occurs: the exchange of property goes in different directions in the two texts. In Gen 24 Eleazar, representing the family of the future husband, gives gifts to Laban, representing the family of the future bride. This corresponds roughly to the biblical *mohar*, or bride-price (Gen 34:12; Exod 22:15–16 [Eng. 22:16–17]). In Tobit, however, Raguel compensates Tobias with an ample dowry.

Casey argues that the difference between bride-price and dowry corresponds to the prevalence of exogamy and endogamy respectively. Among people "organized into clans by descent," such as the Chinese, for example,

> the basic rule of marriage is that of exogamy — that is, one should marry outside the group.... The point seems to be that the patrilineal clan in China constituted a sufficiently defined and important group in its own right, united in the ritual worship of the ancestor.... The fear was that a union of cousins would create more limited and exclusive solidarities which would prejudice the health of the whole.[33]

Endogamy, by contrast, presumes that the daughter as well as the son inherits property. Islam provides a contrast to the Chinese in this respect. The egalitarian fraternity of "true believers" created by Islam destroyed the religious base of the clan. Islam, however, adapted

> the residual strength of clan feeling to the pressing demands of a developed economy, allowing daughters to inherit, but preferring them to keep their inheritance within the clan by marrying their father's brother's son. This is not a rule but a preference, a "noble" or "proper" thing to do, even

---

33. Casey, *History of the Family*, 67–68.

though the reality of family strategy often rules it out in practice.[34]

This connection between exogamy and bride-price on the one hand, and between endogamy and dowry on the other, is subject to a myriad of variations and modifications in various cultures. Nevertheless, the basic connection as described by Casey may help make sense of what is going on in Tobit, where endogamy[35] is strongly linked to dowry. The dowry Tobias receives is, in effect, a down payment on Sarah's inheritance, the remainder of which will fall to them after the deaths of Raguel and Edna (8:21). Tobias is, in turn, beholden to Sarah's family as parents; his filial obligation extends to them (14:12–13).

The appeal of this arrangement to our author is twofold. We have already seen how eager he is to retain the language of tribal lineage with its moral content for the postexilic Diaspora even though the original social contexts that gave meaning to tribal identity had largely disappeared. In such circumstances, endogamy strengthens "the residual strength of clan feeling" in a similar way that Casey adduced for Muslims. A related concern is economic. In a situation where the daughter inherits, the marriage arrangement idealized in Tobit means that the wealth of "good" Jewish families is not diluted; rather, their resources are pooled.

It is, of course, open to question how this emphasis on dowry

---

34. Ibid., 68.

35. Note that here I am using *endogamy* in the sense generally preferred by anthropologists: marriage to cousin or close kin. Sometimes in studies of postexilic Judaism, *endogamy* refers to the ideal of Jews marrying other Jews. This is a very broad (though technically possible) use of the term endogamy, a kind of "endogamy" that was seen as desirable among many ancient ethnic groups.

actually played out in the postexilic Diaspora. Comparison with Aramaic and Greek marriage contracts from the Dead Sea region (ca. 125 C.E.) is illuminating. While the Aramaic marriage contracts make mention of both *mohar* ("bride-price") and dowry, the Greek contracts mention only the dowry brought in by the wife. Even more important is the reinterpretation of *mohar* in the Dead Sea Aramaic documents. At Elephantine, *mohar* was paid by the husband to some person in authority over the wife. In the Dead Sea Aramaic documents, the husband merely stipulates *mohar* as the amount he owes to the wife should the couple get divorced. The only money that actually changes hands at the marriage is, therefore, the dowry. We may conclude that Tobit's depiction of wealthy Jewish families pooling their resources is generally consistent with marriage contracts, the key difference being that the Book of Tobit makes no mention of the possibility of divorce.

Like the situation Casey speaks of among Muslims, endogamous marriage in Tobit is being held up as ideal rather than assumed to be the rule in every case. To be sure, Raphael states that Raguel would incur the death penalty under Jewish law if he gives Sarah to anyone else. But Raguel has already done so seven times — and has remained unharmed each time! I rather think that the legal strictures in this matter are being pressed to underscore praiseworthy behavior. It is doubtful that anyone in Judaism ever died for not marrying his daughter to her cousin.

One anomaly remains: if endogamy is related to dowry, what is its function in Gen 24? There, despite marrying a cousin, Abraham and Isaac (through Eleazar) pay a bride-price for Rebecca, and there is no inference that they are in any way further beholden to Rebecca's family. The answer must be found in the special circumstances of the Genesis narratives, where each family represents a nation. There, to marry outside the family is to marry outside the nation, so it behooves the patriarchs to marry close relatives.[36] But the implication of this for subsequent generations could simply be taken to be "marry one of your people," and indeed this has proved to be the more widespread interpretation in Judaism (cf. the broad use of endogamy discussed above). But Tobit shows that the story could be taken very literally as a model, more literally than originally intended, in a way that dovetails with the author's concern to preserve Jewish families, their wealth, and their values.

Marriage Ceremony and Prayer

Tobit 7:11–14 describes the marriage of Tobias and Sarah as a ceremony over which Raguel presides. The narrative context lends an almost impromptu air to the ceremony, since it is brought on by Tobias's sudden, inspired urgency ("I will neither eat nor drink . . . until you have settled this matter with me"; 7:11). Yet, there are a number of features of the scene that may have been common in the solemnization of Jewish marriages in this period.

That Raguel presides over the marriage of his daughter to Tobias is not surprising; in the Jewish world at this time, marriage did not require the presence of a priest or other religious functionary. In the ceremony, Raguel takes Sarah by the hand and gives her to Tobias, which Carey Moore describes as "a legal act

---

36. For more on the significance of cross-cousin marriage in Genesis, see P. K. McCarter, "The Patriarchal Age," in *Ancient Israel* (ed. H. Shanks; Englewood Cliffs, N.J.: Prentice-Hall, 1988), 4, 14–15; and R. A. Oden, "Jacob as Father, Husband, and Nephew: Kinship Studies and the Patriarchal Narratives," *JBL* 102 (1983): 189–205.

of transfer, a formal 'giving the bride away.'"[37] The marriage is further solemnized by a contract (7:13) and a meal (7:14).

The words that Raguel speaks in this context also have a solemn and formulaic character. Some of these phrases echo phrases found in ancient Jewish marriage contracts. Twice Raguel refers to the marriage being done "in accordance with the law of Moses," a phrase that also appears in the Aramaic marriage contracts from the Dead Sea region.[38] Since, as Joseph Blenkinsopp points out, "there are no biblical laws dealing directly with marriage,"[39] we have here an early instance where the conception of the Mosaic law subsumes custom and interpretation as well as the text itself.

Raguel's words to Tobias, "from now on you are her brother, and she is your sister" (7:11), also have the ring of a formulaic phrase (cf. the phrase "she is my wife and I am her husband" from the marriage contracts at Elephantine).[40] The language of siblings accords well with the idea of marriage as a union of households. But "sister" is also a term of affection, used conspicuously in the Song of Songs (4:9, 10, 12; 5:1, 2); and it is also used this way by the chief male characters in our book: Tobit (5:21; 10:6), Raguel (7:15), and Tobias (8:4). There does not seem to be a corresponding affectionate use of the word *brother* on the part of women. While one of the primary functions of the marriage contract is to secure the financial rights of the wife

---

37. Moore, *Tobit*, 222.

38. E.g., Archer, *Her Price Is beyond Rubies*, 290; Yadin, Greenfield, and Yardeni, "Babatha's *Ketubba*," 79.

39. Joseph Blenkinsopp, "The Family in First Temple Israel," in *Families in Ancient Israel* (by Leo J. Perdue et al.; Louisville: Westminster John Knox, 1997), 58.

40. Kraeling, *Brooklyn Museum Aramaic Papyri*, 143, 205.

in the event of divorce, the spoken words envision an enduring union: "*From now on* you are her brother, and she is your sister; she has been given to you *from this day, and for ever*" (7:11, emphasis added; cf. Tobias's prayer: "Grant that she and I may find mercy and grow old together"; 8:7).

Raguel also invokes God's blessing on the couple (7:11–12); but he does not offer prayer to God. Tobias does, however, when Sarah and he are alone in their bridal chamber. This seems far less typical than the marriage ceremony presided over by Raguel. It gains urgency from the threat of Asmodeus as Tobias exhorts Sarah to get up and pray "for mercy and protection" (8:4). Moore comments on this phrase: "Either the couple was unaware of Asmodeus's permanent banishment [described in 8:3], or they were praying for future blessings."[41] I argue, however, that the author sees the prayer as an essential component of the exorcism. Not only is the prayer juxtaposed with the banishment of Asmodeus, but an exhortation to prayer "for mercy and protection" is part of Raphael's instructions on how to drive out the demon: "But before you consummate the marriage, both of you must first stand up and pray, beseeching the Lord of Heaven to grant you mercy and protection" (6:18).

While offering a prayer immediately before the consummation of a marriage was probably not typical, the prayer itself, which is still read as part of some Christian wedding liturgies, is revealing as an interpretation of marriage. Given the emphasis on family and lineage, it would not have been surprising for the author to hearken back to Gen 1 and the command to be fruitful and multiply. The prayer, however, employs the more intimate language of Gen 2:

---

41. Moore, *Tobit*, 237

> You made Adam, and for him you made his wife Eve
> as a helper and support. . . .
> You said, "It is not good that the man should be alone;
> let us make a helper for him like himself" (Tob 8:6).

At this moment, they are not there to secure a posterity; they are simply there for each other. While some androcentric overtones of the Genesis text remain, the emphasis is on mutuality; Hebrew *kenegdo* in Gen 2:18 is translated "like himself" (*homoion autō*) rather than, for example, the more ambiguous *kat' auton* of the Septuagint.

The prayer emphasizes the companionate joys of marriage that will endure, it is hoped, over the course of a long lifetime. By contrast, the erotic elements of marriage are played down, as Tobit solemnly avers that he takes Sarah to wife "not because of lust [*pornian*], but with sincerity [*alētheias*; lit., 'truth']" (8:7). Yet, since Tobias and Sarah do consummate their marriage that night,[42] it is legitimate to wonder why this contrast is important to our author.

The constraints related to endogamy and arranged marriage that receive lengthy treatment in Tobit are above all matters of loyalty to one's broader family. I have already commented on the portrayal of Tobias and Sarah as two consummately dutiful children. It would be unthinkable for them to harbor the slightest reservation about any lawful marriage their parents should propose. Accordingly, the book cites Sarah's degree of kinship to Tobias's family as the essence even of her erotic attraction: "When Tobias learned that she was his kinswoman,

---

42. Pace Jerome, whose Vulgate translation has Tobias and Sarah delaying the consummation of their marriage until the third night.

related through his father's lineage, he loved her very much, and his heart was drawn to her" (6:18).

Zimmermann calls attention to a rabbinic teaching that condemns "a levir who marries the widow because he admires her beauty, or to indulge in sexual license, or for any ulterior motive."[43] While, as I argue above, Tobias is not a levir, his marriage is desirable from the standpoint of law, custom, and family interest. It is a role he enters upon willingly and with respect for his spouse. This seems to be the essence of the "sincerity" with which he takes Sarah to wife. It is this intent, as much as the burning fish organs, that drives Asmodeus, the embodiment of lust, from the bridal chamber.

Marital Friction

As stated above, marriage is frankly presented in Tobit as a source of tensions that are real and painful, although they are ultimately surmounted. The portrayal of these tensions is obviously filtered through the author's values and sympathies. Yet it is to his credit that the tensions are portrayed at all and that they are not portrayed simplistically, as if one party only was clearly responsible and in the wrong.

The tensions begin to surface with Tobit's blindness. This is hardly surprising. Not only does Tobit's blindness force the family into poverty, but it creates a relationship of extreme dependency that was not there before, especially difficult since the dependent party is accustomed to being head of the household. To be sure, we are told that all of Tobit's kindred are sorry for him, and at first Ahiqar takes care of him. But after two years, Ahiqar

---

43. Zimmermann, *Book of Tobit*, 94.

has to leave Nineveh, and the burden of caring for Tobit falls unrelievedly on Anna and Tobias.

At this point in the narrative, Anna begins to earn money at "women's work." In this case, the work in question is weaving cloth, which she does at home and sends to her employers in return for wages. This is only one of a number of culturally acceptable occupations available to Anna. Rabbinic texts portray women as engaging in a wide range of work (though not as wide as the range for men): "mercantile work, production of textiles and foodstuffs, service work (wetnursing, midwifery, teaching, hairdressing, and innkeeping) and agricultural labor."[44] There is no sense that by receiving wages for weaving Anna is operating outside cultural and Jewish norms, and Tobit's own use of the gendered phrase "women's work" implies that he accepts the suitability of such work for his wife.

Yet Anna is not on the job for long before it becomes evident that the situation clearly makes Tobit uncomfortable. When Anna brings home a young goat as a bonus, Tobit questions the propriety of this, asking overtly whether it was stolen (2:11–13) and perhaps mindful that Tamar was offered the same wage to sleep with Judah (Gen 38:15–17). The situation is full of ethical ambiguity: Tobit's suspicions are based on his moral scruples, yet he is not being fair to Anna, who clearly has not stolen the goat (as Tobit himself tells us in his capacity as narrator; Tob 2:12).

---

44. Miriam Peskowitz, "'Family/ies' in Antiquity: Evidence from Tannaitic Literature and Roman Galilean Architecture," in *The Jewish Family in Antiquity* (ed. Shaye J. D. Cohen; Atlanta: Scholars Press, 1993), 31. Martin Goodman (*State and Society in Roman Galilee*, A.D. *132–212* [Totowa, N.J.: Rowman & Allanheld, 1983], 37 and n. 156) discusses ways Jewish women earned money in Galilean villages in the second century C.E., particularly bread-selling, shop-keeping, and wet-nursing.

We cannot attribute Tobit's uneasiness to the mere fact that Anna is working for wages. The cause of his malaise is more complicated and not explicitly stated in the narrative. It may have something to do with her being the sole breadwinner at this time or with Tobit's dependence and helplessness. The consequence for Tobit is a felt loss of his moral authority to oversee household affairs. He fears that in the absence of such authority his life and the life of his family are tending toward increasing moral confusion.

As often happens in domestic arguments, an accusation by one party leads the other to broach a grievance that has long been festering beneath the daily routine. In response to Tobit's accusation, Anna demands, "And where now are your acts of charity (*eleēmosynai*)? Where are your righteous deeds (*dikaiosynai*)?" (2:14). Anna does not mean "where have they gone?" but rather "what has become of them?" — in other words, what help have they been to Tobit and his family?[45] If her moral judgment and competence as a provider are being questioned, she has a withering rejoinder: Tobit's approach has provided little enough.

Anna's parting shot is ambiguous: *ide tauta meta sou gnōsta estin* (2:14), which literally translates as "behold, these things with you are known."[46] *Tauta* logically refers to the aforementioned

---

45. For similar uses of "where" questions to indicate not the absence but the futility of what is inquired after, see Isa 19:12 and 1 Cor 1:20.

46. So S; BA replaces *tauta* with *panta*, thus obtaining "behold, all things with you are known." The intent of this substitution is probably to make Anna question what knowledge Tobit has to justify the tenacity of his suspicions (so RSV and Goodspeed: "You seem to know everything!"). This is a logical enough tack for Anna to take under the circumstances, but it is a different tack than the one she has begun in asking, "Where are your acts of charity? etc."

acts of charity and righteous deeds; what is known about them with reference to Tobit is that they have not done him any good.

Anna is, in one sense, only fighting back, wounded by Tobit's false accusation. By placing her outburst in this understandable human situation, the author avoids making her as "diabolical" a character as Job's wife. Yet, like Job's wife, she impugns her husband's "integrity."

The effect of her words on Tobit is devastating. Weeping and groaning, with "much grief and anguish of heart," he prays for death. He begins by mentioning all the sins of his ancestors and the corporate punishment of exile, plunder, death, and reproach (3:3–4) and then proceeds to his own sins and sorrow (3:5–6). But the psychological straw that broke his spirit is "that he has had to listen to undeserved insults" (3:6), made all the more bitter because they come from one whom he expects to respect and support him.

But Anna too is destined to be plunged into grief as a result of marital tension before the story is over. The nadir of her grief is reached with Tobias's absence. She never wanted him to go in the first place and apparently did not learn of Tobias's journey until he came to say good-bye. At that point, she weeps and says to Tobit: "Why have you sent my child away? Is he not the staff of our hand, and does he not go in and out before us? Do not rush to add money to money, but let it be a ransom for our son. What the Lord has given us to live on is enough for us" (5:18–20). Two points of tension can be seen here. In the first place, we can see a somewhat stereotypical tension between the viewpoints of mother and father, the former wanting her child to stay at home, the latter more willing to send him out into the world. Second, there is also the question of money. For Anna, any consideration about money is irrelevant if it places their son's life in danger. Moreover, her last remark appears to continue the "discussion" from Tob 2 about her adequacy as a "breadwinner."

Tobit manages to comfort her and secure her assent to the journey. But as Tobias's return is delayed, her misgivings return with a vengeance, and she immediately assumes the worst:

> Anna said, "My child has perished and is no longer among the living." She began to weep and bewail her son, "Woe to me my child, the light of my eyes, that I let you make this journey." But Tobit kept saying to her, "Hush; stop worrying, sister. He is all right. Probably something unexpected has happened there. The man who went with him is trustworthy and is one of our own kinfolk. Do not grieve for him, sister; he will soon be here." But she answered him, "Hush! Leave me be. Stop trying to deceive me. My child has perished." She would rush out every day and watch the road her son had taken, and would heed no one. When the sun had set she would go in and mourn and weep all night long, getting no sleep at all (10:4–7).

Clearly, she blames Tobit for the "death" of their son. Tobit's own responses, though aimed at reassuring her, are also somewhat defensive, and Tobit never acknowledges to her what we learn from the narrative: that he is worried too (10:3).

Like Tobit's grief in Tob 3, Anna's grief also brings her to death's door; even when Tobias returns, her first words are, "Now that I have seen you, my child, I am ready to die" (11:9). She doesn't die; in fact, she and Tobit both live for another half century (14:2, 12). The tensions that emerged in the course of Tobit's blindness are not made into an occasion for repentance by either party; the couple simply sees them through together toward a better future.

Edna Always Cries at Weddings

Greek historian Sarah Pomeroy contrasts the family in the Hellenistic period with the modern family by appealing to the ancient Greek term *oikos* ("house" or "household"), a term that, according to her, "emphasizes property, and ignores affective relationships."[47] In this, she is typical of many contemporary historians of the family, and there is clearly some truth in what she says. Her own study focuses on families whose economic basis was skilled labor, in which children inherited their parents' trade. Viewed in this light, the family does indeed look more like a training ground and business center, less like a "haven in a heartless world."

Yet there are reasons to believe that this contrast between ancient pragmatism and modern sentiment is overdrawn. On the contemporary side, a variety of phenomena, from prenuptial agreements and divorce settlements to the financial investment parents make in their children, show that economic considerations play a large role in the modern family. On the Hellenistic side, there is the evidence of Hellenistic art, with its frequent attempts to tug at the heartstrings, often through familial motifs.

One way that Tobit attempts to elicit an emotional response from its readers is through the frequent depiction of weeping in family contexts. A prime example of this occurs on Sarah's wedding night. As Edna leads Sarah to the bridal chamber she has prepared for her and Tobias, she weeps, tells Sarah to have courage, and prays that God grant her joy instead of sorrow.

---

47. Pomeroy, "Some Greek Families," 155.

Based on this text, Ross Kraemer thinks that it may have been customary for Jewish mothers to escort their daughters to the bridal chamber "weeping (for many reasons?) and praying for their daughter's welfare."[48]

Edna's tears are a demonstration of the bonds of affection between parents and children. Affection is prominently depicted in the many poignant scenes of the departures or arrivals of sons and daughters, all of which involve weeping: Tobias's departure from home (5:17–18), his arrival at the house of Raguel and Edna (7:6–8), the prolonged farewell scene when Tobias and Sarah leave Raguel and Edna (10:8–13), and Tobias's safe return home (11:9). As is often the case with parental tears, it is not always obvious why they are crying, but it is obvious that they care.

Burial

I mentioned at the outset of this essay the importance of the family for the transmission and preservation of Jewish identity. Parental instruction in mores and religion doubtless took place over the entire course of a child's life. The Book of Tobit employs the narrative device of using emotionally charged leave-takings as opportunities for parents to impress the essence of their religious and ethical values upon their children one more, perhaps final, time.

In his farewell instruction to Tobias, Tobit is particularly insistent on two points. One we have already discussed at length: "Marry a woman from the descendants of your ancestors" (4:12). The second is, "Give alms from your possessions . . . for charity delivers from death" (4:7, 10). "Almsgiving" or "acts of charity" are the terms most often used to translate Greek *eleēmosynē*. To-

---

48. Ross Kraemer, "Jewish Mothers and Daughters in the Greco-Roman World," in *The Jewish Family in Antiquity* (ed. Shaye J. D. Cohen; Atlanta: Scholars Press, 1993), 91–92.

bit himself is a model of the advice he prescribes: "In the days of Shalmaneser I performed many acts of charity to my kindred, those of my tribe. I would give my food to the hungry and my clothing to the naked; and if I saw any one of my people dead... I would bury him" (1:16–17).

The most conspicuous act of charity performed by Tobit, the one on which the narrator lays the most stress and the one that costs Tobit the most, is his burial of the dead (1:17–20; 2:3–10). Burial is typically the responsibility of one's near relations. Tobit himself views it as such, when he charges Tobias with the responsibility of burying him and Anna (4:4; 14:10–12). That Tobit extends this responsibility to include any one of his people vividly illustrates the vision behind the author's emphasis on almsgiving: it means Jews treating other Jews as family. Tobit acts out this vision at great personal risk when he undertakes the burial of strangers whose corpses have been left unburied due to political disfavor. The parallel with the story of Antigone from Greek mythology is illuminating. Antigone buries her defeated, treasonous brother and in so doing claims a family loyalty that precedes her duty to the state. Tobit's actions make a similar claim, but the "family loyalty" in this case is loyalty to an entire people conceived of as family.

Conclusion

I began this study of the Jewish family in Tobit by discussing how Scripture and Jewish tradition informed the Jewish concept of family. Now we see that the street runs in the other direction as well: the metaphor of the family informs the Jewish sense of existence. In a number of ways, then, the picture that Tobit draws of Jewish existence is a family affair.

– T E N –

Women as Teachers of Torah in the Apocryphal/Deuterocanonical Books

– Toni Craven –

Constitution as the covenant people, belief in communal survival, hope for political restoration, and expectation of a Davidic heir shape the religious ideas in the eighteen apocryphal/deuterocanonical books.[1] Concern for Jerusalem and the Temple,

---

With deepest appreciation, I offer this work to Walter Harrelson, the teacher of Torah who first opened this literature to me at Vanderbilt University and who continues to enlarge my understanding of it. I call special attention to Professor Harrelson's pieces in *Women in Scripture: A Dictionary of Named and Unnamed Women in the Hebrew Bible, the Apocryphal/Deuterocanonical Books, and the New Testament* (ed. Carol Meyers, Toni Craven, and Ross Kraemer; New York: Houghton Mifflin, 2000) on the various unnamed women in 2 Esdras (=4 *Ezra*) (399–403) and various female representations: "Asia as a Prostitute" (512); "Earth as Mother" (520–21); "Church as Mother and Wet-Nurse" (516–17); "Female Images of God in the Apocryphal/Deuterocanonical Books" (524–25); "Righteousness and Iniquity as Females" (539–40); and "Weeping Woman — Jerusalem/Zion as a City Being Built" (542–43).

1. No women are mentioned in the Prayer of Azariah, the Prayer of Manasseh, and Ps 151. Unnamed women appear as community members, brides, widows, wives, mothers, daughters, nurses, servants, prostitutes, and worshipers in the other fifteen apocryphal/deuterocanonical books: Tobit, Judith, Esther with Additions, Wisdom of Solomon, Sirach, Baruch, Letter of Jeremiah, Susanna, Bel and the Dragon, 1 Maccabees, 2 Maccabees, 1 Esdras,

as well as differing patterns of life governed by Torah, are regularly expressed. Adherence to Torah does not depend upon obedience to static norms, but rather upon maintenance of its tradition.[2] Torah embodied in sacred Scripture, instruction, guidance, and revelation defines both public and private behavior.[3] In the Jewish pluralism that emerged between 200 B.C.E. and 100

---

3 Maccabees, 2 Esdras (=4 *Ezra*), and 4 Maccabees. For details regarding the unnamed women, see the canonically ordered listings in *Women in Scripture*, part 2 (358–406). Seventeen named women are found in nine books: Tobit includes Deborah, Anna, Sarah, Edna, and Eve of Genesis; Susanna and Judith are the only named women in their books; Baruch refers to Hagar of Genesis; Greek Additions to Esther names Esther, Vashti, Zosara (Zeresh in Hebrew Esther), and Cleopatra; 1 Maccabees mentions another Cleopatra (Cleopatra Thea); 2 Maccabees names Antiochis; 3 Maccabees refers to Arsinöe; and 1 Esdras names Agia and Apame. Female personifications occur in five books: 2 Maccabees refers to two goddesses, Nanea and Atargatis; 2 Esdras represents God, and in some instances the church, as mother, nurse, hen; 2 Esdras personifies Earth, Zion, Babylon, Asia, Righteousness, and Iniquity; 2 Esdras, Wisdom of Solomon, Sirach, and Baruch depict Wisdom as a woman. See the various alphabetic entries in *Women in Scripture*, part 1, on named women and in part 3 on female personification.

2. See Walter Harrelson, "Life, Faith, and the Emergence of Tradition," in *Tradition and Theology in the Old Testament* (ed. Douglas A. Knight; Philadelphia: Fortress, 1977), 11–30.

3. Torah faithfulness in its origin and development is essentially a combination of sources played out in covenant stories and laws, though not systematic speculation, that wrestle with God as "merciful and gracious, / slow to anger, / and abounding in steadfast love and faithfulness, / keeping steadfast love for the thousandth generation, / forgiving iniquity and transgression and sin, / yet by no means clearing the guilty, / but visiting the iniquity of the parents / upon the children / and the children's children, / to the third and the fourth generation" (Exod 34:6–7 NRSV). Bruce C. Birch et al. (*A Theological Introduction to the Old Testament* [Nashville: Abingdon, 1999], 447) point out that in the diverse biblical literature from the Persian and Greco-Roman periods "the theological beacon of Torah remained primary. Torah piety was necessary to accommodate the needs of Jews living both in and outside the land. Yet, the very notion of Torah was a flexible one, since it involved far more than the Pentateuch." See also Hans-Joakim

(or 200) c.e., Torah and its interpretation, circumcision, observance of the Sabbath, fidelity to dietary laws, and repudiation of
idolatry assumed great significance. Monotheism, based on the
existence of no God save Yhwh, the God of the ancestors, became a tenet of faith for which the faithful were willing to suffer
torture and even death.

In the idealized world of the apocryphal/deuterocanonical
works, the solidarity of the Jewish family, with its concerns for
the maintenance of economy, reproduction, nurturance, and education, served as the cornerstone for a religion that endured
and survived the radical cultural changes, warfare, and poverty
of the Hellenistic and Roman eras. Because so much of this literature is didactic fiction, constructed in support of various ideals
of postexilic Jewish piety, it is unclear how these works square
with the social realities of the period. It is clear, however, that
women assume roles of special prominence, that "motherhood"
is more than biological, and that three of the eighteen books are
titled by the names of women: Esther, Susanna, Judith.

Although there are notable exceptions, androcentric stereo-
types are supported throughout. For the most part, social
structures are patrilinear (i.e., with descent reckoned through
the male line) and patrilocal (i.e., with women joining the
households of their husbands). Inheritance is generally through
the father or husband. It is the duty of all to have and care for
children, teaching them obedience to Torah and respect for parents. Explicit and implicit teaching roles are ascribed to women
and men, who through their words, deeds, or the voice of their
narrator, maintain and shape religious identity. Generally, al-

---

Kraus, *Theology of the Psalms* (trans. Keith Crim; Minneapolis: Augsburg,
1986), 34–35.

though not always, women exercise teaching roles within the family or the larger Jewish community. Texts from the books of Tobit, Judith, Susanna, and 1, 2, and 4 Maccabees offer counter-testimony to the later talmudic position forbidding women to study, much less teach, Torah.[4]

Tobit

Tobit structures his life on the ordinances decreed "in the law of Moses and according to the instructions of Deborah," the mother of his father (Tob 1:8).[5] Deborah, Tobit's grandmother, teaches her orphaned grandson. The substance of her teaching is not fully detailed, but its fruits are evident in Tobit's righteous life and the values he later hands on to his and Anna's son, Tobias. Tobit instructs Tobias to bury the dead, honor his mother, revere the Lord, give alms, seek endogamous marriage, avoid idleness, and practice the commandments (see especially 4:3–19). Later rabbinic literature will maintain that if a father failed to teach his son the law, the son was supposed to teach himself (Mekilta, *Pisha* 18). But "Tobit, who is presented as scrupulously observant of the law, seems proud of his knowledge and unashamed of how he got it."[6] Beverly Bow rightly states: "The

---

4. Beverly Bow ("Deborah 3," in *Women in Scripture,* 68) points out that some rabbinic authorities were adamant that women not be allowed to study Torah (Jerusalem Talmud *Sotah* 3:4; Babylonian Talmud *Yoma* 66b) and even claimed that teaching a daughter Torah was equivalent to teaching her obscenity (Babylonian Talmud *Sotah* 20a). The Babylonian Talmud mentions only one woman, Beruriah, who was learned in the law (*Pesahim* 62b; *Eruvin* 53b). This wife of the second-century C.E. Rabbi Meir is likely a legendary character.

5. Unless otherwise noted, biblical quotations are from the NRSV.

6. Bow, "Deborah 3." See also Beverly Bow and George W. E. Nickelsburg, "Patriarchy with a Twist: Men and Women in Tobit," in *"Women Like*

author does not indicate that there is anything odd about the way in which Tobit receives his education. . . . Perhaps what Deborah did was not, after all, as uncommon as later traditions have led us to believe."[7]

Another woman in Tobit, Edna, offers instruction to her child. On the eve of the marriage of Sarah, Edna and Raguel's seven-time widowed daughter, to Tobias, this mother offers prenuptial consolation to her daughter Sarah: "Take courage, my daughter; the Lord of heaven grant you joy in place of your sorrow. Take courage, my daughter" (Tob 7:16).[8] Although initiated at her husband Raguel's command (7:15), Edna's words address Sarah's distress and uphold hope in a future whose features are as yet undisclosed. Such beliefs are characteristic of Torah ideals fundamental in the exodus tradition and the laments of the Book of Psalms: God will provide.

Judith

In the book titled by her name, Judith, a childless pious widow from Bethulia, summons the three male town officials (Uzziah, Chabris, Charmis) to her house in order to chastise their testing of God and their five-day postponement of surrender to the Assyrian enemy (Jdt 8:1–27).[9] She demands, "Who are you to

This": New Perspectives on Jewish Women in the Greco-Roman World (ed. Amy-Jill Levine; Atlanta: Scholars Press, 1991), 127–44.

7. Bow, "Deborah 3," 68.

8. See John J. Collins, "Marriage, Divorce, and Family in Second Temple Judaism," in *Families in Ancient Israel* (by Leo J. Perdue et al.; Louisville: Westminster John Knox, 1997), 104–62.

9. Toni Craven, "Judith 2," in *Women in Scripture*, 104–6. On the complexity of interpretation of Judith, see Denise Dombkowski Hopkins, "Judith," in *The Women's Bible Commentary* (ed. Carol A. Newsom and Sharon H. Ringe; 2d ed.; Louisville: Westminster John Knox, 1998), 279–85.

put God to the test today, and to set yourselves up in the place
of God in human affairs?" (8:12). She tells them that God can
deliver or destroy, reminding them that faithfulness demands
waiting for deliverance. Her radical proposal, "Let *us* set an example for *our* kindred, for their lives depend upon *us*, and the
sanctuary — both the temple and the altar — rests upon *us*"
(8:24, emphasis added), falls on deaf ears, yet it suggests a vision of inclusive gender roles in modeling and thus teaching a
community a way through calamity. When collaboration is not
possible, Judith goes on single-handedly to destroy the Assyrian
enemy. To God, she voices her single desire that the "whole nation and every tribe know and understand that you are God,
the God of all power and might, and that there is no other who
protects the people of Israel but you alone!" (9:14). That God
hears her prayer is evident not only from her great victory in
beheading the enemy general, but also in her actions being the
cause of people rediscovering their own theological moorings.
The book closes with the note that "no one ever again spread
terror among the Israelites during the lifetime of Judith, or for
a long time after her death" (16:25). Judith successfully mod-
els maintenance of right relationship with God that combines
prayer and action. Her assurance that God is with the people,
seeing those things that bind them and willing to deliver them,
rests in the ideals of the exodus tradition. By word and deed, Judith teaches fear of God that puts in balance fear of any other.
She, a widow, is thus metaphorically mother to Israel.[10]

---

10. See Margarita Stocker, *Judith, Sexual Warrior: Women and Power in
Western Culture* (New Haven: Yale University Press, 1998), 207, for parallels
with Mother Judith as "the conduit of essential Jewishness to her grandson"
in André Schwarz-Bart's 1959 Holocaust novel *The Last of the Just.*

Susanna

The narrator of Susanna notes that "her parents were righteous, and had trained their daughter according to the law of Moses" (Sus 3).[11] Raised in an observant home, Susanna marries into a household dedicated in a public way to the maintenance of the law. The garden of Joakim and Susanna's Babylonian home functions as a courtroom of sorts where frequently two elders served as judges (4–6). When these legal leaders attempt to have intercourse with Susanna, saying that unless she lies with them they will testify that she was with a young lover (19–21), she chooses not to do it (23). Her trial, at which the law does not entitle her to speak, results in her death sentence (41b). She, however, cries aloud to God that she is innocent (42–43). And "the Lord heard her cry" (44), sending the young Daniel to her vindication (45–62).

"In the Book of Susanna, Susanna represents the community besieged by internal problems."[12] While she does not stand against the legal practices of her community, she does teach through her example that faithfulness to Torah is more important than life itself. When propositioned by the wicked judges, she says, "I am completely trapped. For if I do this, it will mean death for me; if I do not, I cannot escape your hands. I choose not to do it; I will fall into your hands, rather than sin in the sight of the Lord" (22–23). Torah undergirds her logic and informs her actions. Her narrative is didactic, even if fictional. Her double characterization as a "very beautiful woman and one who

---

11. On Susanna, see Toni Craven, "The Greek Book of Daniel," in *The Women's Bible Commentary* (1998), 312–14.

12. Jennifer A. Glancy, "Susanna 1," in *Women in Scripture*, 158.

feared the Lord" (2) suggests that she, like Judith who is similarly described (Jdt 8:7–8),[13] is a teacher of right behavior.[14]

1, 2, 4 Maccabees

Circumcising Mothers

In 1 Maccabees, a story of Jewish struggle for national liberation, religious-political oppression represents the economic, cultural, and religious consequences embodied in the ideological conflict of the Hasmonean revolt against Hellenism. Antiochus IV Epiphanes' subjugation of Jerusalem included prohibitions against temple worship, observance of Sabbaths and holy days, circumcision, and the keeping of Torah. Following his desecration of the temple on the twenty-fifth day of Chislev (1 Macc 1:59), Antiochus orders the execution of certain Jewish mothers:[15]

> According to the decree, they put to death the women who had their children circumcised, and their families and those who circumcised them; and they hung the infants from their mothers' necks. But many in Israel stood firm and were resolved in their hearts not to eat unclean food.

---

13. See Toni Craven, *Artistry and Faith in the Book of Judith* (SBLDS 70; Chico, Calif.; Scholars Press, 1983), 85–112.

14. Glancy ("Susanna 1," 158) maintains that "on the one hand, Susanna's resistance to rape and adherence to the Mosaic law is laudable. On the other hand, Susanna's understanding of her dilemma unfortunately supports the problematic notion that victims are somehow themselves guilty. For these reasons Susanna is an ambiguous heroic figure for some contemporary feminists."

15. Ronald S. Kline, "Women/Mothers with Circumcised Sons," in *Women in Scripture*, 385.

They chose to die rather than to be defiled by food or to profane the holy covenant; and they did die (1:60–63).

Antiochus's act is meant to destroy the community, its traditions, and its future. Ironically, in the Maccabean context, stories of such epic horror do just the opposite. This hideous illustration of mothers with their circumcised infants hung around their necks is also found in 2 Macc 6:10 and 4 Macc 4:25.[16] In 2 Macc 6:10, two circumcising mothers are publicly paraded with their babies hanging at their breasts and then hurled from a wall. The deaths of these two unnamed Jewish mothers — which is the first in a series of martyr stories, followed by Sabbath observers assembled in caves, an old man (Eleazar), seven brothers and their mother (6:7–7:42) — illustrate the writer's point that God disciplines the faithful, but never withdraws mercy (6:12–17).

---

16. Second Maccabees is not a continuation of 1 Maccabees, but it covers some of the same material about Judas Maccabeus and the mid-second century B.C.E. revolt of the province in Judea against the Seleucid Empire. Two letters (2 Macc 1:1–2:18), prefixed to a compiler's preface (2:19–32), introduce an abridgment of a five-volume history by an otherwise unknown Jason of Cyrene that concludes with an eloquent epilogue (15:38–39). In 4 Maccabees, an introductory historical preamble (3:19–4:26) briefly summarizes 2 Maccabees, while martyr stories occupy fourteen chapters (4 Macc 5–18). Fourth Maccabees is in no sense a history of the exploits of the Maccabean leaders. A philosophical exercise on the subject of devout reason's mastery over the emotions, it is so thoroughly Greek it is not usually regarded as a product of Palestine; rather Alexandria in Egypt, or more likely Antioch in Syria, is held to be the place of its composition. There is no other biblical book like this first-century C.E. work of a loyalist Jew of the Diaspora who completely embraced Greek thought and utter faithfulness to Jewish tradition. Fourth Maccabees is called, variously, a specimen of synagogue preaching, a lecture, a commemorative address (delivered on the site of the martyrdoms at Antioch), or a diatribe celebrating the virtue exemplified by the deaths of celebrated Maccabean martyrs. See Hugh Anderson in *OTP* 2:531–43.

In 4 Macc 4:25, the deaths of the circumcising mothers are given only passing notice as one of the savage measures of Seleucid King Antiochus IV against Jews in Jerusalem to destroy respect for Jewish law. These unnamed circumcising mothers stand as teachers of resistance to domination. The mothers, as well as the other martyrs, serve as examples of Antiochus's inability to destroy the community or its future.

Martyred Mother with Seven Sons

The martyrology in 2 Macc 6:7–7:42 (the first of its kind in the Bible) lists stories of those who choose death over apostasy. The last martyr is an unnamed mother who dies after witnessing each of her seven sons cruelly tortured. Her family story appears both in 2 Macc 7 and in a considerably expanded version in 4 Maccabees.[17] Exactly where the martyrdoms take place is unclear. No scene other than Jerusalem and Judea is ever established, yet Antioch is a possible setting since King Antiochus IV seems so thoroughly on his own turf.

The 2 Maccabees version of the martyr family story opens with the arrest of the seven brothers and their mother, who are beaten in an effort to force them to eat swine's flesh (prohibited by Lev 11:7–8). The first six sons each defy the king and are cruelly tortured one by one: tongues are cut out; scalps, hands,

---

17. See Robert Doran, "The Second Book of Maccabees," in *The New Interpreter's Bible* (ed. Leander E. Keck; Nashville: Abingdon, 1996), 4:179–299; Jonathan A. Goldstein, *II Maccabees: A New Translation with Introduction and Commentary* (AB 41A; Garden City: Doubleday, 1983); Robin Darling Young, "2 Maccabees" and "4 Maccabees," in *The Women's Bible Commentary* (ed. Carol A. Newsom and Sharon H. Ringe; 2d ed.; Louisville: Westminster John Knox, 1998), 322–25, 330–34; and idem, "The 'Woman with the Soul of Abraham': Traditions about the Mother of the Maccabean Martyrs," in *"Women Like This,"* 67–81.

and feet are cut off; bodies are fried. The six brothers' exchanges with the king (2 Macc 7:2–19) build a coherent argument, which is arranged chiastically:

A Jewish refusal of the king's command results in suffering and death (7:2–6).

  B Jewish hope in eternal life is born of serving God, *the King* (7:7–9).

    C Jewish belief in bodily resurrection makes suffering meaningless (7:10–12).

    C′ For the Gentile king there will be no resurrection to life (7:13–14).

  B′ This mortal king's abuse of authority will be righted by God's retribution (7:15–17).

A′ The king's "fight against God" will not go unpunished (7:18–19).

Measure for measure, what Antiochus is doing shall be returned to him, for God, not this Gentile king, is in control.

Attention next turns to the mother (7:20–23), described as "especially admirable and worthy of honorable memory" (7:20). Because her hope was in the Lord, she had encouraged each of her sons, in Aramaic or Hebrew, to persevere: "Filled with a noble spirit, she reinforced her woman's reasoning with a man's courage" (7:21). Addressing these sons — not Antiochus — she claims not to comprehend how life came to them in her womb, even as she expresses confidence in the Creator, who "will in his mercy give life and breath back to you again, since you now forget yourselves for the sake of his laws" (7:23).

Antiochus interprets her words, which he cannot understand

since they are not in his language, as reproach and so appeals
to her seventh and youngest son that he will make him rich
and will befriend him if he abandons the ways of his ancestors
(7:24). When the youngest will not listen, Antiochus calls the
mother and urges her to persuade her son (7:25). The mother
leans close to her remaining child and counsels him to "accept
death, so that in God's mercy I may get you back again along with
your brothers" (7:29). Three matters in the mother's words merit
notice: (1) she speaks only to her family members, never to the
king; (2) she remarks that she nursed her son for three years; and
(3) she argues that God creates out of nothing, which may reflect
the philosophical argument *creatio ex nihilo,* or more likely, with
7:11, 22–23, belief that life comes from the Creator of the world.

While his mother is still speaking, her youngest says to the
king, "What are you waiting for? I will not obey the king's command, but I obey the command of the law that was given to our
ancestors through Moses" (7:30). The seventh son claims that
the king will not go unpunished, that suffering is discipline for
human sinfulness, and that reconciliation with God is at hand
(7:31–36): "I, like my brothers, give up body and life for the
laws of our ancestors, appealing to God to show mercy soon to
our nation and by trials and plagues to make you confess that he
alone is God" (7:37). Antiochus falls into a rage and treats the
youngest brother more harshly than the others (7:39): "So he
died in his integrity, putting his whole trust in the Lord" (7:40).
Only a brief statement records the mother's death: "Last of all,
the mother died, after her sons" (7:41).

Antiochus's brutal efforts and ideology are completely ineffec-
tive. Death has no power in the face of obedience to the laws of
the ancestors and belief in God's mercy and the resurrection of
the dead. Adherence to such traditions cancels fears of earthly

death for faithful Jews. The author's claim that the mother bore the deaths of her sons with good courage because of her hope in the Lord and the reinforcement of "her woman's reasoning with a man's courage" (7:21) reflects the Greek cultural norm, mediated through Hellenism, that courage and control are distinctively masculine virtues. Thus praise comes for being like a man. This mother, unlike her counterpart in Jer 15:5–9, did not swoon, nor is she disgraced by her children or her own actions. She is mother of a martyr family that was unified in facing death. No husband or father offers protection. The unexplained absence of her husband makes her a virtual widow. Courage such as hers and that of her sons won God's mercy and made possible the victories of Judas Maccabeus (2 Macc 7:37–38; 8:3–5).

Drawing upon various ethical philosophical traditions and wedding Greek philosophy to Jewish religion, the parallel story of the martyred mother with seven sons in 4 Maccabees reshapes the two-chapter martyrology in 2 Macc 6:7–7:42 into fourteen chapters (4 Macc 5–18).[18] Details fill out what is essentially the same story, giving greater attention to rational promotion of rigorous adherence to Torah. The mother is "aged" and her sons are "handsome, modest, noble, and accomplished in every way" (4 Macc 8:3). One by one they endure hideous torture — described in gruesome detail — for the sake of Jewish law and tradition. Fourth Maccabees develops the supremacy of devout reason over emotions or passions (such as anger, envy, jealousy, grief, fear, love). The death of the mother, told in one verse

---

18. The author of 4 Maccabees is generally described as benefiting from a number of philosophical influences, especially Platonism and Stoicism. For a listing of important primary and secondary texts, see David A. deSilva, *4 Maccabees* (Guides to Apocrypha and Pseudepigrapha; Sheffield: Sheffield Academic Press, 1998), 74–75.

in 2 Macc 7:41, is presented with great detail (4 Macc 14:11–17:6). Praised as of "the same mind as Abraham" (14:20) and as a "daughter of God-fearing Abraham" (15:28; cf. 18:20), the 4 Maccabees mother displays mastery over love of offspring and physical life. She teaches Torah through word and example as wife and mother, here referring to the death of her husband and crediting him while alive with the education of their seven sons (18:10). The writer praises her prudence in overcoming limitations as "the weaker sex" (15:5) and displaying rational rather than emotional logic (cf. 1:15–19).

Following a long section praising the seven brothers' courage, piety, and endurance for the sake of religion (13:1–14:10), the death of the mother as narrated in 4 Maccabees forms the climax of the oration (14:11–17:6). Written as an encomium, a tribute to the mother, the author emphasizes her terrible torments and her great mastery of her passions. In the end, by throwing herself into the flames (17:1), the mother's suicide prevents her being touched by a Gentile, and thus she dies with no violation of her chastity.[19] According to the logic of 4 Maccabees, Antiochus violated physical bodies, but he could not touch the true life of the community or, in the end, this woman.

Hailed as the "mother of the nation, vindicator of the law and champion of religion" (15:29), the mother of seven sons is "more noble than males in steadfastness, and more courageous than men in endurance!" (15:30). This "guardian of the law," though flooded by emotion, withstood like "Noah's ark, carrying the world in the universal flood" (15:31–32). The martyred mother

---

19. The mother's displaced last words to her sons (4 Macc 18:6–19; the seventh son died in 12:19) make her — even in death (she died in 17:1) — the final spokeswoman for the supremacy of the Jewish religion and family values in 4 Maccabees.

is heroic according to the standards of both Jewish piety and Greek virtue. Her obedience to Torah even unto death confirms that "devout reason is sovereign over the emotions" (1:1).[20]

Conclusion

In the apocryphal/deuterocanonical books, Deborah, Edna, Judith, Susanna, unnamed circumcising mothers, and one martyred mother with seven sons embody Torah's traditions by doing all that they understand God to command. These women know and teach right relationship with God and others as they conserve and construct Jewish religious identity. In so far as "biblical narrative is Torah" that both persuades and imparts "teachings powerful enough to affect an entire people,"[21] the telling and retelling of stories about women such as these reports a past in which women knew and took responsibility for the maintenance of Torah. These women teach wisdom, courage, piety, mastery over passions, devout reason, and abhorrence of all that hinders justice. Anchored by Torah, they participate in forming and informing individuals and community, giving heart to the next generation.

---

20. "In the philosophical aspect of his discourse, the author has already made a remarkable achievement. He has given to the keeping of the Jewish Torah the status of an ethical philosophy dedicated to fulfilling the highest ideals of virtue"; so deSilva, *4 Maccabees*, 74. Jan Willem Van Henten argues further that "the Jewish philosophy in 4 Maccabees measures up to Greek philosophy in every aspect. And because of its divine origin it surpasses Greek philosophy" (*The Maccabean Martyrs as Saviours of the Jewish People: A Study of 2 and 4 Maccabees* [Journal for the Study of Judaism Supplement 57; Leiden: Brill, 1997], 294).

21. Tamara Cohn Eskenazi, "Torah as Narrative and Narrative as Torah," in *Old Testament Interpretation: Past, Present, and Future: Essays in Honor of Gene M. Tucker* (ed. James Luther Mays, David L. Petersen, and Kent Harold Richards; Nashville: Abingdon, 1995), 23.

ELEVEN

Critical Themes in the Study
of the Postexilic Period

– Walter Harrelson –

Many of the issues and themes of critical importance for understanding the postexilic period were already important in the time of exile (598–539 B.C.E.), but they continue on or become of even greater weight during the period following the return(s) of exiles to the homeland. In this connection we should remember that those exiles who remained in exile probably continued to deal with these themes in their own ways.

Chief among such issues, in my judgment, are the following: the place of Torah (God's teaching, instruction) in Israelite life, Israel's place among the nations (universalism and particularism), prayer and personal piety, diversity and variety in Israel's life and witness, and the significance of Zion in God's purposes.

Many of these themes are treated in the essays above. I wish to offer only a few paragraphs suggesting texts that illuminate these themes and offer a few observations about them.

Torah

Evidence for the importance of Torah in the postexilic period is overwhelming. That the books of Genesis through Deuteronomy become known as "Torah" is itself a valuable reminder of what the term has come to mean. It is the Torah of Moses, the record of the beginnings of the universe and of Israel, and the story of Israel's first exile in Egypt, redemption from Egypt, and entrance into the land of Canaan. Moses must have written it, with a bit of help from Joshua in recording Moses' death — or so the tradition claimed. Torah defines who Israel is, specifies the bond that unites God and people, and makes clear God's investment in and commitment to Israel's future.

Torah's relation to Wisdom is reflected on and specified in two texts of the Apocrypha: Sir 24 and Bar 3:9–4:4.[1] The identification with Wisdom shows that Torah, like Wisdom, is becoming a distinct entity, a reality intimately close to deity, sharing characteristics with God. Torah/Wisdom is present with God at the creation (as in Prov 8; Sir 1; 24). It/she is present throughout the entire creation (Sir 24; Wis 7) and is guiding the course of world history (the theme of the entire Book of Wisdom).

These later developments build upon the understanding of Torah found in Ps 1; 19:8–15 (Eng. 19:7–14); and 119. Psalms 1 and 2 form a complementary introduction to the entire Book of Psalms, with Ps 1 indicating that fidelity to Torah and meditation (*hagah*; 1:2) on its delights produce happiness, while Ps 2 portrays that God's order established over the nations of earth, though murmured against (*hagah*; 2:1) by the nations, holds firm through the agency of Zion's anointed king, who must of course live by the demands of Torah (Deut 17).

Fidelity to Torah is pleasing to God and brings delight to those

---

1. See my essay "Wisdom Hidden and Revealed according to Baruch (Baruch 3:9–4:4)," in *Priests, Prophets and Scribes: Essays on the Formation and Heritage of Second Temple Judaism in Honour of Joseph Blenkinsopp* (ed. Eugene Ulrich et al; JSOTSup 149; Sheffield: JSOT Press, 1992), 158–71.

who observe it, as Ps 19 makes clear.[2] The two parts of Ps 19, in fact, relate the praise to God rendered by the creation itself and the praise due God for the gift of Torah. Psalm 119 goes even farther, using each letter of the Hebrew alphabet to apostrophize the glory and mystery of Torah. "Oh, how I love your Torah," the psalmist can exclaim (119:97).[3] Such praise of Torah displays how near to one another are God and this special gift of God. Torah brings God very near indeed to those who claim the way of Torah as their way. Small wonder that the teachers of Israel later on will speculate whether Torah was created or has been eternally with God. How could there have been a time when there was no Torah?

Universalism and Particularism

God's call of Abraham has in view "all the families of earth" and their welfare (Gen 12:3).[4] God's gifts of peoplehood, land, and blessing bring distinctiveness to the people of the covenant, but all such gifts have the world's welfare in view. Israel's election may easily be misconstrued, as biblical texts make clear (Deut 7–8; Amos 3:2; 9:7), but it should not be. God has the world's future in view, and Israel's testimony to God is intended to keep that universal perspective in focus.

---

2. See my essay "Psalm 19: A Meditation on God's Glory in the Heavens and in God's Law," in *Worship and the Hebrew Bible: Essays in Honour of John T. Willis* (ed. M. Patrick Graham, Rick R. Marrs, and Steven L. McKenzie; JSOTSup 284; Sheffield: JSOT Press, 1999), 142–47.

3. Biblical quotations are the author's own.

4. See my essay "Universalist and Particularistic Texts on Zion (Jerusalem) in Biblical Texts," in *Christian Faith Seeking Historical Understanding: Essays in Honor of H. Jack Forstman* (ed. James O. Duke and Anthony L. Dunnavant; Macon, Ga.: Mercer University Press, 1997), 76–90.

Several postexilic texts do so. Isaiah 19 speaks of a day to come when a highway will connect Egypt and Assyria. When that happens, God will pronounce blessing upon the three peoples, Egypt, Israel, and Assyria:

> Blessed be Egypt, my people,
> Blessed be Assyria, the work of my hands, and
> Blessed be Israel, my heritage! (19:25).

Isaiah 35 also speaks of a highway, a highway that will lead back to Mother Zion all the hurt and wounded and despised of earth:[5]

> A highway will be there, a way;
> It will be called the Holy Way.
> The unclean shall not pass it by [Hebrew *'br*];
> It shall be for them as well.
> No travelers, not even the simple ones,
> Shall lose their way (35:8).

The Book of Zechariah has additional texts with universalistic themes. In one of the visions of the prophet (2:5–9 [Eng. 2:1–5]), a figure appears ready to measure the length and breadth of the city of Jerusalem, which is to be restored. Another figure, however, calls back the first and cancels the mission. Zion is not to have walls but is to lie open. No one can know just how extensive Zion will have to be in order to accommodate those for whom God will see fit to make a home in Zion. The author of 2 Esd (=4 *Ezra*) 3–10 uses these chapters to indicate that the Zion to come will have massive foundations suitable to support

---

5. I have discussed this text in *Language, Theology and the Bible: Essays in Honour of James Barr* (ed. Samuel E. Balentine and John Barton; Oxford: Clarendon, 1994), 247–60.

a multitude of those who will find blessing there.[6] Since the number of those whom God will spare is the central subject of 2 Esd 3–10, the answer received is a contradiction of the view that only the few can or will be spared in the last days.

A second universalistic theme appears in Zech 14:16–21.[7] There, the unknown author envisages a time to come when all the nations of earth will be required to worship the Lord in Zion. As they do so, the entire area will become a sacred locale. Bells on the harnesses of the horses will be inscribed "Holy to the LORD," and worshipers need not be concerned about the sanctity of vessels with which to make their offerings, for every pot and vessel will be holy. This culminating celebration of the Festival of Booths will unite the peoples of the earth around God's temple in Zion. Interpreters often assume that the text depicts a gathering of Diaspora Jews for the Jewish festival. On the contrary, the text seems rather to stem from the same community of believers responsible for Isa 19:23–25. The nations must celebrate the Jewish festival, which has become a universal festival.

Other texts speak of the triumph of Israel at the expense of the nations that have mistreated Israel. Some of these texts come from the time of exile, but others date to the postexilic period. Isaiah 60:4–22 and 61:5–7, for example, look toward the day when Zion will be glorified with the riches of the nations, with Israel's enemies now required to honor and serve their former

---

6. See my essay "Ezra among the Wicked in 2 Esdras 3–10," in *The Divine Helmsman: Studies on God's Control of Human Events, Presented to Lou H. Silberman* (ed. James L. Crenshaw and Samuel Sandmel; New York: Ktav, 1980), 21–40.

7. See my essay "The Celebration of the Feast of Booths according to Zechariah xiv:16–21," in *Religions in Antiquity: Essays in Memory of Erwin Ramsdell Goodenough* (ed. Jacob Neusner; Leiden: Brill, 1968), 88–96.

captives. Other texts stress the centrality of Israel or Zion in the divine purpose but make it clear that God's purpose in Israel's election has the health of the entire universe in view. Memorable postexilic texts that declare the universal design of God include Isa 56:6–8, which affirms that foreign converts to Israel may bring their offerings to the temple in Jerusalem, "for my house shall be called a house of prayer for all peoples." The divine covenant with Israel is to bring blessing to "all the families of earth" (Gen 12:3), as noted above. Israel has many perspectives on the question of how such blessing is to reach the nations of earth. It is unmistakable, however, that one of those ways is through the agency of a glorified and transformed Zion and a glorified and transformed people of the covenant.

Prayer and Personal Piety

The prayers of the Book of Psalms continue to be a central part of the life and worship of postexilic Israel, of course. In addition, marvelous prayers appear in the biblical and apocryphal literature of the period. Ezra 9 and Neh 9 include great prayers by Ezra, and a similar prayer appears in Dan 9. The apocryphal or deuterocanonical writings contain many notable prayers. In Greek Esth 13–14, for example, the prayers of Mordecai and Esther for divine aid are notable examples. Tobit's prayer for God to take his life (Tob 3) is a bit petulant, overstated, and self-serving, but it is all too familiar. Sarah's prayer in far-off Ecbatana, offered simultaneously with that of Tobit, powerfully states the plight of one who cannot understand why she has become the bearer of death to those betrothed to her (3:11–15). Sarah's prayer sharply points up the shallowness of Tobit's complaint against his wife Anna, whom Tobit has falsely accused of wrongdoing. Sarah has a grievance, while Tobit is ready to die because of wounded vanity. One also thinks of Jonah's plea for death because his shade from the sun was taken away (Jonah 4:6–8).

Another great and memorable prayer is that of Judith as she prepares to risk life and honor in order to save her people (Jdt 9). Her prayers reveal an almost naïve trust in God's active involvement in human affairs, a readiness on God's part to hear and heed the prayers of those who earnestly seek that help. That same spirit shines through the prayer of Sirach (Sir 36:1–22), where the sage prays for Israel to prosper and Israel's enemies to come to grief. The same sentiment appears in the long prayer with which the Book of Sirach ends (Sir 51). Susanna's brief prayer for God to save her from the false charges of the elders is yet another example (Sus 42–43).

The best window on postexilic piety is found in Tob 4. The words of Israel's prophets shine through the practical counsel given by Tobit to his son Tobias as the latter prepares for the long journey he is to undertake for his father. Almsgiving, care for the needy, marriage within one's extended family, avoidance of fornication, greed, pride — the catalogue includes these and more. Long before the appearance of the Pharisees, the community of postexilic Israel is well grounded in Torah's day-to-day import for all aspects of life within the community.

Fidelity to Torah even at the risk, or the cost, of one's life is perhaps the basis for the community's piety. The stories of Daniel and the three youths (Dan 1–6) give vivid pictures of how the Jewish community is to hold fast to Torah in exile or in foreign lands. Judith illustrates that fidelity, as do Mattathias and his sons (1 Maccabees). The most striking example appears in the stories of those who undergo the severest kinds of torture and give their lives rather than recant their faith. The martyrs of 2 Macc 7 set an example that will prove to be particularly valuable to early Christians when they face similar tests of faith. Fourth Maccabees uses the stories of the martyrs to demonstrate how devout reason is able to — and should — rule over the emotions. These martyr stories inform the piety and the daily life of faithful Jews and Christians for centuries to come.

Diversity and Variety in Israel's Life and Witness

One of the chief features of postexilic Jewish life is its variety, its diversity of life and witness. Survival in exile had helped to produce such variety, of course, for Jews had found themselves caught up in public service among the successive empires of Mesopotamia and Egypt, able to preserve the community by following the advice of Jer 29:6–7: build houses, plant gardens, take wives and have children, and seek the welfare of the land. This counsel concluded with the remarkable assertion that "in its [the land of captivity] welfare you will find your welfare." And so it proved to be.

The return from exile left a flourishing community of Jews that did not return. Jews continued to settle in other parts of the world as well, especially in Egypt, where their numbers would reach hundreds of thousands during Hellenistic times. Postexilic literature reflects this spread of the Jewish people and the varieties of interests and concerns that occupied them. Many of the texts of the Apocrypha reflect this wider world of Judaism. Sirach, the Wisdom of Solomon, and 3 Maccabees belong to the world of Egypt, while Greek Esther, Additions to Daniel, Baruch, the Letter of Jeremiah, Tobit, and 1 Esdras reflect the

Persian world of Mesopotamia. Much of the literature actually comes from the period of Hellenistic control of Mesopotamia, Anatolia, and Egypt.

Varieties of occupations, living arrangements, languages, and customs characterized postexilic Judaism. By the second century B.C.E. the variety in religious outlook was also notable. Commitment to Torah was basic, and the community's hopes surely included the promise of land, divinely appointed leadership, and a central sanctuary, Zion. The ways of working for the realization of these, however, surely differed widely, as the literature reveals. Most writers today speak of the several forms of Judaism that existed by the dawn of the Common Era.

This variety of outlook and culture is a good caution against reading the New Testament references to "the Jews" carelessly. The Dead Sea Scrolls make unmistakable the extraordinary variety of ways in which Jews lived, prayed, believed, and hoped during postexilic times. Studies of the social world of the various documents from postexilic times have underscored this variety. Jeremiah's counsel was taken seriously, and the results were varieties of ways by which Jews lived in covenant with the one God, in various lands and under various forms of government.

Mother Zion

It may be that too little has been made of the image of Mother Zion for understanding what held Judaism together as one community in the midst of the variety. I listed several of the Zion texts above and spoke about their significance. Here I want to focus upon one feature of Zion's significance for understanding postexilic Judaism: Zion as mother of all. While the term comes from 2 Esd (=4 *Ezra*) 10:7–8, the reality is widely reflected in biblical and apocryphal literature.

Ezekiel 16 vividly describes the foundling girl born of mixed parentage who was abandoned by the roadside. The Lord came by, did the duties of a midwife, and secured life for the girl. She grew up, became beautiful, and the Lord came by and betrothed the girl. She, however, turned against her beloved and proved utterly faithless. God's judgment will fall heavily upon Zion, but God will remain true to the covenant and will forgive Zion and restore her at the end.

It is this Zion that is destined to become the center (lit., "navel") of the universe (Ezek 38:12), described in Isa 2:2–4 and Mic 4:1–4 as the goal of the nations' pilgrimage, where at last they will lay down all weapons of warfare and thenceforth arbitrate their disputes according to God's Torah. This Zion is the object of the mourning found in the Book of Lamentations, sometimes mourning for itself. This is also the one for whom prayers are offered in the Book of Baruch (4:5–5:9), and she sometimes speaks for herself/itself. Zion is the object of psalmists who see it as "beautiful in elevation, . . . the joy of all the earth" (Ps 48:3 [Eng. 48:2]), firmly planted, protected by God, and the site of peace and blessing for earth (Ps 46). The city also waits on tiptoe, watching for signs of the exiles' return (Isa 40:1–11), and stands as the very presence of deity, causing the heart to long for it as "the deer longs for flowing streams" (Ps 42:2 [Eng. 42:1]).

The image of Zion as mother stands out especially in Isa 35 and 2 Esd (=4 *Ezra*) 9–10. Zion welcomes her children in Isa 40:1–11, offering comfort and consolation. In Isa 35, however, Zion offers more. She is particularly concerned about the wounded, the afflicted, the ones who otherwise have no hope

at all. Zion is the sign of God's love for those who are neglected, overlooked, pushed aside, or despised among earth's
creatures. The highway to Zion will not be denied to any, not
even to those who are charged by the community to cry out as
others approach, "Unclean! Unclean!" Those who are simple,
unlearned, or naïve are also welcomed to join the highway that
leads to Zion.

Second Esdras (=4 *Ezra*) 9–10 carries out this theme with
its parable of a woman who appeared to Ezra in a field, grieving
her heart out, and told her story to Ezra. She and her husband
could have no children, though they prayed to God night and
day. Finally a son was born, grew up, and was betrothed. On the
marriage night the son fell down dead. The mother has come
into the field to weep until she dies. She will no longer live, now
that this son of her old age has died.

Ezra chides her for weeping so violently over the loss of a
single son, while Zion, the mother of us all, lies desolate, her
children scattered, her temple and altar in ruins, her people's
hopes utterly dashed. Suddenly, the woman shakes, cries out a
cosmic cry, and is transformed into a city under construction,
with massive foundations, a city so wide that none can doubt
that it will accommodate all the orphaned of earth, all the troubled and grieving, all those who will come to find shelter with
the mother of all.

This parable is the answer for Ezra to his persistent question throughout 2 Esd (=4 *Ezra*) 3–8: can God not find a way
to bring the lives of sinful, failing, unjust humankind into the
blessedness prepared for the righteous? The text seems to affirm
that the most central image for the fulfilling of God's purposes for
the whole of humankind is a locale, a structure erected on earth,
a place of community and commerce and social/cultural activ-

ity, one with the qualities of the best mother anyone ever had. Jesus' weeping over Jerusalem comes into clearer focus (Matt 23:37–38) in light of the texts portraying Mother Zion.

This picture also offers a corrective to the Zion of Rev 21–22. That city is lowered to earth from heaven, while the Zion of 2 Esdras (=4 *Ezra*) is built upon earth, over time, to accommodate those who lived their lives awaiting the community that Zion affords. The heavenly city of the Book of Revelation denies entrance to those whom the earthly Zion's arms welcome in Isaiah 35 and 2 Esdras.

Finally, Mother Zion is a potent metaphor for all cities, all communities that set up barriers to keep out the undesirable. Like the Zion of Zech 14:16–21, which welcomes all worshipers and requires no special utensils or offerings to be brought along, so also Mother Zion is simply ready to receive her children because they are her children.

Postexilic Jewish life and literature amply and splendidly continue traditions developed before and during the exile. The essays in this collection demonstrate that assertion, and it is time for this period of Israel's history, literature, and thought to take its due place in the world of biblical scholarship and Christian worship. The Jewish community has rarely undervalued this period and its literature. Until recently, the Christian community has rarely failed to do so.

Contributors

Niels-Erik A. Andreasen is President of Andrews University, Berrien Springs, Michigan, and author of *The Old Testament Sabbath*.

Jon L. Berquist is Academic Editor of Chalice Press. His books include *Judaism in Persia's Shadow: A Social and Historical Approach* and *Reclaiming Her Story: The Witness of Women in the Old Testament*.

Toni Craven is Professor of Hebrew Bible and Director of Ph.D. Studies at Brite Divinity School, Texas Christian University. Together with Carol Meyers and Ross Kraemer, she edited *Women in Scripture: A Dictionary of Named and Unnamed Women in the Hebrew Bible, the Apocryphal/Deuterocanonical Books, and the New Testament*.

Katheryn Pfisterer Darr is Associate Professor of Hebrew Bible at Boston University School of Theology. She is the author of *"Far More Precious than Jewels": Perspectives on Biblical Women* and *Isaiah's Vision and the Family of God*.

John C. Endres is Associate Professor of Sacred Scripture at the Jesuit School of Theology at Berkeley and the Graduate Theological Union, Berkeley. He is the author of *Biblical Interpretation in the Book of Jubilees* and *Temple, Monarchy and Word of God*.

Walter Harrelson is Professor Emeritus of Hebrew Bible at the Divinity School of Vanderbilt University and Adjunct University Professor of the Divinity School of Wake Forest University. Major writings include *Interpreting the Old Testament*, *From Fertility Cult to Worship*, *The Ten Commandments and Human Rights*, *Jews and Christians: A Troubled Family* (with Rabbi Randall M. Falk), *The Making of the New Revised Standard Version of the Bible* (with Bruce M. Metzger and Robert C.

Dentan), and *Jews and Christians: In Pursuit of Social Justice* (also with Rabbi Falk). He is editor of the forthcoming *New Interpreter's Study Bible*.

LAMONTTE M. LUKER is Professor of Hebrew Scriptures at Lutheran Theological Southern Seminary, Faculty Associate in the Department of Religious Studies of the University of South Carolina, and Adjunct Professor of Old Testament at the Jerusalem Center for Biblical Studies in Israel. He is the author of *Doom and Hope in Micah: The Redaction of the Oracles Attributed to an Eighth-Century Prophet.*

LEO G. PERDUE is Professor of Hebrew Bible and President of Brite Divinity School, Texas Christian University. His books include *The Companion to the Hebrew Bible* and *Families in Ancient Israel* (with Joseph Blenkinsopp, John Collins, and Carol Meyers).

PAUL L. REDDITT is Professor of Old Testament and Chair of the Department of Religion at Georgetown College, and the author of *Haggai, Zechariah, Malachi* and *Daniel* (both New Century Bible).

WILL SOLL is Director of the Library at Sanford-Brown College, and Reference Librarian of the Eden/Webster Library of Webster University and Eden Seminary. He is the author of *Psalm 119: Matrix, Form and Setting.*

MARTI J. STEUSSY is MacAllister-Petticrew Associate Professor of Biblical Interpretation at Christian Theological Seminary. She is the author of *Gardens in Babylon: Narrative and Faith in the Greek Legends of Daniel* and *David: Biblical Portraits of Power.*

Index of Ancient Sources

All biblical citations are based on the English versification. Differences in Hebrew versification are noted in the text. General references are included for the Apocrypha, Pseudepigrapha, and Dead Sea Scrolls where the specific references would not direct the reader.

OTHER ANCIENT SOURCES

RABBINIC LITERATURE

Index of Subjects

priests (continued)
  as leaders of Second Temple, 39, 40,
    41, 42, 45
  legitimate, 126
  as ordering principle of time of
    worship, 209
  organization by David, 163
  pagan, 146
  people of Zion as, 96
  as the real postexilic Israel, 102
  and rebuilding of the temple, 7
  relation to Levites, 188
  return from Babylonian exile, 121
  and Sabbath duties, 194
  sacrifices by, 167n, 172, 187
  sanctity of, 200
  as teachers of Torah, 3, 8
  as trumpet players, 164, 167, 168,
    173, 175
  view of Persian domination by,
    187–88
  Zadokite. *See* Zadokites
protoapocalyptic literature
  in Ezekiel, 92–94, 117
  failed expectations in, 94
  Isaiah (chaps. 24–27), 97–98, 117
  Isaiah (chaps. 56–66), 95–97, 116
  Jerusalem in, 91–102
  in Joel, 99–100, 116
  the temple in, 91–102
  Zechariah (chaps. 1–8), 95
  Zechariah (chaps. 9–14), 100–102,
    116–17
prophecy
  birth of classical in Amos, 15
  and eschatology, 91
  function of, 214
  and Hebrew monarchy, 15
  and origins of apocalyptic literature,
    15, 82, 83, 84, 90, 91, 98, 101,
    101n, 102–3, 105, 106
  and the worshiping community, 8
  universalizing of, 15
  vitality of, 1–19
  waning of Hebrew, 10, 15, 205–6

resurrection, idea of, 17, 17n, 107, 110,
  114, 285, 286

Sabbath, the
  in apocalyptic literature, 201, 202,
    202n
  as a basis for inclusiveness, 193–96
  broadening of concept, 208
  as a call to genuine religion, 4, 4n,
    197–99
  defilement as a cause of exile, 200
  delight of, 199–200
  as formative for Israelite worship, 190
  as a gathering for prayer, 194
  as a holy day, 207, 207n
  negligence of as thwarting salvation
    history, 207
  as an ordering principle of life, 201,
    202, 209
  and refraining from work, 194
  relation to synagogue, 189–90, 191,
    192, 206–7, 208
  and the sanctity of Israel, 198, 200
  as a source of tension with other
    ethnic groups, 236, 282, 283
  as a symbol of the world to come,
    201–2
  and vitality of postexilic Israelite
    religion, 19, 191–92, 202–3, 205,
    277
  worship on, 189–90, 194, 202
Shabbat. *See* Sabbath, the
story
  Bel and the Dragon as a case study of,
    215–41
  the complexity of, 214–15
  importance of, 212, 241
  modern importance of, 241
  as a source of Jewish identity, 213–14
songs, use of in worship
  before the ark, 166, 177
  in Chronicles, 161–62, 165, 168, 171,
    175, 187, 188
  correspondence to sacrifice, 171–72,
    179